TRU
NOR

Gavin Francis is an award-winning ~~~~~~~~~~. He is the author of ten non-fiction books, including *Island Dreams*, which was shortlisted for the Waterstones Book of the Year 2020; *Adventures in Human Being*, which was a *Sunday Times* bestseller and won the Saltire Scottish Non-Fiction Book of the Year Award; *Empire Antarctica*, which won Scottish Book of the Year in the SMIT Awards and was shortlisted for both the Ondaatje and Costa Prizes; and *Recovery: The Lost Art of Convalescence*, which was a *Sunday Times* bestseller. He has written for the *Guardian*, *The Times*, the *New York Review of Books* and the *London Review of Books*. His work has been translated into nineteen languages, and he is a Fellow of the Royal Society of Literature. He lives in Edinburgh, Scotland.

'*True North* is a wonder-voyage – an *immrama* – out into the land-scape of the northern regions, but also down into the mindscape of those many travellers who have been drawn irresistibly north-wards over the millennia – Gavin Francis among them. Fluent, subtle, tough and often beautiful, *True North* stands alongside Peter Davidson's *The Idea of North* and Joanna Kavenna's *The Ice Museum*, as a significant recent addition to the Arctic canon'
Robert Macfarlane

'Returning from a frostbitten world, Gavin Francis describes land-scapes few of us have seen and narrates stories almost none of us have heard. He is a true traveller'
Daniel Kalder

'Thank goodness for people like Gavin Francis who are prepared not only to visit our northerly neighbours, but write about them in a way that shows how much of their history is our history too'
Roger Cox, *The Scotsman*

'An accomplished teller of travellers' tales . . . really gets under the skin of Europe's magical North'
Sunday Herald

TRUE
NORTH

TRAVELS IN ARCTIC EUROPE

GAVIN FRANCIS

CANONGATE

This Canons edition first published in Great Britain,
the USA and Canada in 2024
by Canongate Books Ltd, 14 High Street, Edinburgh EH1 1TE

Distributed in the USA by Publishers Group West
and in Canada by Publishers Group Canada

canongate.co.uk

First published in Great Britain in 2008 by Polygon,
an imprint of Birlinn Ltd

1

British Library Cataloguing-in-Publication Data
A catalogue record for this book is available on
request from the British Library

ISBN 978 1 83726 195 6

Typeset by SJC

Printed and bound by CPI Group (UK) Ltd, Croydon CR0 4YY

This book is dedicated to Esa,
who doesn't mind sleeping on the ground

Contents

Maps

Introduction

Colin Thubron

As early as a century ago doomsayers were forecasting the death of travel writing. The genre was losing its interest, wrote Joseph Conrad, while Claude Lévi-Strauss lamented that the magic of journeys had been lost forever. Evelyn Waugh, Kingsley Amis, even Susan Sontag lined up to announce the end of a kind of writing that had existed since the Babylonian *Epic of Gilgamesh* four millennia earlier. It was being rendered obsolete by tourism, some said, by television or by satellite photography. And today its putative killer is the Internet, which makes everywhere seem accessible, enacting travel by illusion, and thus shrinks Time and the World.

Yet the travel book, wrote Jonathan Raban, is 'a notoriously raffish house where very different genres are likely to end up in the same bed', and its perennial robustness may lie precisely in this promiscuity. Its sheer diversity eludes easy definition. It transforms and borrows from nature writing, history, sociology, anthropology, even politics. It evokes a land less by study and analysis than through lived experience: the feel of an unfamiliar terrain, the prolix lives of humans on the ground.

So the travel book lives stubbornly on, and flourishes above all on the variety of its obsessions. In a world that has become superficially more travelled and known, a dizzying range of compulsions and individual quests surfaces. The journey has become more personal, more introverted, more various.

With its daunting reach, its immersion in early and little-known histories and its telling human encounters, Gavin Francis's *True*

North: Travels in Arctic Europe exemplifies why travel writing survives. The author's fascination is above all with those who have preceded him in these harshly magnificent lands. The ancient Greek explorer-astronomer Pytheas, who claimed to have discovered Thule, the northern edge of the Earth (perhaps Iceland), creates a teasing leitmotif. Then there is the sixth-century Irish monk St Brendan whose ox-hide coracle may have reached the American continent while seeking the Land of the Promise of the Saints. His voyage westward, however far it went, touched on lonely anchorites surviving in a scattered archipelago of landfalls far across the North Atlantic. All phenomena, of course, were witnessed in the light of his faith. The spitting fires of an Icelandic volcano (perhaps) were a demon-ridden outcrop of Hell; the gulls and auks that thronged a cliffside became fallen angels that spoke to him; and when the monks sighted a crystal pillar floating alone in the ocean, they circled it reverently as a wonder of God.

Above all Gavin Francis evokes the world of the least accessible of protagonists: the heroes of Norse saga. Eirik the Red, Hrafnkel, Gunnlaug Serpent-Tongue: his fascination for their epics becomes intimately linked to his passion for the wilderness they traversed and inhabited, and which he so richly describes. He follows their trails, seeks out the ruins of Norse farms and settlements, even their hilltop cairns.

But almost uniquely, in travel writing there is another person in the narrative: the writer himself. A whole sub-genre of the discipline describes voyages as therapy, as if the journey might yield up a lost homeland or its hardship cleanse the spirit.

Gavin Francis's concerns, however, are directed passionately elsewhere. The travails of his journey are lightly borne. He often hitchhikes (in these lands, no problem) and above all he walks. 'I have never thought so much, existed so much, lived so much, been so much myself,' wrote Rousseau, 'as in the journeys which I have made alone and on foot', and the same heightened vitality shines off these pages. A tent, a portable stove and a sturdy constitution carry Francis along with buoyant ease. A Scottish trainee doctor with little money, he escapes the censure that foreign travel is a post-colonial imposition on less privileged peoples. His interlocutors are his equals, and in this lonely land hospitality is the norm. He questions them without judgement and listens raptly to their native languages.

Sometimes, after Francis's fleeting but pithy encounters, the reader may wonder what happened to these people. What of the artist who abandoned his studio to paint storms in his dinghy off the Shetland coast? Has the penurious artist, encountered in the Faroe Islands, now realised her dreams of creating theatre? Did the man who built his hotel on a storm-lashed fjord in the Faroes at last exchange it, as he hoped, for a cruise ship in the Caribbean?

Reactions to these lands range from disillusion to the profound enchantment of Francis himself. In the space of four pages we encounter the oldest inhabited wooden house in Europe and its highest sea cliffs (a bulwark of almost three thousand feet) and hear of the underwater mountain range, the biggest such barrier in the world, that divides the Arctic Basin (and its deep-water fish) from the Atlantic.

But his journey never strays into a nostalgic wonderland. He is acutely conscious of moving through a world of climatic turmoil, of declining populations and stagnant economies. Ruefully he discusses the thawing Arctic Ocean with researchers in Svalbard, watches with misgiving a retreating ice-cap in southern Iceland and hears the rumbling of glacial shift in Greenland. Some of the land's changes carry almost personal hurt. The warming North Sea has driven the seabirds of Shetland and Orkney to near-starvation.

Yet the sheer beauty of these unforgiving lands still catches the heart. The book is threaded with moments of infectious joy. Wandering by a river-fed lake near the western littoral of Greenland, Francis comes upon the stone-lined barrier laid by Norsemen to divert the current for fishing. Using makeshift spinners, he pulls up three plump char and eats them poached in their own water, garnished with cloudberries. The silence is broken only by the cries of ptarmigan and the footfalls of passing caribou, while the sun sets and a half moon rises over the lake.

In such passages, where the past and the land and the writer elide, travel writing properly endures.

Prologue

I began to dream of the North in an African hospital ward. I had just started work in a village hospital on the shores of the Indian Ocean. Pus stained the bedsheets of cots that contained three or four children each. Vomited milk was splashed over the blue walls. Disinfectant had been slopped on the floor, and flowed lazily out through channels cut in the concrete. The smell, and the sound of children crying, was at first overwhelming. On my first morning a colleague stood over a cot and pointed out one of the toddlers. The boy had cerebral malaria, and was jerking with epileptic seizures. 'This one is not responding,' he said. 'Sometimes they get here too late.' As we stood by the bed I noticed a fleshy worm creeping out of the child's anus. I was new to Africa, and stared at the worm, horrified, then pointed it out to the doctor. 'Oh that,' he said calmly. 'They come out when the child is too hot, or starving, or too anaemic.' It was the first of many lessons that I learned there.

Soon after arriving I had met Anna, an Icelandic woman who told me that she came to Africa to work because she loved the contrasts with her home in the North Atlantic. She described the empty beauty of Iceland, how starkly it contrasted with the heat and the lushness around us. She invited me to an evening barbecue on the beach, and with the sound of the ocean swells breaking over the reef we talked into the night about life on the edge of the Arctic. She said she had come to realise she needed both extremes in her life; the Arctic and the tropical. She wanted to work out a sustainable and ethical way to live with both.

After that first shocking morning I continued to work during the heat of the day at the hospital, but after particularly difficult days would recover by casting my mind out to imagine that cooler northern world, where the environment could be harsh, but seemed less cruel somehow. In the dripping equatorial heat it would cool me down to think of the Polar Circle. When the sun set like a dropped stone and the afternoon glare fell to darkness, I enjoyed thinking of a land where the sun slipped gently into the ocean and where in summer it shone throughout the night. It was only by living and working somewhere so far removed from Europe that I gradually began to think about how little I knew about that other extreme, the far north. I realised that from the perspective of the tropics, Europe itself bordered on the Arctic, and I thought about how little I knew of the northern lands at my own back door. By the time I left Africa I had decided that I would not return to the tropics until I had explored Arctic Europe for myself.

Soon after my return I began to do some research. As I read into the history of the Arctic I saw that leaving from Scotland I would follow a route that Europeans had taken towards what they once saw as the very limits of the world. It would lead me across the many different landscapes, languages, and cultures of the northern fringes of Europe. Beginning in Shetland in the Classical period I found traces of Greek mariners whose stories were burnt with the Library at Alexandria. Reaching the Faroe Islands in the Dark Ages I came across storm-tossed men of God, praying and fasting in isolation. Then came the bloody fury of the Viking expansion through the Middle Ages that reached Iceland, Greenland and North America. There were stories of greed, murder and starvation in the struggle for discovery of northern merchant routes, and Svalbard, through the sixteenth and seventeenth centuries. Finally there was the surge of understanding as the Enlightenment gave way to the Industrial Revolution, and exploration turned in on itself in Lapland (among other places), evolving into the world-wide tourism that we know today. As I moved north my journey would mirror Europe's own self discovery.

Hidden within it were the themes that drive human exploration itself.

I wanted to follow the journeys undertaken by these explorers, imagining for myself their reactions on seeing these new landscapes, and recording how Europe's northern lands and their people are dealing with the modern world. The polar fringes of Europe have become backwaters to many of us in the 'south'. Off the top of most of our maps and thinly populated, they are often forgotten by nations and societies that look increasingly to large cities for their answers. But it has not always been that way and in my journey I hoped, as a European, to find out a little more about the peoples and the history of the North.

Note to the Reader

While researching this book I have used a variety of sources. Rather than fill the text with excessive numbers of notes and footnotes which would be of interest only to a few readers, information on the source of quotations and further background reading can be found in the Notes on Sources at the end, under the chapter and page number in which the quotation is found.

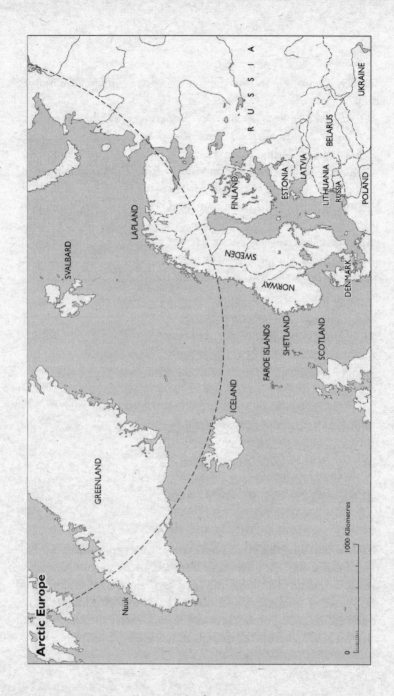

Arctic Europe

Shetland
ULTIMA THULE

✴

MOVING PATCHES OF cloud-shadow and light merged and diverged on the hillside like patterns in a kaleidoscope. They set the landscape in motion the way the wind moves the sea. I was standing on the northern cape of Unst, the northernmost of the Shetland Islands. Far into the Atlantic Ocean, bordering the North Sea, this was the furthest outpost of the British Isles. For years I had paid it homage in maps and atlases, its name so un-British, un-Scottish, it seemed to hint of a wilderness beyond normal reckoning.

On the ferry to get here I had stood out on the deck, gazing at the sea and the sky. There were very few passengers on board, and the ticket inspector had called me up to the bridge to point out a school of dolphins passing by. The ferry had turned to follow them for a while. The slow and graceful swell of the islands broke the sheen of the sea like the backs of sleeping whales.

The landscape had unexpectedly seemed to become softer the further north we had sailed; barren blasted moors had given way to heath and fertile pasture. As I had arrived on the island the wind had eased and I had quickly hitched a lift that had brought me up to the northern end. The driver had lived all over Shetland for twenty years before settling on Unst, she told me. Of all the islands she loved this one best. 'It's a Viking word, "unst",' she had said. 'I think it means "closest".' She explained that for the Vikings it was 'closest' because it was their first landfall when they arrived over the sea from Norway a thousand years before.

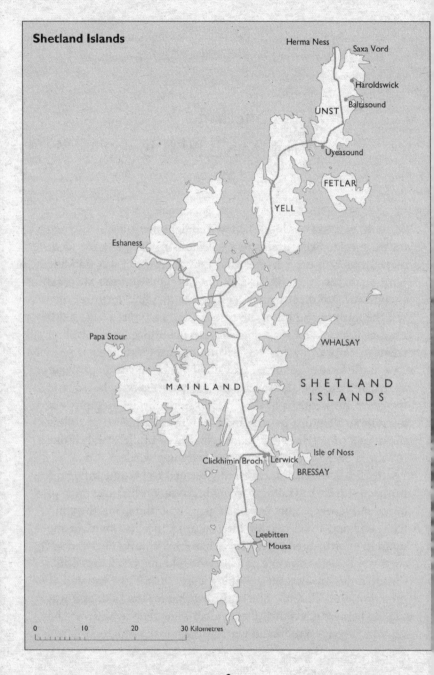

Shetland Islands

Herma Ness
Saxa Vord
Haroldswick
UNST
Baltasound
Uyeasound
FETLAR
YELL
Eshaness
Papa Stour
WHALSAY
MAINLAND
SHETLAND
ISLANDS
Clickhimin Broch
Lerwick
Isle of Noss
BRESSAY
Leebitten
Mousa

0   10   20   30 Kilometres

The RAF had just closed a Cold War listening post on the island. It had been designed to listen to the Russian jets passing back and forth to Cuba. She had pointed it out, hunkered down on one of the two hills forming the north end of the island, its huge dish antennae facing down the Arctic Ocean. In Shetland lore the two hills were once giants, Saxa and Herma, petrified into hills after being caught by the rising sun. When Saxa, to the east, was poured with concrete and circled in barbed wire for the RAF, Herma to the west was left to the birds. The hill and the whole peninsula is now part of the bird reserve of Herma Ness.

I stood on the cliff at Herma Ness. Nesting skuas and oyster-catchers swooped over my head in the brittle spring air. It was May, and the heath and moor, sea and sky seemed to shimmer with the anticipation of summer. The cliffs teemed with birds. Fulmars spun in dizzying aerobatics, gannets hovered on the breeze and fell out of the sky onto unseen shoals of fish. There were puffins too, tumbling from the cliff tops and beating their absurdly tiny wings. The grass was warm and comfortable, kept short by a few sheep, and mixed with delicate flowers of sea-pink. The smooth skin of the sea was broken only by a lobster boat lifting its creels, and the hum of its engine in the distance was the only noise other than the cries of the birds. On an island crag to the north stood Muckle Flugga, the light-house at the end of Britain.

I took off my pack at the cliff's edge and sat down on the grass in the sun. This place, I thought, was the furthest north I had ever been. My journey was finally beginning. I took a book out of my rucksack and, lying down on the grass, began to read about the explorers who had first started to sail north out of the Mediterranean over two and a half thousand years before.

*

A long time ago when the earth was flat and the sun was a blazing chariot in the sky, the first literate explorers of the North were the Phoenicians. Their maritime empire extended the length and breadth of the Mediterranean, and according to Herodotus in about 600 BC they rather casually circumnavigated Africa. They were no strangers to the North Atlantic, sailing regularly to Cornwall to trade for tin. A Phoenician captain called Himilco was the first to write about the northern limits of what he called the great 'Encircling Ocean,' (the word 'ocean' itself comes from an ancient proto-Sanskrit word, *a-çayana*, meaning 'that which encircles'). Sometime in the sixth century BC he wrote that the Atlantic could not be crossed and that it was a dead, sluggish sea, filled with monsters and clogged with weeds. For centuries his descriptions dissuaded anyone else from attempting the voyage, which was probably what he had intended. Less shipping on the ocean meant less competition for trade.

As the Phoenicians pushed out into the Atlantic, Greek culture was on the way up. For centuries Homer and Hesiod had been trusted by the Greeks to provide accurate descriptions of the earth. The Homeric vision of the earth was as a flat shield with ocean running around the rim. This is *The Odyssey* on the geography of the North Atlantic: 'We had attained Earth's verge and its girdling river of Ocean, where are the cloud-wrapped and misty confines of the Cimmerian men... an endless deathful night is spread over its melancholy people...' In short, it was the sort of place that should be left well alone.

Greek culture had developed an elaborate belief system about what probably lay in the North, and took its clues from Africa. It was thought that the people who lived furthest to the south were the Ethiopians, and frankly, they were a terrifying bunch. They were feared as god-like men, formidable in war, who mocked the gold and purple robes worn by the 'civilised' Greeks. It was reported in the marketplaces of Athens that not only had they beaten the Persian army, they had yelled 'DUNGEATERS' at them because unlike the nomadic Ethiopians they ate cereals grown from fertilised land. They considered the Ethiopians an early prototype of Rousseau's 'noble savage' and assumed that they must have their northern counterpart: a fearsome people who lived *beyond* the north wind, or *Boreas*. It was thought these 'Hyperboreans' must be a race of perfect men, living by the 'stream of Ocean,' itself. It was said that they had lived near the Greeks once, but had left the depraved centres of the earth (such as Athens) to live in the North free from disease, famine, and war. Pindar wrote of them: 'In truth Apollo delights in their festivals most of all… neither sickness, nor baneful old age, mixes with this holy tribe; far from toils and battles they dwell.'

Herodotus was the first man to challenge this Homeric view of the world. A Greek from south-west Asia Minor writing around 500 BC, he thought that Homer invented 'Ocean' and complained that there was no evidence for it. He pointed out that the Caspian Sea had been discovered to be land-locked meaning that Asia itself could extend to the ends of the earth. A man of reason, he changed the Greek world view from that of boundaries beyond which men should not go, to unknowns that men should explore.

The Greek expansion through the Mediterranean was gathering pace. Colonies were founded on Sardinia, Corsica and along the southern coast of France. In the fourth century BC, not long after the Celts crossed the Alps and sacked Rome, a man was born in Massalia (Marseilles) who became the greatest astronomer, mariner and explorer of his time. Pytheas was the first European to write about the tides being related to the waxing and waning of the moon. He knew the Mediterranean and the Black Sea well, and his astronomy was so accurate he was able to calculate that the Pole Star was very slightly displaced from true North, a difference of only fractions of a degree. Marseilles today counts him as one of its founding fathers, and a statue of the old Greek looks out over the Vieux Port from the top of the Chamber of Commerce there. I had visited it a few weeks before leaving on my journey and had asked inside for more information about the background of this man, one of the first explorers in the modern sense of the word. No one was able to help me. The only traces I found of the world that he knew were amphorae pulled from the sea-bed in the bay and exhibited in the Musée de la Marine et de L'Economie. Even the ancient Greek *agora* behind the museum had been walled in by modern apartment blocks.

Pytheas' account of his travels was called *Peri Okeanou* or 'Concerning the Ocean'. No copies of it survive, so we only know of the book from its fierce critics. Strabo of Pontus, for example, witheringly wrote of it in his *Geography* (AD 23): 'Pytheas asserts that he explored in person the whole northern region of Europe as far as the ends of the world – an assertion which no man would believe, not even if Hermes made it.'

There were other less critical commentators. Pliny the Elder quoted Pytheas in his *Naturalis Historia* (AD 77), telling us that he reached an island called Thule, 'six days voyage north of Britain'. Because it lay at the very edge of the world it became known as *Ultima* Thule. Hipparchus was a geographer who took the sun-sightings of latitude recorded by Pytheas in his book and converted them into the system of measurement by degrees that we use today. He tells us that Pytheas landed on the British Isles and took sightings at 54° (Lancashire?) and at 58° (the Outer Hebrides?) As his journey continued northwards we hear that he reported forty 'Orcades' (the Orkney Islands). The accuracy of the figure hints at a lengthy stay there. He also described the waves reaching up to 80 cubits (35 metres) which is not unknown when storms beat against the cliffs of Orkney and Shetland. The last sun sighting recorded by Pytheas on his journey north corresponds to a latitude of 60°, where day at midsummer lasted 19 hours. And at that latitude lies Shetland.

When Pytheas set out from Massalia no one in the Greek world knew answers to questions like: How far north could people really live? How cold would it really get? Could the trend for increasing length of days during the summer extend to 24-hour sunlight? Was there a place beyond which climate improved again, a climate in which the Hyperboreans could be living? Could the world have an 'edge' at all? Pytheas' answers to these questions were so out of keeping with the established beliefs of Classical Europe that his critics labelled him a fabulist and a charlatan. He denied the misconceptions of the North then currently held in Greece, such as that one-eyed Arimaspians danced with the Hyperboreans there, and stole gold from the nests of gryphons. He said that on the contrary the Britons were people like the Greeks. Though they had to thresh their corn indoors because of the rain they lived reasonably well, had a trading economy, and even managed to brew a sort of beer.

He has been remembered largely because of his claim to have been led by locals to an island that he called 'Thule', six days sail north of Britain. In this place barbarians had indicated where the sun went down for only two or three hours in summer. From Thule Pytheas claimed that it was only one day's sail to where the sea became frozen. Though scholarly debate over the whereabouts of Thule has dragged on for centuries, the most likely candidate is Iceland. So although we know for sure from his surviving sun-sightings that he made it as far as Shetland, there is a lack of evidence to show how much further he really managed to go.

*

As I lay reading on the grass it had become cold, and all around me the puffins were returning to their burrows in the hillside after a day's fishing. A fulmar hovered on the cliff's up-draughts less than an arm's reach away, eyeing me suspiciously, the wind ruffling its pinion feathers. The birds looked strong and healthy to me, but I had read that sea-birds on Shetland were experiencing an un-precedented crisis. They had recently suffered their worst year on record, when the skuas, Arctic terns, guillemots and kittiwakes of both Orkney and Shetland were thought to have suffered almost complete breeding failure. Scientists agreed that global warming was to blame; climate change had warmed the waters of the North Sea by up to two degrees over only twenty years, and the cold-loving planktons that drive the sea's ecosystem had shifted north. Without plankton the small sandeels that feed on them had all but disappeared, and the seabirds that depended on sandeels for their diet had starved. An ornithologist friend had told me that in Orkney she had found kittiwakes choking on pipefish, a sandeel substitute that filled the birds' bellies but had almost no nutritional value. She asked me to look out for abandoned pipefish around the breeding grounds in Shetland, as signs that the birds were desperately seeking alternative foods.

I unfolded a map of the island and began reading the names of the features of the coast. I was sitting on the Taing of Looswick. Nearby were the Kame of Flouravoug and Shorda Hellier, names that spoke of a rich overlay of Norse and Scots heritage. To the south broken stacks and needles of rock stretched in a shattered mosaic towards Yell and the mainland. With my finger on the map I followed the route I would take back through the Shetland Islands. Pytheas came this way so long ago that there were no traces of his passage. There are, however, still remnants of the peoples who lived here when he passed. They were Picts, builders of brochs, the double-walled towers found all over the northern and western isles of Scotland. There were two particularly famous brochs in Shetland that I wanted to visit, both the centrepieces of villages when Pytheas had passed by 2,300 years before. One was in Lerwick, the capital town of the islands. The other was on Mousa, an island off the south-east coast of the mainland. I sat up thinking about the world that Pytheas knew and watching the light on the waves change from peach to crimson until the sea slipped into darkness.

The next day I started back towards Yell and the mainland. The hillsides were dotted with ruined homes, abandoned by crofters during the nineteenth and early twentieth century. The 'North Isles' folk of Britain (Shetlanders and Orcadians) have always defended their separate identity from that of their southern neighbours, whom Shetlanders refer to as 'Scots', a quite different nation. In the nineteenth century there were still people in the North Isles who spoke

'Norn', a language descended from the Old Norse of the Vikings. They had different property laws, and they did not suffer clearances in the way the Highlanders did, but were gradually pushed out by worsening economic opportunities and the pull of the colonies of the British Empire. Now, the owners of these houses and their descendants would be buried in the graveyards of Glasgow, Sydney and Toronto. Among the ruins lay old boots, tools, iron hearths and rusting bedsteads. Grasses grew thick over the fertilised plots and sheep grazed on ridges of topsoil gathered to make the most of the poor earth. The process was ongoing – I had met people who told me that the depopulation of the islands was continuing despite schemes and incentives to encourage the children to stay and the incomers to arrive. It was a story I was to hear all over the North.

That night I found a hostel in Uyeasound, at the southern end of the island. It was empty, and a sign told me that the attendant came around once a day to collect her fees. I went to the kitchen and had started to make some dinner when I heard a knock on the door. She must have seen me coming down the hill and followed me in.

She was wiry and slight, and peered at me through horn-rimmed glasses and the smoke that rose from the cigarette at her mouth. Her accent was lilting but abrupt, the words clipped short by years of stern pragmatism. 'Sit yourself down,' she said, 'and I'll make you a cup of tea. And you can tell me what has brought you up to Shetland.'

'I want to travel right round the edge of Europe,' I told her. 'Right up from here into the Arctic.' I hesitated, wondering if perhaps she thought this was a silly idea. 'I thought Unst was a good place to start,' I added.

'Oh that's a long way. And what do you think of our island so far?'

'It's beautiful,' I said.

'Aye, it's a beautiful place to live in the summer,' she said, 'but bleak in the winter. Aye, bleak and depressing.'

I asked if she had lived here all her life. 'Oh no!' she gasped, as if I had suggested something unthinkable. 'I was born in Haroldswick, in the north of the island, and moved down here when I married!'

Outside the rain started to drum against the windows. She sat down with the tea to talk about what it was like to live at the furthest-flung corner of Britain. 'It's a pity that so many of our young folk don't stay on, but there's no work, you see.'

I nodded and said that it was a story I had heard before in other parts of Scotland. I realised my mistake too late.

'But we're not Scottish up here!' she replied briskly, 'Oh no, we're Shetlanders! And where would you be from?'

'Edinburgh,' I told her.

'I've a grandson in Edinburgh, he went down to the university there and became an engineer. Maybe you know him.' She told me his name but I had to admit that I had never met him. I wondered if he loved the anonymity of living in the city, and dreaded going back up to Unst. Or maybe he longed to come back, but was caught in a job and lifestyle that trapped him.

She seemed disappointed that I had not met him. 'I suppose there are a lot of people living in Edinburgh. But there used to be a lot of people here too. A century ago this island had over two thousand souls. We had mines, and the biggest herring fishery in the world. Now there's just a few hundred.' She shook her head and her voice filled with sorrow at the thought of families that had packed up and driven south, the schools run down and closed, and the gardens left to overgrow.

I went south-west to Eshaness. I had met Paul and Claire Whitworth only briefly before, after an introduction through a friend of a friend. If I was ever up in the north of Shetland, they said, I should certainly look them up. Theirs was an inspirational story. Paul was an artist, and seven years before the couple had left their home in Lincolnshire with their baby son Jacob, to start a new life in Shetland.

That night I put up my tent in their garden, facing west. The swell rolled in from the ocean, hitting a reef just outside the bay with seismic booms I could hear from a mile away. Paul and Claire invited me in for dinner, and after their four children had gone to bed we began to talk about what had brought them to Shetland. 'I was living down in Lincolnshire,' Paul began, 'as a manager in a factory, and painting in my spare time. I hated the factory, hated the shifts, and more and more I started painting these landscapes of low brown and green swells, of valleys and bays, but never any people, never any trees. They were like dreams for me. I felt I needed somewhere without people, some space to think, somewhere easy on the eye. Lincolnshire landscapes are so *busy*. People would ask me what they were paintings of, and I couldn't tell them. "They're in my head," I'd say, and I started making them more and more austere, more and more empty.

'At about that time Claire was pregnant, and I was having real problems at the factory. I remember the World Cup was on, and some of the lads had smuggled in a telly, and had barricaded themselves in the staff room and were watching matches instead of doing any work. I broke in and ordered them back to work. They refused, so I told them I'd have to sack them unless they did the work they were paid to do. One guy just came at me with a knife. I ran for it, managed to lock myself into the manager's office. I heard him battering on the door, then he shouted, "I know where your wife lives!"

'That was it – I phoned Claire, told her to lock all the doors and windows. I phoned my parents, who went round to the house, then phoned the police. The guy never did show up but we were badly shaken. And when I took it up with my boss he told me I did not have the authority to threaten those guys with the sack, and that I should just get on with coaxing them along.

'I was still painting those landscapes, and we saw an advert for a croft in Shetland. I've got a farming background so thought I'd give it a go, and we drove up here. The croft was a wreck, and over-priced, but as soon as we drove off the ferry and looked at the island Claire said, "This is it! This is the landscape you've been painting so often!" She was right. On the ferry we'd met a couple who offered to put us up and we were just so struck by how everyone wanted to help us, our venture became the venture of everyone we met and told about it. And so we didn't buy that first croft, but it wasn't long until we found this place. And we haven't looked back.'

'Well, we did look back once,' said Claire. 'That first winter was really difficult. The roof leaked, Jake was just a baby, there was no heating. Paul had to cut peat and carry it all himself and we seemed to eat nothing but porridge made from our own oats. If we'd had any money maybe we would have left that first winter, but we couldn't afford it.'

They told me that that first spring they had turned one of the outhouses into a gallery, and Paul had started painting again. He and Claire ran the croft part-time, bought some sheep, brought up some pigs from down south and started to breed them, and gradually fixed up the house. But his skill as an artist was quickly recognised in Shetland, and the gallery began to do well. Some of his pieces were selling for good prices, and to buyers not only in Scotland but to collectors in London.

Paul told me that he loved Shetland because there was so little between him and nature. 'In the cities you're so buffered, so pro-tected from what is real in nature. You're surrounded by things that are man-made, to man's convenience. I find that after a while I get so stressed it makes me ill. Out here you're surrounded by things that are God-made, if you like, they're part of the natural world, there's room to breathe and think, room to live your life the way *you* want, not the way some advertising executive wants.'

Paul had recently become fed up with the niceties of painting in the studio, the ease of it, which was so in contrast to what he saw as the power and sometimes the rage of nature around him. He had taken to rowing his little dinghy out into the winter storms, anchoring it, and trying to paint the storm from his boat while being thrashed around in it. 'I love the way the sea and the rain interfere with the oils and become part of the painting,' he explained. Not content with this, he had started experimenting with painting in blizzards too, allowing snow and ice crystals to embed themselves in the paint.

He and Claire talked excitedly about his next project. He had long been fascinated by the influence of the environment on art, and during the winters in Shetland had done a lot of reading about different art forms around the globe, how they had developed according to the climate: the tropics, the deserts, the poles, the steppe. He was trying to synthesise it all in his mind.

*

The children were fast asleep upstairs. I thanked Paul and Claire for their hospitality, and for giving me so much insight into their lives and the choices that they had made in Shetland. It was late, but a dusky light from the northern horizon lit my way back to the tent. My head was buzzing with ideas about the North, and our retreat to it, and the perspectives that it can reflect back onto the South. Despite depopulation there were still people like Paul and Claire who were drawn here because this landscape and community had something to offer them. I fell asleep with the pounding of the ocean swell in my ears.

*

The shores of the North Atlantic are dotted with places like Lerwick; harbour towns cluttered with high, brightly-coloured warehouses, thin cobbled streets and dark workshops.

The port was small until the development of trade on the high seas in the sixteenth century. The Dutch used to come through it on their way home from the East Indies rather than brave the English warships in the Channel. By the early seventeenth century the town was so overrun with them that it was illegal to sell a Dutchman beer, and all the town's brothels were demolished. Now its bars are filled with the *nouveau riche* of the Norwegian and Aberdonian oil industry, and a few northern fishermen.

Down in the harbour I noticed a bar called 'Thule'. The sign was faded and peeling, and over a black door marked 'No dogs' a buxom Nordic maiden with pleated golden hair and a serpent wound around her shoulders was being gently bleached by the sun. The sign indicating the opening hours was in Norwegian. It was early afternoon and the bar was nearly empty. A group of drunks in the corner shouted about how often they argued with their wives.

There was one other man at the bar. I ordered a beer, sat down beside him and mentioned the sign outside. I asked him why they had called it Thule.

'Shetland used to be thought to be the farthest north in the whole world,' he explained. 'That's what they called it then, "Thule".'

What he said was not strictly true, but I drank my pint in peace: no one likes a smart aleck. But as I sat at the bar I thought about how the idea that Shetland and Thule were the same place could have come about. When Pytheas wrote 'Concerning the Ocean' he stated quite clearly that Thule was six days sail north of the British Isles, which could not possibly mean Shetland.

After Pytheas the historical trail of exploration in the North went cold for over three hundred years. It was not until the arrival of the Romans in the first century AD that literate people would try again to sail so far into the ocean, and it was the Romans who mistook Shetland for Pytheas' Thule. Less than a generation after they crucified Jesus of Nazareth they had been pitched into their last battle to quell Caledonia once and for all. By then Pytheas' report had become myth. Because Britain lay across a stretch of ocean (the English Channel), the expanding Roman Empire thought it was the southerly tip of a whole new world. One Roman elegist wrote in praise of Claudius' early conquests in Britain after the invasion of AD 43, 'Ocean, the bounds of the world, is no longer bounds to our Empire.' I liked to think of those Romans standing where

Calais stands today, and thinking that instead of Kent, they were looking onto a magical New World.

A few decades later they had yet to capture Caledonia. By AD 80 it was clear that Roman expansion *had* been stopped, there *were* bounds to their Empire. Buoyed up by his early successes the Governor of Britain, General Julius Agricola, undertook an expedition to circumnavigate the British Isles. A brilliant military strategist, he wanted to claim all of the islands for Rome and explore the North from the water. Agricola's son-in-law, a bookish historian named Tacitus, reported on the journey. In his *Agricola* he wrote that as they rounded the northern cape of the British Isles, '… even Thule was seen in the distance, but their orders bade them go only so far; and besides, winter was coming on. But they did report that the sea was sluggish and hard to row against, and was barely stirred even by the winds.'

It is unclear whether they saw Orkney or Shetland in the distance. Either way the Romans chose to believe that they had sighted the Thule that Pytheas had described, and so reached the bounds of the Classical World. Tacitus thought that this one region would be forever closed to Rome as the edge of the earth had checked their progress, rather than an army.

Another attempt was made in AD 83 to conquer the whole of Britain. Confident after a victory on the banks of the river Forth near Edinburgh, one of Agricola's generals declared, 'We must drive deeper and deeper into Caledonia and fight battle after battle until we have reached the end of Britain!' They made it to a place they called 'Mons Graupius', probably in the Cairngorm Mountains, but were forced back by the miserable climate, the unforgiving terrain and the unanticipated ferocity of the Picts. Troops were needed for the German frontier, and so they gave up and turned south. Agricola himself was recalled to Rome in AD 84. They reassured themselves that they had seen the end of the earth, and did not need to go looking elsewhere for their Thule. The policy would be containment, not conquest – apparently the North was not worth fighting for.

Skirmishes continued across the border from Scotland into the Roman administered north of England throughout the rest of the Roman era. Their capital was Eburacum, now York, and it was repeatedly threatened by the Picts. In AD 120 the Emperor Hadrian gave orders to build his famous wall between Scotland and England to keep them out. A legend has survived, famously dramatised by the children's author Rosemary Sutcliff, surrounding the last attempt by the Romans to subdue the North. The Ninth Hispanic legion had distinguished itself in the German campaigns and in the conquest of the Iceni tribe of southeast England, led by Boadicea. Formed in Spain around 20 BC, it was one of the most feared legions of the Roman army. Chosen in the years around AD 140 to lead a final campaign to subdue the 'Caledonians', the entire legion crossed Hadrian's wall and then disappeared without trace. None of its soldiers were ever heard from again.

I was thinking about the Romans when my companion at the bar began to talk. He had red hair, freckled cheeks and sea-deep eyes. He had grown up surrounded by the sea, he told me, and his childhood was one of endless horizons and the high, free sound of gulls on the wing. As a youth he had joined the merchant navy and seen the world: the Persian Gulf, the South China Sea, the Malacca, Hormuz and Magellan Straits. Once in Buenos Aires after too much to drink he had joined in with a rabble of sailors and gone to a bordello. The next day he had stood in the shower scrubbing himself and vowed he would never see another whore. His tattoos were signed by a beautiful Australian artist he had met in Singapore. In the dusty, sticky heat of Calcutta and Antofagasta he had dreamed of Shetland.

'I've been in some horrible places,' he said, taking a long drink from his pint. 'My family's always been on the sea – my uncles were whalers in the Southern Ocean, they were all Shetland men down there.' His voice was slow and steady, paced with memory and self-assurance. His words were peppered with dialect that seemed as much Norse as English, and at times I strained to understand. He told me that a good job meant four months at sea, two months off. For years he had spent his leave on the family croft, working the peaty soil that had supported his family for generations. When his leave was over he had returned to the tankers of Arabia, Venezuela, Brunei.

One year on leave he met a girl from the Isle of Whalsay at a dance. The four months at sea began to drag more than ever. The partings became too much for him and he decided to come back to Shetland to stay. The family croft became his, and one bright morning he and his Whalsay girl married.

'Do you think you'll ever move anywhere else?' I asked.

'Oh no,' he replied, his face calm with the knowledge of his love for these islands. 'I'll die here'.

*

Outside the bar along the harbour were berthed a series of luxury Norwegian yachts. The Vikings had run out here from Bergen with an easterly wind in just under two days, and these yachts could do it faster. The men that crewed them were tall and self-assured, with blonde hair and wraparound sunglasses. I walked by the harbour admiring their yachts and listening to their speech, so similar in intonation to the accents of the Shetlanders. Climate change had made its mark here too; I heard of plans by the local council to raise the sea-defences of the harbour, to protect it against a rising sea level. The road was being cleared for a procession. Shetlanders take pride in their Norse ancestry and celebrate it once a year at Up Helly Aa, a festival in January where the men of the town dress as Vikings and set fire to a wooden ship. Today was one of their preparation marches – an opportunity to show off their magnificent costumes then retire to a pub to drink the rest of the afternoon away like true Vikings. The Norwegians in the yachts seemed thoroughly bemused by the whole display.

I wandered away up the hill to the Lerwick Town Library and Museum. It was a stiff concrete box of a building, but a new one was being constructed down by the harbour. Outside the door, carved panels of Pictish designs were propped against the wall. Inside Bronze Age pots were exhibited together with modern local sculptures. Norse weapons of war lay side by side with Scottish whaling harpoons. But the most interesting relics of Shetland lay in the landscape all around.

Clickhimin broch, one of the ancient towers used in the time of Pytheas, stood in a park just down the hill behind the museum. I sat on the turf, my back against the ancient stones, the sun warm on my face. Starling chicks cried out from nests deep within the broch walls, while their parents whirred in and out of the stonework around my head. The broch community may have been quite new in Pytheas' time, and I tried to imagine how the valley looked when he came by. Perhaps the people rowed out in their skin boats to meet his ship. Maybe they led him ashore, fascinated and afraid, hoping for a trade of fine cloth, metals, or the chance of some exotic foods. I imagined him striding taller than the people here, well dressed, with a retinue of guides and interpreters. He may have brought gifts, maps, rumours and stories for them, before beginning to ask about the length and harshness of the winters.He would have asked for tales of fishing and whaling expeditions that had been swept off course, and any lands they might have seen to the north.

It is a modern misconception that these people or their ancestors could not have known how to sail to Iceland or beyond. Pictish excavations on Shetland reveal traces of boats and indicate a success at whaling that imply they would have been easily capable of crossing the 160 miles of open sea to the Faroe Islands and the 240 miles from there to Iceland. The Pacific archipelagos were populated by people with inferior technology who were forced to make jumps between islands three and four times more distant. Bird migration routes would have passed over their heads leading to Iceland, and mirages caused by the layering of cold Arctic air can cast images of Iceland and the Faroes into the sky, making them visible hundreds of miles away. The Pictish Shetlanders could well have known about 'Thule' and guided Pytheas there.

So far there has been little evidence found in Iceland of any settlements of pre-Norse people: a few third-century Roman coins found in the sands of the south-east of the country (which may have arrived later), a moment's mention in the Norse mediaeval annals that there were Irishmen living there before the Vikings arrived. But the evidence of Pytheas' book should not be doubted on that basis alone – people may have only travelled to Thule seasonally, perhaps to hunt or take part in the easy harvest of eiderdown.

Only the drone of cars on the main road in the distance reminded me of the twenty-first century. The starlings had probably been nesting in these walls for millennia, the hillside was likely to have been as bare then as now, and the view over the fine sheltered bay the same.

The broch is in a relatively poor state. The winter storms and expanding ice have slowly worn it down and it was difficult to imagine how people lived in it. But a few miles down the coast lay another broch that was said to be the best preserved in the world. Standing on an island with few predators it has been taken over by one of the world's biggest storm petrel colonies. The 'stormies' are very timid birds that only come inland to feed their chicks during the short Shetland nights. A friend had told me that an evening spent watching and hearing the storm petrels returning to the broch was one of the most magnificent of his life. To get a better idea of Shetland as it looked to Pytheas, I wanted to see Mousa next.

*

Mousa is famous not only for being the best preserved broch in the world, but also because it was well known to the Vikings. *Egil's Saga* of the Icelanders describes how in the tenth century a Viking raider, Bjorn Brynjolfsson, abducted his lover Thora 'of the Embroidered

Hand' and eloped across the North Sea, with the wrath of Thora's father following fast behind them. On their way to Dublin they were shipwrecked on Mousa. The saga reports that, 'they were married there in Shetland, and spent the winter at the fort in Mousa'. When they set off again in the spring they were again blown away in a gale, this time all the way to Iceland. The Shetland and Orkney Islands have their own saga too, the *Orkneyingasaga*. A Shetland chieftain called Erlend the Young is described eloping to Mousa with Margaret, widow of the Earl of Atholl (the saga calls her a 'very forward woman'). The Earl of Orkney was her son, and he organised a siege to get her back. The lovers Margaret and Erlend withstood the siege and in the end were allowed to marry. Drama and intrigue seem bound into the history of Mousa Broch.

I hitched down to the ferry at Leebitton to catch one of the midnight tours to see the petrels. Down at the pier Tom Jamieson, boatman for the last thirty years, was ushering visitors onto his boat. I tiptoed past a baby seal sleeping on the beach. The coast and the gentle swell of the hills that rose above it were cut into a crisp silhouette, and a tense silence built between the passengers.

We arrived on the island before the adult petrels and walked the path from the jetty out to the broch in the twilight. It stood silhouetted against the sky, like a watchtower. Some petrels had nested between stones deep under the shingle beach and so the ground reverberated with a low chirrup and hum of petrel chicks calling out in expectation of their feed. Looking closely at the ground to avoid any chicks, I found a few of the tell-tale pipefish. Half-digested and then regurgitated, they were a sign that already, early in the season, some of the local seabirds were struggling to find enough food.

We crept inside the broch, its walls alive with the calling of the birds, using filtered torches so as not to upset them. It was over two thousand years since it was built, and a thousand since it had sheltered the fugitive Vikings, but the walls were still solid and the staircase that ran inside them intact.

At the foot of the broch the birds had started to return. I lay on my back, head to the wall and looked up as first a few, then hundreds, of the birds returned to their nests. They seemed too tiny to survive their migrations that bring them each year to Shetland from the seas off West Africa. In a fractal swirl their bodies danced around and around the broch, the sound of their wing-beats a susurration. In the northern sky I thought I could make out the softest hint of the aurora borealis, washing a gentle green glow into the sky. The Inuit believe that you can hear the Aurora, and lying there in the darkness I could not hear where its sound might have ended and that of the birds began.

*

The next stage of my journey was to follow the direction that Pytheas must have taken when he set out for Thule. After gathering what information he could he may have set off with another local guide, secure in the new knowledge that six days sail to the north there was new land, a land where the summer night was an hour or two at most, and from where he may have hoped to find news of land still further north. He took to the sea again, in search of the Hyperboreans. But another archipelago lies between Shetland and Iceland, one that does not seem to have been mentioned by any of Pytheas' critics in their attacks on his book. We will never know if Pytheas himself described it. The earliest written evidence we have of the Faroe Islands being visited is a few centuries later, when they seem to have become the home of a few fervent believers of a new religion coming out of the East.

The first literate peoples to have described the Faroes were Irish monks. Following an early form of Christianity that reached Ireland with St Patrick in the fifth century they took to their leather boats and established tiny monasteries throughout the Atlantic shores of Europe. The next stage of my journey would take me by ferry to the Faroes where I would follow their story.

The Faroe Islands
A DESERT IN THE OCEAN

※

It was two in the morning before I boarded the *Norrøna*, the ferry that ploughs the seas between Denmark, Norway and Iceland. I had been warned not to expect an easy crossing. The forecast was for dead calm, but once a year the Faroese senior high school pupils take over the ferry and travel to Denmark and back for an alcoholic blow-out on a scale that only Scandinavian teenagers seem to contemplate. By the time the ferry arrived in Shetland they had been drinking for well over twelve hours, and looked like continuing on all night. From the gangway I stumbled into a maelstrøm of drunkenness. Blonde teenage girls falling out of their dresses vomited over the deck. Young spotty guys hung in packs, smoking, and bumping into the walls. Weaving between bleary-eyed young men holding cans of lager I found the information desk and noticed that as well as information, they provided bulk-buy quantities of hangover remedies and condoms.

I found my way down five decks below to the bunks in the depths of the ship, near the keel, where rooms without locks had nine bunks each. I picked my way between piles of rucksacks and discarded underwear, and found an empty space to unroll my sleeping bag.

The next morning I stood at the rail on deck and watched the islands climb gradually over the horizon into view. After the gentle curves of Shetland they looked fearsomely steep. I wondered if I was going to have trouble finding enough flat land to camp on. My plan was to explore the islands by hitch-hiking and camping,

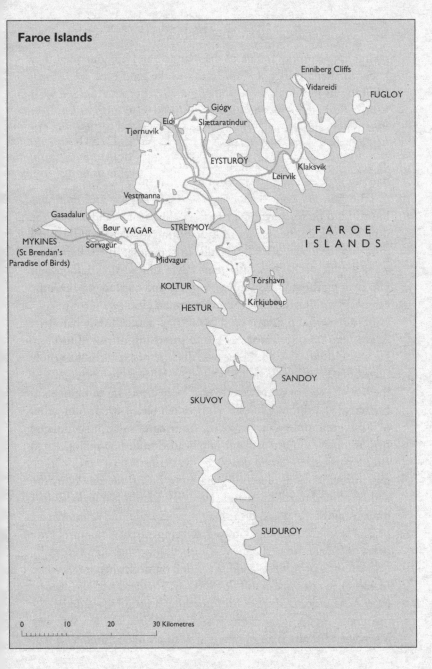

Faroe Islands

Enniberg Cliffs
Vidareidi
FUGLOY
Gjógv
Eldi
Tjørnuvik   Slættaratindur
EYSTUROY
Klaksvik
Leirvik
Vestmanna
FAROE
ISLANDS
Gasadalur
Bøur   VAGAR   STREYMOY
MYKINES
(St Brendan's   Sorvagur
Paradise of Birds)
Midvagur
KOLTUR
Tórshavn
HESTUR
Kirkjubøur
SANDOY
SKUVOY
SUDUROY

0   10   20   30 Kilometres

23

taking opportunities to talk to the islanders and find out what they
knew of their history. I wanted to see the landscape for myself,
climbing its mountains and walking its beaches, but also see what
I could find out about the Irish monks who were supposed to have
discovered, and named, the islands fifteen centuries before. The
Faroes have a strong Viking history too, and they are still inhabited
by a Scandinavian people. I hoped that the strength of that culture
had not washed away all traces of its earlier inhabitants.

The *Norrøna* drew into a large south-facing bay and then into
the harbour of Tórshavn, the capital of the Faroe Islands. From the
deck I could see the queues of cars waiting to board and be taken
onto the next port of call, Iceland. In the midst of the cars there
was a double-decker bus with 'Jesus Loves You' written in foot-high
letters along the side. As soon as we were tied up alongside and the
gangway was down, I made my way towards it.

Its driver was a reformed dipsomaniac, saved by the Salvation
Army, who had dedicated his life to preaching the word of God.
He was a slight man, with blue eyes that did not blink and a yellow
tinge of cigarette smoke in his white hair. He had been preaching in
the British Isles for over twenty years, he told me, and now went by
the name of Brother Clifford. He was not ordained, or a member
of a monastic order, but preached the word of God in the unique
manner that the Lord had communicated to him many years ago
after a particularly severe relapse of his alcoholism. It was a sort of
pilgrimage, he said; preaching had saved him from his addiction,
and he wanted to tell the world. The Faroe Islands had been his first
foreign ministry. I asked him what he would like to do next and he
paused before answering, 'Go back to my Lord. As we all will.' One
of his assistants then explained in hushed tones that he was actually
on his way to preach the 'good news' in Iceland. He had had a warm
reception in the smaller isles of Orkney, Shetland and the Faroes.
Now he was going to take on something a little bigger. In reaching out on a pilgrimage across the North Atlantic, he was in a way
repeating what the Irish monks had done a millennium and a half

earlier. I asked him what he thought of the North as a modern place to which to take a pilgrimage, but he replied obliquely. He looked away, ran his tar-stained fingers through his hair and then turned back to me. 'You see, I don't think about these things,' he sighed. 'The Lord leads and I follow.' His assistant ushered me off the bus. The queue of cars had begun to move forwards. 'I'm sorry, we're in a bit of rush, about to get on the ferry. Do you have a Bible?'

I shook my head.

'Here, take this.' Into my hand he pressed a small cloth-bound edition of the New Testament and Psalms. 'I've highlighted a few of my favourite passages. You should never travel in a foreign land without one.'

I thanked him and stood back from the bus. The door closed with a hiss, and Brother Clifford climbed into the driver's seat. His expression as he drove off spoke of absolute conviction, and the knowledge that there were still an awful lot of souls out there to save.

*

Tórshavn feels like a village that has outgrown itself. Its streets and brightly coloured houses clamber up the hillsides from the harbour, spattered like paint on a landscape that seems barely to tolerate them. Near the centre of town sheep graze by the traffic lights and pizza parlours. The mountains rise sheer out of the sea around the bay, looking as if in an afternoon they could shrug off the evidence of a thousand years of human habitation. Caught in the middle of weather systems sweeping the Gulf Stream, the islands are soaked in a caliginous fog for much of the year. Though their winters are mild, Atlantic depressions spin around them in every season. Their storms are legendary.

I walked up from the ferry terminal towards a fortress, built by the Danes to protect their interests against Basque pirates over three hundred years ago. Old brass cannons now aim at Russian trawlers and passenger ferries steaming back and forth across the bay. By the side of the fort a group of boys had found a starling nest. Shooting an air pistol and squealing with laughter they threw the fledgling at one another. It cried and tried to flap away from them, but it was not fully fledged, and soon fell silent. Once they were sure it was dead they ran off shrieking into the town.

I lay on my back in the grass overlooking the bay, and opened a translation of the *Navigatio Sancti Brendani Abbatis* or 'The Voyage of St Brendan the Abbott', first written in Latin in the eighth century but describing events that took place two hundred years earlier. It is often known by scholars as simply, the *Navigatio*. The story is one of the most extraordinary examples both of early mediaeval literature and of the exploration of the North Atlantic. It also includes the first written descriptions of the Faroe Islands. It follows on from the Celtic tradition of the *Immram*, or magical journey, but it is also rich in factual and geographical detail. It seems that Brendan did sail across the North Atlantic sometime in the early sixth century AD. Some believe that he made it to North America, and the descriptions in the *Navigatio* point to his reaching at least as far as Iceland. I knew that travelling around the Faroe Islands it would be difficult to link exactly the places mentioned in the *Navigatio* with places today, but I was optimistic I would be able to find some connections. Among other leads there is a description in the book of an island that was almost certainly Mykines, one of the smallest and westernmost of the Faroes, and I wanted to try and reach it. There were two islands, the Dímuns, whose names are related etymologically to Old Irish, not Norse. There was also a valley in the north where traces of the same type of oats used by the Irish in the Middle Ages have been found, farmed there centuries before the Vikings arrived. But as much as the places to visit, there were modern themes that I had started to pick up on in Shetland and wanted to explore in the Faroes, of a people rooted in an unforgiving landscape, of the threat of depopulation, of the North as a place that people still seek out as part of a search for peace, as Brendan did.

His journey was not unique, it is just that sadly most accounts of sea-pilgrimages undertaken by his contemporaries are lost. We know that throughout the early mediaeval period the monks spread out from Ireland both south and north in boats of tanned ox-hide. They often left their destination to the wind and the waves, and many must have drowned. Some settled on the west coast of Scotland (such as Columba who settled on the small island of Iona). Brendan himself was reputed to have founded a monastery on the Hebridean island of Tiree. From there they reached the Orkney Islands and beyond. Through their name of *Papar* or 'Fathers' they left their legacy scattered throughout the islands they visited. Often it is the smallest and most barren of them that still bear their name: in Orkney Papa Westray and Papa Stronsay, in Shetland Papa Stour, in Iceland Papos and Papey. Even on the thin soils of the North Atlantic the layers of history lie thickly on the land.

The so-called 'Dark Ages' were a time when Europe seemed to forget about the gains that had been made by Greek and Roman scholarship and looked in upon itself again. During the sixth and seventh centuries AD the Irish monks were some of the few literate Europeans who still tried to look outwards, and at a crucial point in history managed to keep some of the older knowledge traditions alive. They had read Pliny and Aristotle, knew Tacitus' accounts of Agricola's campaign, and that the earth was round like 'a well-formed apple.' Though they knew the sea and were skilled navigators, it seems that they lacked the desire to map the ocean and record the currents and winds to help those coming later. Like the Immrama before them they considered their journeys on a magical level, as pilgrimages of the soul, not voyages of exploration. As a result their stories are catalogues of wonders recalled after years at sea rather than ships logs. Reading them is an exercise in the imagination, and in faith.

*

Reading between the lines of the *Navigatio* it shines through that Brendan was a powerful man, loved by all who met him, whose soul knew no rest and whose eyes seemed to burn with the glory of God. Since becoming a Christian he had sailed the whole coast of Ireland and Wales, shared Holy Communion with Columba on Iona and tutored Malo, the Breton saint. Apparently Brendan was to be understood as a man of the sea as well as a warrior of Christ. He and his contemporaries believed with the ardour of the newly converted and were inspired by tales of the Desert Fathers that arrived muted and distorted by the long passage from the Holy Land. Ireland of the sixth and seventh centuries was apparently too comfortable, too fertile, too busy. But on their doorstep lay uncharted archipelagos of islands stretching out into the north, and in lieu of a drier desert to retreat to they called these islands 'the desert in the Ocean'. Some of them made a profound impression on the places they ended up in. For example, one of Brendan's contemporaries, Columbanus, is known to have set himself adrift from Ireland in an ox-hide boat before eventually washing up in Brittany. He wandered through what is now France, Switzerland and Italy for decades before setting up a monastery at Bobbio, south of Milan. His monastic rule survives and his town is thriving today (and he has recently been declared the patron saint of motorbikers).

But Brendan's story begins rather differently. He did not fall upon his voyage by chance, he planned for it as meticulously as modern explorers make preparations. The *Navigatio* explains how.

Barinthus, the abbott of the monastery of Drumcullen, and a relative of Brendan, came to see him as he was 'engaged in spiritual warfare' on a meadow near his home at Clonfert. He brought news of a land he had found over the seas, a land he called 'the Promise of the Saints'. Brendan listened carefully to Barinthus' tale of how he had sailed westwards until he came to great fog banks on the sea. Beyond the fog banks he had found a land where precious stones were strewn on the ground, every tree was a fruit tree, night never fell and in fifteen days of walking he could not find the farther shore.

Brendan meditated and prayed on Barinthus' words all through the night before he reached a decision. The next day he gathered together fourteen of his most faithful monks and addressed them:

'My most beloved co-warriors in spiritual conflict. I beg you to help me with your advice, for I am consumed with a desire so ardent that it casts every other thought and desire out of my heart. I have resolved, if it be God's will, to seek out that Land of the Promise of the Saints which our father Barinthus described. What do you think of my plan? Have you any advice to offer?"

They replied, 'Father, your will is ours too. Have we not left our parents and set aside our earthly inheritance in order to put ourselves completely in your hands? We are prepared to come with you, no matter what the consequences may be. We seek to do one thing alone – the will of God.'

He and his monks then observed a series of fasts for forty days in preparation for the dangers of their voyage. Only then did they set to work on their boat.

> Brendan and his companions made a coracle, using iron tools. The ribs and frame were of wood, as is the custom in those parts, and the covering was tanned ox-hide stretched over oak bark. They greased all the seams on the outer surface of the skin with fat and stored away spare skins inside the coracle, together with forty days' supplies, fat for waterproofing the skins, tools and utensils. A mast, a sail and various pieces of equipment for steering were fitted into the vessel; then Brendan commanded his brethren in the name of the Father, Son, and Holy Spirit to go aboard.

This account in the *Navigatio* of how Brendan built his boat was so detailed that in 1976 it inspired the writer and explorer Tim Severin to try to replicate their journey. Severin's career reads like a Boy's Own story. While still a student at Oxford he followed by motorcycle the route Marco Polo took to China. He has re-enacted Sinbad's voyage from Arabia to China, floated a bamboo raft across the Pacific, followed Jason and his Argonauts in rowing a galley across the Mediterranean into the Black Sea, and ridden Crusader routes from Europe to Jerusalem on horseback. He has received medals from the Scottish and the British Royal Geographical Societies and has become a successful novelist, setting a trilogy in the Viking Age. One of his more dangerous projects was what he called 'The Brendan Voyage'.

He found that even the smallest details described in the *Navigatio* were necessary to make a boat of hide successfully. As an example, the text specifies that the ox-hide must be stretched over oak bark. Severin experimented with the properties of ox-hide and found that tanned in this way it became two to three times more resilient to seawater than hide tanned in any other way. He heard that in the west coast of Ireland boats similar in shape and design to these *curraghs*, or coracles, were still used (though made of modern materials), and he went there to learn how to sail them. In Cornwall he found a tannery that was still able to tan ox-hide to his specifications – and he needed 49 hides to make a sea-worthy boat. The frame needed to be strong and light, and in Ireland he searched out ash trees growing in shaded, rocky soil which grew slowly enough to given the wood the supple strength it needed. The frame was lashed together with leather thongs. Though the *Navigatio* mentions only one sail, Severin found that without two it was impossible to handle, and so he altered the design. With a crew of only three, as opposed to Brendan's fifteen, he set sail in spring from Brandon's Creek on the Dingle peninsula of Ireland's west coast.

Severin sailed directly from Ireland to the Outer Hebrides in Scotland, and from there crossed over to the Faroe Islands, missing out Orkney and Shetland. This may well have followed Brendan's route, as it is not clear whether some of the earlier islands he visited were in the Hebrides or in the Northern Isles. He found that the coracle handled beautifully in most weather conditions. The leather seemed to muffle the slap of the waves against the hull, and flexing itself at the joints, it seemed to mould itself to the sea. He found that whales seemed to be fascinated by the boat, perhaps by its unusual acoustic properties, and he was visited regularly by schools of dolphins. The *Navigatio* too mentioned numerous encounters with whales and 'great fishes'.

In the Faroe Islands Severin arrived at the island of Mykines, which Brendan called 'the Paradise of Birds' because of the gulls and auks that he found nesting there. He describes guiding the coracle through clouds of birds feeding in the waters around its cliffs. In the Faroes too he picked up another crew member, Tronđur Patursson, whose skills at navigating through the storms and tidal rips of the Faroes proved invaluable later on (Tronđur was also to prove himself as an Argonaut on Severin's later 'Jason Voyage'.) They reached Iceland by late summer, and after wintering the boat there, returned in spring to complete the journey past Greenland and through the ice-fields of the Davis Strait to make landfall in Newfoundland.

Before Severin proved it could be done, it had been doubted that Brendan's 'Land of the Promise of the Saints' could really represent North America. It was assumed that such a fragile boat would be destroyed by the months at sea, or the pack ice that flows down out of the Arctic. At one point Severin's craft was actually holed by ice, but with simple materials he and Tronđur managed to patch the hole almost immediately; the *Navigatio* specifies that Brendan packed spare hides to make repairs. His success provoked a reappraisal of the legend, and won him a famous reputation. His book of the Brendan Voyage inspired a music album (one track is dedicated entirely to the sound impressions of the birds on approaching Mykines) and the journey is something that as a lecturer he is still asked to comment on, more than thirty years later.

*

Up the hill behind the town was the Faroese National Museum. It was an uninspiring grey rectangle on an industrial estate. The receptionist told me that it had been converted hurriedly from a furniture warehouse after rising Faroese nationalism had demanded the return of national treasures from the museums of Copenhagen.

The Danish seemed to have acquiesced unexpectedly quickly and caught the museum organisers on the back foot. The warehouse was the only available building which could take the air-conditioning required to preserve the delicate cloths and wood carvings that were to be exhibited there. One day, she told me, they would build something a little more impressive.

I was the only visitor. Much was made of the Viking heritage of the islands; jokingly it was said to have been settled by Norsemen on their way to Iceland who had found themselves too seasick to complete the journey. In sequence around its walls, crudely carved runestones of the first settlers gave way to the artefacts of mediaeval Catholicism, which in turn led on to the history of the islands as a protectorate under the Danish Empire. There were elaborate friezes depicting the severity of life in the nineteenth century, with mannequins dressed in coarse woollen cloth mending nets or hunched over fireplaces. Sepia photographs of workers and fishwives showed a strong community of lively faces, weatherworn and prematurely aged.

Displayed in the subdued lighting of the basement were treasure hoards hidden and never recovered by Norsemen that suggested trade networks stretching from Greenland to the Islamic Caliphate. There was a remarkable sequence of carved wooden pews that had been preserved from the fires of the Reformation, and a display of traditional fishing boats. But there was no sign of Brendan. The only hint of Irish influence I could find was a display showing three stuffed sheep, and a notice explaining that the Faroe Islands may have originally meant 'the Islands of Sheep' in Old Irish. These three, it explained, had been shot on Lítla Dímun in 1860, and it was thought that they were the last of a very primitive breed that was first brought to the islands from Ireland well over a thousand years before. Analysis of their bones has shown they were related to other primitive breeds such as the *loaghtan* of Shetland and Man, the wild short-tailed sheep of St Kilda, and even show similarities with the sheep bones that have been found at the Bronze Age settlement of Skara Brae in Orkney. Across Europe these primitive sheep have now been interbred with fatter, woollier cousins, but on Orkney I had once visited a flock of about a thousand still living on the remote island of North Ronaldsay. They survived because rather than be killed off and replaced during the agricultural 'improvements' of the nineteenth century they were instead forced off the green pasture onto the beach. They survived by eating seaweed, and remarkably evolved to cope with the poor mineral content of their diet. I was told that one of these primitive sheep cannot now survive a normal pasture because they extract so many minerals from the grass that they poison themselves. They are also unnaturally long-lived, prompting a Japanese firm to investigate the properties of alginates in Atlantic seaweeds as an elixir of youth.

I turned back to study the stuffed ones. They were wiry and goat-like, with thick black wool and powerful legs for springing up and down the cliffs. Looking into their glass eyes I felt closer to the lives of Brendan and his monks, imagining the hillsides around grazed by flocks of these animals that survived here almost to the present day. There was sadness, too, that with the death of the last one something of those Irishmen was gone forever.

The receptionist could not give me any more information about Brendan or whether there were any more traces left in the islands of the passage of the first Irish settlers. 'But there is someone who might be able to help you,' she said, taking out a map of the town. 'You need to go down to the other museum.'

I stepped out of the warehouse into the sunlight and followed the path she had sketched on the map. It skirted over a couple of fields and across the main road out of town before dropping down to the shore.

A collection of traditional wooden houses stood near the beach. Chickens and geese scratched in the yard, protesting noisily as I walked through the middle of them. I knocked on one of the doors and went in. The house had been restored to show a traditional Faroese home of about a century ago. It was dark inside, and smelled of pine and smoke. The curator sat at what would have once been the kitchen table, scored with decades of knife-cuts. He nodded and gestured to my boots and I saw that I should take them off and leave them at the door. Light fell in from the window casting the lines of his face in relief, and adding a silver edge to his white hair.

'I'm wondering if you can help me,' I said. 'I've heard that there were Irish monks here in the Faroe Islands before the Vikings arrived, and I wondered if there are any traces of them left. Someone at the other museum told me you might know.' There was a lengthy pause. A grandfather clock in the next room ticked loudly.

'Yes yes, you're quite right' he said at last. 'There were Irish here, maybe even still living alongside the Norwegians and marrying with them after they arrived.'

'And the book, the Voyage of St Brendan, do you know it?' I asked.

'Of course.'

'Is it known where he went here in the Faroes?'

'Not so much, not so much, we have to guess a bit. Have you a map?'

I took out my map and laid it on the table. 'So, you see this place?' He pointed out a small bay marked as 'Brandans vik'.

'"Brendan's Bay"; "vik" means bay, like "Vik-ings." They called themselves that because they went robbing and stealing in bays.' He sighed as if in mild disapproval of the violence of his ancestors. 'Brendan's Bay. So maybe he was there. I don't know how many centuries ago it was given this name.'

I saw on the map that the bay was next to the oldest church in the islands, and the ruined cathedral. 'Was there an old church there before the present one,' I asked, 'an old Irish chapel that the Norse would have built their own church on top of?'

'Now, that I don't know. Excuse me a moment.' He took a mobile phone out of his pocket and with great deliberation punched in a number from a crumpled piece of paper. After a pause I heard the connection and he began to speak. Listening to a language of which you have no knowledge at all can be like following music in a style you've never heard. Faroese had none of the flat vowels of Danish; the consonants were soft and the vowels rounded, rising up suddenly through the words like bubbles. I recognised only a few words, 'Brandan', 'Ireland', 'Vestmenn'. He hung up.

'We don't think so. I don't think traces of a chapel have been found there. But there is a town further up, see here,' he indicated on the map, 'called Vestmanna. That's what we call Irishmen, the men of the West. It's likely that they did go on living here. Someone did a study of the Faroese people and found that genetically we were all a mix-up of Irish and Norwegian.'

'How did they manage to work that out?' I asked.

'There's a way you can tell if the gene comes from the mother's line or the father's line, and they found a strange thing. That of the ones that come from your father 80 per cent were Norwegian and 20 per cent Irish, but the ones that came from your mother were the other way round, 80 per cent Irish and 20 per cent Norwegian. I think that's what they found. And no one knows if it's because of all the Irish that were living here, or because the Vikings brought slaves and wives back from Ireland, or because in the early days the Irish monks could have women with them. But it's very interesting nonetheless.'

'And where do you think I should go?' I asked him. 'To see the places that Brendan probably saw.'

'Oh I don't know for sure, but take your time and see the islands. We've got the highest cliff in Europe here you know, up in the north, and you could see a lot of the islands from up there.' His finger traced over the map. 'And this is Mykines and Vágar, where he probably went, and you should certainly go and see the church at Brandan's vik.'

'And where was it they found the pollen of the Irish oats?' I asked, as I had read about traces of Dark Ages agriculture that had been discovered in the islands.

'At Tjornuvik, here.' He pointed at another small bay, up at the

end of one of the long ridges that stretched like a finger out towards
the Arctic Ocean. 'But there's not much special to see there at this
time of the year, just another pretty little village. In the autumn you
can go there on *stakksdagur*, the day that they start the slaughter of
the rams that are left out all summer. But I don't think there is a lot
there for you to see right now.'

'It's a pity I won't be here in the autumn,' I said to him. 'You've
been a wonderful help,' I added, going to the door and starting to
put on my boots. 'Thank you very much.'

'Don't mention it. Just make sure you enjoy visiting our islands.
There's nowhere else quite like them.'

*

I went down to the harbour to look at the yachts. One had sailed all
the way from Melbourne. Another that looked too small to brave the
North Atlantic flew a Swedish flag. I reminded myself that Severin
had proven just what was possible with a small boat, and on second
thoughts it looked a lot more comfortable than a coracle.

It had just started to rain. A man standing nearby turned to
me and pointed at the boat. 'Do you want to buy it?' he asked me.
'It's for sale. The Swedish girl who owns it has fallen in love with
an American here. They're selling it to get something bigger.' For a
moment I was tempted.

'Do you know how much they are selling it for?'

'Oh, 40,000 kroner I think,' he said. It seemed like a bargain, but
I decided against trying to sail from here to Iceland. I would never
complete my journey in a season if I tried to find a crew and sail it.
'Maybe one day,' I said to him, 'but I don't think I would make it
back home anytime soon and would probably get myself killed.'

He laughed. 'Where is your home?' he asked.

'Scotland,' I said.

'A Scotsman! And why have you come to visit our rainy set of
islands?'

'Well…' I wondered where to start explaining.

'Why don't you tell me over some dinner,' he said. 'Would you like to come and meet my wife?'

*

Peter Hjørleif was a Faroese patriot. He drove me to his house, and his wife Berlina spread out a feast of rye bread, cheese and Faroese jam for us to eat. Their daughter Elin joined us too, and together we talked about holidays we had taken both in Scotland and all over Europe. They preferred bus tours to flights and loved to travel, but they were always glad to get back to the Faroes. Peter told me his ancestry: his grandfather was from the small island of Hestur and his grandmother from the even smaller island Koltur but he himself had grown up on Sandoy, one of the main Faroese islands to the south. 'You must go to visit all these places if you can!' he said, his enthusiasm infectious. He remembered the men from Koltur coming over to his island to cut peats, and then he would help them carry the peat back as it had a community of only forty in those days. 'And you know now it has only one,' he shook his head. 'But you know every Faroese has the right to electricity. So that one man is paid to maintain and run a generator. He is given free fuel, but then he has to pay his electricity bill like the rest of us! It's a wonderful system we have here in the Faroes.'

He trained as a fitter, and at twenty years old started work as a stoker on trawlers in the North Atlantic and over in the Davis Strait. Later he joined the merchant navy as an engineer, based in Copenhagen, and told me a story about taking cargo from the American military airbase of Thule in Greenland to Virginia, and then taking on new cargo for the Americans down to the Panama Canal and on to Tierra del Fuego. 'And we never did find out what we were carrying for them.' One spring afternoon in Copenhagen a friend confided in him that it would break Berlina's heart if they were never to return to the Faroes. He resigned the next day, and took a job teaching back in the college in Tórshavn. Berlina smiled at the memory and filled my teacup.

'Living in Tórshavn is wonderful, it's a perfect size, and everyone is friendly. We have a very strong community here,' she said. 'It was the right decision.'

I had heard that the Faroese still practised whale hunts as a community. These islanders who have embraced the modern world in so many ways had hung onto some of their oldest traditions, including the pilot whale hunts which are called *grind*. I asked Peter about them.

'You want to ask about the grind. What can I say…' He spread his hands out on the table and a slow grin stretched across his face. 'I love to eat whale! And you must know that eating whale is good for you!'

Pilot whales move in schools, he explained, and sometimes they become confused and stray into the blind-ended fjords that slice like axe-wounds deep into the Faroes. When a school of grind are sighted (the whale and its hunt have the same name), a call goes out through the village and the men take to their boats. They form a fence behind the school, and cutting the backs of the whales from the boats with special knives designed for the purpose they drive them up onto the beach. The whales flail around in the shallows while the men run between them, trying to kill the whales humanely by quickly cutting through the neck of each one. In each community the whale meat is shared out fairly between all the members, with a little extra going to whoever first sighted them.

'One of my ancestors came over from Denmark as a Lutheran minister in the eighteenth century,' Peter went on. 'The people still practised Catholicism in secret and because he had studied medicine before entering the ministry he was called on more as a doctor than a churchman.' In those days, he explained, there was only one doctor walking and sailing around the islands slowly through the cycle of seasons, visiting each settlement on a rotation, and staying until he had seen each of the villagers. Scrupulous records of these visits were kept.

'The records show that whenever a village was lucky enough to

lure the grind into their fjord, the health of everyone improved,'
he said. 'And we have a saying in the Faroes, "A knifeless man is a
lifeless man!"'

In a beautiful photographic book about the Faroe Islands by
Gunnie Moberg and Liv Schei I had read of a tradition that the
hunt will be unsuccessful if women or clergymen watch from the
shore, and of a song that the men sing while butchering the meat
which translated goes something like, 'Strong lads are we, to kill
the grind that is our joy!' Environmental activists have understand-
ably taken a dim view of the grind, and the devolved Faroese government have been the target of quite a few campaigns to ban it.
Their defence is admirably succinct: for centuries the islands have
relied on the slaughter to supplement a poor diet, and foreign governments and liberal urbanites should mind their own business.

The conversation moved on, and I told them that I was interested in finding out more about St Brendan. They knew of Tim
Severin's Brendan Voyage, and told me they were related to Trondur
Patursson, who is father-in-law to their son Pauli. 'You must have
a look at his latest book,' Peter said, and brought out a recently
published coffee-table volume of Trondur's paintings. Thirty years
since the Brendan and Jason Voyages he was now an established artist. There were several photographs of the artist in various stages of
his career. In one he was standing on Severin's ox-hide coracle beset
by ice off Canada, caught by the camera in the act of throwing a
harpoon at a whale. He looked like a man who would be as happy
to move backwards in time as forwards. His paintings and sculpture
were varied in style, often abstract in form, and seemed to speak
more of his character and that of the elements around him than of
the subject of each work. His approach is diverse; I heard about the
light installations he placed deep in the tunnels of the Faroes, and
looked through photographs of his paintings and sculpture. They
were untamed, like the weather of his islands and the hair and beard
that he wore. It was difficult to imagine his work without considering the context of the islands that had formed him.

'But you should meet him!' Berlina said. 'He would like the idea of your journey very much.'

'No, he's off the island at the moment,' said Elin. 'He's in Denmark.' I was disappointed to have missed meeting one of only three men who have sailed the North Atlantic as Brendan did, in a little leather boat.

Outside the rain was easing. Peter and Berlina showed me out, past framed prints of more of Trondur's paintings. I gave them my address in Edinburgh, and told them they were welcome to come and visit me any time. 'I will hold you to that,' Peter smiled. 'You know we are like cousins, the Scots and the Faroese. Together we are a mix up of Vikings and Irishmen!'

I slept at the campsite and next morning shouldered my rucksack again and wandered through the town. Tiny alleyways sloped off from the streets at improbable angles. Many of the houses were turf-roofed and built of wood, a precious commodity in those islands. Peter had told me that nothing beats turf for cutting out the sound of an Arctic storm. In many of the restaurants I saw *Lunda*, or puffin, on the menu. I asked if I could try some but was told that it was not the season. I'd need to wait until their chicks had fledged and then the islanders would maybe start catching them. No one knew if the sandeels would be scarce this year and the puffin numbers would suffer. It had been noticed that when they had a bad breeding year the lack of guano fertilising the hillsides had a knock-on effect on the sheep, which might weigh as much as ten pounds less when the time for slaughter arrived. The balance of nature in the North Atlantic seemed so delicate.

From the hill over the headland I made my way across a bare scree and rubble plateau. To the north, fog was rolling in over the islands, cloaking the hillsides in a net of gossamer that slipped gently towards Tórshavn. To the south the sky was much clearer. When I reached the crest of the hill I saw the sun shining down on the

sheer slopes of the southern islands, their cliff faces soaring over
a calm ocean. Hestur and Koltur were the first islands across the
sound, their names meaning 'horse' and 'colt', and I saw at once
how they seemed to trot along together, heading west out of the
sound. Koltur looked more of an improbable fantasy than a real
island of rock and grass, a pillar of stone towering over the waves.
Before me a path fell steeply down towards Brendan's Bay, and the
old church of Kirkjubøer.

The church was built in the eleventh century, and from a distance it seemed to lie against the shore like a beached ship, its hull
overturned, bleached by the centuries. Beside it, to the south-east,
I could make out the grey, ruined cathedral which was a couple of
centuries younger, and to the north-west a small harbour.

Once down at the shoreside I saw that the old church's immense-
ly thick walls were whitewashed and interrupted by only four plain
windows angled out over the sound to the south. Inside there was
a deep silence, broken only by the distant and occasional beats of a
hammer coming from one of the fishing boats tied up in the harbour
outside. An old crozier from the cathedral's days as a bishop's seat lay
in a glass cabinet beneath the altar. It had been found buried beneath
the cathedral. Above it hung an abstract painting of Christ calming
the waters. It was difficult to imagine the generations of people who
had worshipped there; from the mediaeval monks through all the
ages of European history, this building supporting a community that
depended on the sea and had reason to pray for it to be merciful.
I stood between the intricately carved wooden pews and looked out
across the waters, where so many had anxiously watched, and prayed,
for the return of loved ones. If there was an Irish chapel on Faroe in
Brendan's day I thought, it may well have stood here.

The few surnames in the graveyard told of a small, tight community, rooted in this earth. Many of them bore the surname of Patursson, and Peter had told me that Trondur's family had been living
in the turf-roofed house overlooking the graveyard for seventeen
generations. He himself had designed and made the churchyard

gate. He had built a cross modelled on an early Norse symbol found etched on a stone nearby, framing it in steel and inlaying it with blue glass. With the sun high in the sky it channelled and filtered the sunlight, sprinkling an ocean's iridescence on the dry earth.

The Patursson family still used part of the old house, known as the *Roykstovan* or 'smoke room,' but most of it was made into a museum. After paying into the honesty box I wandered in rooms made of ancient driftwood, and caught a glimpse of a life that had lain unchanged by the passing storms of history, its rhythms instead governed only by the winds, seas and tides of the North Atlantic. It is the oldest inhabited wooden house in Europe, having been built nine hundred years before as the bishop's residence. Now its corners were stacked with whaling harpoons and fishing gear, an old stove and a display of knives that must have seen the deaths of hundreds of *grind*. The smoke-stained beams were low and dark, but a column of light fell from a modern window that had been cut into the roof.

Outside the main room a series of models showed the cathedral as it evolved over the centuries, never being finished, before falling into ruin following the Reformation. An avalanche in 1772 from the cliffs above had destroyed the western wall. There were plans to restore it, and a gantry had been constructed over the whole structure to preserve it from the wind and rain. Afterwards I walked in it but it felt only cold and empty. It had none of the strength or the simplicity of the old church by the bay.

✳

I hitched a lift north with Bjorn, a Faroese lawyer who worked for the World Trade Organisation in Geneva. While his work took him to Japan, Latin America, Greenland, and China, he returned to the Faroes with his son once a year. He wanted his son's Swiss-French sophistication grounded in the earth and seas of his ancestors.

'His name is Hugin,' he told me. 'One of the old god Óðin's ravens.' The teenage boy shifted uncomfortably in his seat. 'Óðin and Hugin travelled the whole world together.' He looked down at the boy and smiled. 'I hope his name will inspire him to travel far.'

We drove through green valleys hemmed in by grey cliffs, past more small homesteads with turfed roofs. But for the occasional bus shelter the landscape looked as if it had been unaltered for centuries. Bjorn told me he had studied in Copenhagen.

'Is it normal to leave the islands to study?' I asked him.

'There is a small college here where you can study agriculture and fisheries, they are teaching more and more here as years go by. But yes, for most university subjects you have to leave.'

'And do many people stay away?' I wanted to find out if the Faroese were facing the same problems as the Shetland Islanders.

'Sadly yes, like me, many people stay away. But there is a scheme now, all students who leave to study are given a return ticket home by the government, from anywhere in the world! It's a way to try and keep people connected with the Faroes.'

We moved on to talk about the education system, and he told me that traditionally they have always had to study Danish at school, but there is more and more of a move towards studying English as a second language and making Danish optional. It was part of a growing trend towards independence from Denmark. They were keen to have closer ties with the UK too. For many years the Faroese shipping line, Smyril, had connected them to Denmark, Norway, Shetland and Iceland but never mainland Scotland. In Shetland I had heard rumours that Smyril were going to stop calling in Lerwick altogether and call only on the Scottish mainland instead. Shetlanders were outraged because their council had recently invested several million pounds in the link, and the Shetland Development Trust are themselves the biggest shareholders in the Faroese shipping line. Despite having just arrived from Geneva, Bjorn knew all about the dispute, and told me it was a hot topic in Tórshavn too.

'Every time they call in Shetland they lose money, they spend more in harbour fees than they ever get in passengers or freight.

It's just bad business. Calling in Scotland would change that. We could build stronger trade links with them, and they're our closest neighbours after all.' (On getting back to the UK a few months later I read in the newspaper that a compromise had been reached. The *Norrøna* would call in first at Thurso in the Scottish Highlands and then at Lerwick after all. For a few years at least.)

'But about a quarter of the money here comes as direct funding from Denmark,' he added. 'Too much independence from them could be a dangerous thing for the economy here.' He gave an example of a recent crash in the North Atlantic fisheries. With no fish, the Faroese had almost nothing to export, and had depended on handouts from Denmark to survive. Recently the whole saithe fleet had been asked to stop fishing altogether. But oil fields were being explored in Faroese waters since then. As they were deep and under areas prone to storms, it would be difficult oil to extract and would be unlikely to turn the Faroe Islands into another Gulf State. But it might be enough to safeguard their economy for a few decades.

'I think we'll be alright, here in the Faroes,' Bjorn said. 'We've survived out here in the ocean for a thousand years, not bothering others, and nobody has bothered too much about us.' He crinkled his eyes in a smile. 'I think we've got another thousand or so.'

The next day I reached the northernmost point of the Faroe Islands, which also happen to be the highest sea cliffs in Europe that the curator in Tórshavn had told me about. The cliffs are called Enniberg, great bulwarks of basalt nearly three thousand feet high, torn into needles by the winter storms which come shrieking out of the Arctic. I had struggled up the slope, ducking skuas which swooped down on me, but was rewarded with a magnificent view from the top. I sucked icicles broken off the cliff face and swung my legs over the edge. Far below my feet the waves frothed on the rocks, a distant smudge of cream on the slate-grey stone. Near the water's surface, seven hundred metres below, fulmars circled on the up-draughts of air like motes of dust in a column of light. The cliffs faced onto the Norwegian Sea, fanning out into the Arctic Ocean where the sea, sky and horizon were merged together in layers of soft blue.

Behind me to the south were the eighteen islands of the Faroes; separated by narrow and broad sounds, joined by innumerable tunnels, bridges and ferries, fracturing the sea around them like a broken mirror. An old Norse legend said that they had been formed from the fingernails of a god who had dropped them out of the skies into the ocean. The truth was only a little less striking – they were the peaks of an underwater mountain range called the Wyville-Thomson Ridge. Despite being unheard of in most geography classrooms this ridge deserves a renown to match the Andes, Himalayas and the Alps: it forms the biggest underwater barrier between bodies of water anywhere in the globe. To the north of it lies the Arctic basin all the way to the Bering Straits, and to the south the Atlantic which joins and mingles freely with the Pacific and the Indian Oceans. The Wyville-Thomson has divided them for millions of years so successfully that the types of deepwater fish on either side have evolved quite independently. The channels between the Arctic Ocean and the Atlantic had been coming under ever greater scrutiny in recent years not only for the different types of fish they divide but for the clues they might give to the future climate of the whole of the North Atlantic. Flow through the Faroe Bank Channel that divides the Faroes from Shetland has been found to be in decline. Not only that, but the water that is flowing down into the Atlantic has been found to be becoming steadily less salty due to meltwater from the gradually warming Arctic. Senior oceanographers and climatologists, such as Bogi Hansen of the Faroese Fisheries Laboratory, have published warnings that these changes could soon tip the delicate balance of the ocean's currents and divert the Gulf Stream itself. They believe that the lighter, fresher water from the Arctic may soon start to form a thin cold layer, floating *on top of* the warm, dense, saltier water that arrives from the Tropics with the Gulf Stream. This could have catastrophic cooling consequences for both western Europe and the north-east of the United States and Canada. Some predict that within a few years of the breakdown of these currents (collectively known as the Oceanic Conveyor) the warming of the Arctic could suddenly reverse, like a switch turning, and average temperatures of the North Atlantic could plummet (although the rest of the planet will continue to heat up). The loss of the circulation of water, and the gases and nutrients that it carries, could also have unpredictable effects on marine life and commercial fisheries. It was difficult to imagine how changes in the movements of water below my feet could have global repercussions on our climate and our future.

I started to think about Brendan again, and how he saw these islands when he arrived in the sixth century. He came at a time when climatologists have told us the North Atlantic was experiencing one of its warmer phases. It is likely that the islands were populated with small communities of monks back then, monks that had set off from Ireland decades earlier and had been scraping a life with their sheep and oats, fishing in the rivers and fjords. The *Navigatio* is filled with short vignettes of the anchorites that he encountered, either living alone on tiny islands or in scattered small communities across the North Atlantic, much as the Greek Orthodox *skiti* still do in the Aegean today. I opened it to the page that describes their arrival on the Faroe Islands.

*

The coracle of Brendan and his disciples was well provisioned. If they were struck by adverse winds or beset by fogs they could sail back and forwards for weeks without sight of land. Brendan himself had taken a vow of vegetarianism and gathered only fruit, shoots and roots for these voyages. The others were not so abstemious, and after weeks of being, 'borne hither and thither over the face of the deep,' eating and drinking only once every two days, it was with great joy that they sighted the Faroes, or 'the Islands of Sheep' as Brendan called them. The streams seemed to be stocked with fish, and great flocks of docile and fattened sheep 'big as bulls' grazed on the hillsides. This first landing could well have been at Brendan's Bay, facing as it does out towards Scotland.

It was Maundy Thursday. Like any self-respecting mediaeval monks they began to prepare their Easter feast. The islands had at first seemed deserted of people, but on Easter Saturday a man approached their camp and hailed them in Irish. He introduced himself as their 'Procurator', prostrated himself before Brendan and presented gifts of fresh bread baked in ashes. 'What have I done, you pearl of God,' he addressed Brendan, 'to deserve the honour of providing meat and drink for you by the sweat of my brow during this holy season?' Brendan raised him and kissed him, then reassured him; 'Our Lord Jesus Christ himself has indicated the place in which we are to celebrate His holy Resurrection.'

The Procurator showed signs of remarkable clairvoyance; telling Brendan that they would sail to a small island close by, and then west to another island known as 'the Paradise of Birds' where they would remain until the octave of Pentecost – nearly two months away. He went on to tell them that they would have to wait there until he arrived to resupply them for the next stage of their voyage.

After an adventure on an island that turned out to be the back of a whale, they climbed one of the islands' summits facing westwards over the sea. From the top they saw another island close at hand across a narrow strait. The island was carpeted in grass and wild flowers, and its slopes hinted at an interior of luscious glades. I had studied the map and it seems most likely that the peak they climbed was 'Arnafjall', one of the westernmost summits on the island of Vágar. It fits the description of overlooking Mykines, which Brendan identified as the Paradise of Birds.

They climbed back down the mountain again and took to their boat. They sailed around this new island, and Brendan noted that it had a stream running from its interior down to its southern shore, as Mykines does. The monks pulled him up the stream while he remained sitting in the coracle, and he declared that the water of the island was so pure that they would scarcely need any other nourishment during their stay there.

Brendan was a driven man, holy and piously devoted to his God but possessed of a fervour to understand God's wonders that was unusual among his contemporaries. His faith was not meek and accepting, it was allied to a fiercely incisive intellect. His behaviour on the Paradise of Birds offers a glimpse of this side of his personality. On a tree 'with a trunk of colossal girth' near the stream were settled thousands of white birds; so many that its branches and leaves were obscured. The monks were enchanted, mystified by why so many pure white birds could have flocked to one place. Brendan dropped to his knees, and tears flowed down his face as he prayed: 'O God, to whom nothing is unknown and who can bring to light every hidden fact, you see how anxious I am. I beseech your infinite majesty to deign to make known to me, a sinner, this secret design of yours which I see before me.'

His emotion passed. God would provide the answer. He sat back in the boat and marvelled at the sight, until one of the birds flew down towards him. The sound of its wings was like the ringing of bells. It alighted on the prow of the coracle and began to speak to him.

'We are fallen angels,' the bird said to Brendan in a human voice, 'like the other messengers of God, we wander through the air, over the bowl of Heaven, and upon the earth, but on Sundays and holy days we take on this physical form and tarry here to sing the praises of our Creator.'

The bird told the monks that they had now been at sea for one year, and six more years of their journey remained until they would find the Land of the Promise of the Saints. After it had spoken the bird flew away, and the air was filled with antiphonal choruses as the whole flock began to sing vespers: 'Thou, O God, art praised in Sion: and unto thee shall the vow be performed in Jerusalem.' The plangent beating of their wings harmonised with their voices in an elegy so beautiful it made the monks weep.

Throughout the week following Easter the birds continued to sing for them. At the end of the first week when the monks' feasting was near an end the Procurator arrived by sea with a boat full of supplies as promised, and after being blessed by Brendan went away again. The monks remained listening to the birds until the octave of Pentecost, sometime in June, when their servant returned again. This time he came with supplies for the voyage ahead, including dry bread which he told them would keep for a year. It seemed they had a long trial ahead of them.

✳

The history of the transcription of mediaeval manuscripts is a catalogue of misinformation and misinterpretation. It is difficult to be sure of any details recounted in texts such as these, now nearly 1,500 years old. At some point in Brendan's travels he may well have encountered a colossal tree filled with white birds, but with the context of this island lying so close to the well-known 'Islands of Sheep' it seems much more likely that he is describing a great cliff covered by birds nesting on its ledges so thickly, 'that there was hardly a branch, or even a leaf, to be seen.' The volcanic columns and fissured ridges of the basalt can look surprisingly like the corrugations of bark, and over time the simile may have become metaphor. Alternatively, the story may have been exaggerated in order to impress its listeners in what was for its first couple of centuries part of an oral tradition. Holy trees were immersed in the Irish cults of fertility as part a tradition much older and stronger than the new Christian one.

The great Celtic scholar Kenneth Hurlestone Jackson translated many ancient Celtic manuscripts into English. The similarities between the more magical details of Brendan's voyage and these older pagan traditions are striking. Some of the following passages that Jackson translated from the ancient texts suggest that the monks were building on this much older tradition of the magical journey when they finally wrote down the account of Brendan's voyage.

There is an island far away, around which the sea-horses glisten, flowing on their white course against its shining shore; four pillars support it.

There is a huge tree there with blossom, on which the birds call at the hours; it is their custom that they all call together in concert every hour.

There are three times fifty distant islands in the ocean to the west of us; each of them is twice or three times larger than Ireland.

Do not sink upon a bed of sloth, do not let your bewilderment overwhelm you; begin a voyage across the clear sea, to find if you may reach the Land of Women.

All along the southern coast of Vágar there are great colonies of kittiwakes. In Brendan's day they may easily have been tens of thousands of birds strong. They are gentle birds, with brilliant white plumage and dove-grey wings. The noise of a few thousand of them in the Easter breeding season may not resemble a sung mass, but can be beautiful nonetheless. Their harsh cries of 'kitti-wake kitti-wake' as they call to their mates and fend off others from their nests may well have impressed the monks, who would have been at a loss to explain such numbers of them. Given that they interpreted everything they encountered as a gift from God, and in the light of their holy pilgrimage, it is not surprising that the birds were held to represent fallen angels.

Brendan filled the coracle with provisions, and pushed it down the stream towards the shore. The monks now knew that they had six years ahead of them of continuously voyaging on the ocean. One of their number had already died and two more were to leave their company: one to join another monastic community with which he fell in love, and another to be dragged into the pit of hell in front of the helpless monks' eyes.

But that was ahead of them now, and they put to sail to the

sound of the birds chorus: 'Hear us, O Lord, thou that art the hope of all the ends of the earth, and of them that remain in the broad sea…'

✳

The Faroese were kind to me, picking me up in the rain that beat across the islands, driving me far out of their way. I never had to wait long by the road, and was given lifts by sheep farmers, fishermen, businesswomen, and mothers on school runs. One day a Member of the Faroese parliament gave me a lift up to the town of Eiđi. He had been a schoolteacher before entering politics and had lived for many years in a remote community in Greenland. He loved it there and would have stayed but when his sons reached adolescence he wanted them to have a good secondary education. 'Sadly,' he said, 'that's not yet possible in Greenland.' He told me that many Faroese people go to Greenland. The Danish administration there ensured there was not too much red tape to cut through if you wanted to make the move, and they had a need for educated professionals. That the Greenlanders were obliged to learn Danish as a second language helped too. It was fascinating to me that just as Brendan had sailed west from the Faroes, trying to reach the North American continent, many local people here were still making the same journey. It was a natural progression, following the winds and currents that had also made Severin's crossing achievable.

✳

In Eiđi I looked across at Tjornuvik, the bay where traces of the Irishmen's oats had been found, grown 1,500 years before, and I met another man who had gone west to seek his fortune.

He was a self-made man, a parvenu of conservative Faroese society. As a boy of fourteen he had gone to work the shrimp boats off the coast of Greenland. Working the nets for years in temperatures as low as minus forty degrees had gnarled and cracked his hands. He told me chilling stories of the brutality of the weather and the terrors of working through the Greenlandic winter. But he had made money.

In the summers he had sailed the swift running channels and braved the tidal rips of the Faroes. He fished locally as well, but all the time he was out in his boat he was dreaming of escaping the cycle of the seasons that he saw destroying other men. With a couple of years' wages he bought a small plot of land overlooking the Sundini, the fjord which divides the Faroe Islands in two main groups, and ignoring the jeers of the villagers he started to build.

'This place has the best view in all the Faroes,' he said.

The winters on the shrimp boats came and went, and each time he saved enough money to build more. He borrowed books from the library in Tórshavn on masonry, plumbing, wiring. He attended summer school in Denmark in catering and accountancy. Over ten years his hotel took shape. But it was not enough – he needed to advertise abroad. He taught himself French, English, German, and learned the ways in which Norwegian and Swedish differed from his native Danish and Faroese. His business grew.

Every winter now instead of sailing across the Denmark Strait for shrimp, he and his wife flew across the waves and ice-fields to reach the Caribbean. While the worst of the Atlantic storms raged over his hotel the two of them meandered among the archipelagos of the New World. One day, he said, they would stay there. He had great love for the Faroes but his love for sunshine was still greater. Over an imported Danish lager I sat in the bar he had built himself listening to his plans for selling the hotel and becoming established as the owner and manager of a Caribbean cruise ship. His eyes shone as he showed me the size of the fish he had caught there. Brendan had been enticed by tales of shores littered with jewels, where every tree was a fruit tree. In the Caribbean, he told me, the sand sparkled like diamonds and a man could live like a king and eat mangos in the sunshine all year round.

He let me set up my tent in the garden of his hotel. I awoke to a clear morning where the sunlight bleached the grasses and cut the islands into sharp relief, and made my way to the top of the Faroes' highest mountain, Slættaratindur, which towered over the village. *Slættar* means 'flat'. It isn't. Billowing clouds of Arctic terns mobbed me when I strayed by accident into their nesting area. When I finally got past them great skuas fell from the sky as they had at Enniberg, swooping at my head and plucking at my hat, their wings tearing the air around my ears. I fell onto my belly and scrabbled along the ground looking for a stick to wave at them. They were defending their nests among the tussock grasses of the lower slopes, and left me alone when I had made it to the frost-shattered ice-fields of rubble nearer the summit.

The Faroe Islands looked small from up there; a few folds of leaden rock, carved by the last ice age, dusted with green. The ocean stretched to the northern horizon, glittering in the tinselled light. I dropped down over a mountain path and into a wide and serene valley of rich pasture, then on over a ridge to the settlement of Gjógv. A few houses dressed in primary colours were clumped together in a narrow ravine, hemmed in by cliffs and the sea. Dead gulls swung in the breeze on garden posts, as grim totems of warning and a deterrent to gull raids on the chickens that scraped over scraps of earth nearby. I asked at the youth hostel if there was any space for the night, but was told that it had been hired out for a week. A large party from a private art college in Denmark had taken over the whole building. I carried on down the hill to the beach, where I set up my stove and began to make some dinner.

'Where are you from?'

The speaker had climbed down the path behind me. She waited for a response; a broad-boned expectant face, sun-burnished skin, blonde hair caught in the wind.

'Scotland,' I said.

'Sorry you were told we were all full up, that was very rude. Would you like to come and have dinner with us?'

Low smoke-stained beams were draped in drying clothes. Their sour smell mingled with that of fresh bread; dough was proving by the fireplace. Light filtered through skylights in the turf roof, cutlery clinked as tables were set for dinner, and around the room lay men and women of all ages stretched out over contact sheets, canvases and manuscripts.

Paula, my new friend, showed me to the table and we sat down together. She was explaining her art: 'I want to show how the clouds change the lighting here, how the uniform greys and greens are cast into so many hues by the patchiness of the sunlight.' She paused, wondering perhaps if she was boring me. 'I think I'm going to concentrate on monochrome photography, using blocks of water-colour next to the prints.' Her accent in English was meticulous, groomed by summers spent caring for privileged children in the Home Counties of England. Her eyes were hooded and looked half-asleep, dozing beneath a nest of yellow hair. A Swede from Gothenburg, she had travelled the world working and saving money to pay the fees for the art school. This was a brief college trip as part of a six-month course based in a mansion in the Danish country-side, with tutors in abundance and eccentricity and freedom of ex-pression encouraged. 'One day,' she confided, 'I'll become a theatre scenographer. This is just the first step'.

During a lull in the conversation one of the Danish tutors ex-pounded her views on Faroese nationalism. 'They can never leave us,' she declared, 'they love their Queen too much. The Queen of Denmark comes here every year and is in love with the Faroes. The people of the Faroes love her.'

'But surely it's more complicated than that,' I said. 'Some of the people I've met seem to think that they would love their independ-ence more.'

'But they can never survive on their own, economically they would never make it,' she said.

'I don't know, but surely it's up to them if they want to try,' I said.

'What do you mean, "It's up to them". You British can't talk, look at what you did in India, South Africa, Australia, the "Great British Empire".' Her voice was curt with sarcasm.

She had a point. The British did not have much of a history of allowing peoples to make their own choices. And nationalism in all its guises had a nasty habit of leading to bigotry and violence. I did not want to antagonise her, and fell silent. I wondered if the Faroese people would ever become violent in the cause of their nationalism. From the little that I had seen of them so far it seemed unlikely, they seemed much too sensible. Around the table the chatter went on and I listened, catching the odd Danish phrase. The freshly baked bread was delicious.

*

After dinner I picked my way through rooms that had been converted into studios, looking at half-completed canvases and stepping over grey bundles of wrapped clay and rolls of cardboard. On one of the floors, surrounded by cassettes and contact prints of portraits, crouched a young woman with a kind face, diffidently beautiful, who blushed when I asked about her project.

Over a decade ago she had left the mountains of Norwegian Lapland for the lush fields of Jutland and her art was inspired by a conflict that ran deep within her. 'We can't ever leave behind our love for our home,' she said, choosing her words carefully. She reached for a tape recorder. 'The landscape of our childhood is where we first learn and grow, but there is something else that moves us, something so powerful driving us on out into the world, into new landscapes.'

'Listen,' she said, and started the tape. 'This is what I want to bring out in my work.' I heard a thin voice, broken, in halting Danish, 'Vejen kom i tresserne og tog alle væk.'

'"The road came in the sixties and took everybody away"; it's one of the old ladies who lives here in Gjógv, she doesn't speak Danish very often. She told me that before they built the roads and the first tunnels here, each of the villages was more or less isolated but they were *alive*. Now the population here is falling fast, and although the people are proud of their children making new lives in Tórshavn and Copenhagen, the life of the villages is draining away.'

Her photographs were in black and white. They showed an ageing population with bright intelligence in their eyes, but in their smiles a sadness that I had seen before, in the face of the old lady I had met on Unst.

*

I went for a walk. The late evening light softened the mountainsides in a wash of indigo. Three children played in the creek, paddling makeshift boats deftly at an age when most children have barely mastered a bicycle. Their shouts and giggles broke the dense silence. Scuffed on the pavement was the chalk outline of an earlier game they had been playing: shapes were scratched on the tarmac representing different countries of the world, and I recognised France, India, and the USA. At the centre of them all was written Føroyar, the Faroe Islands. Following an obscure set of rules they had been jumping back and forwards between the powerful nations of the earth, but always returning to their home. After hearing the recording of the old lady, they seemed like the last children of Gjógv. I wondered whether any of them would stay.

One of the tutors had invited me to stay in the youth hostel overnight after all. Early in the morning I packed up my things and tiptoed out as the students snored gently around me. Outside the air was still cold, and as I climbed up out of the village the valley filled with a saffron light.

*

At some time there must have been Irishmen living in the settlement of Vestmanna, coeval with the Norsemen, either as slaves or freemen, and the name has stuck. It is a small fishing port now, and slumped by the harbour is the ferry terminal serving the island of Vágar. Shortly after I was there a tunnel was due to open, but I was glad to be one of the last ones to have to sail there, as Brendan must have.

I crossed over to the island on the ferry, left the coastal road and climbed into its interior. I was heading for the mountain Arnafjall, the one that Brendan and his monks probably climbed to see over to Mykines. Before me stretched a rolling moorland, dull and rocky, punctuated by thin sheep-tracks and streams with names like lullabies: Áin á Flatum, Kvígandalsá, Áin á Fjøllum, Tunguáin. The clouds had cleared and the sky was a flawless nursery-school blue. High in the air a pair of great skuas fought with a pair of Arctic skuas. The Arctics were smaller, sleeker, faster and meaner. They spun through the sky, locking talons and butting their adversaries into graceless tumbles. Brendan had seen gryphons fighting in these skies, and I wondered whether these birds had inspired the legend.

From the top of the plateau two ridges slid towards the west. Between them in a broad, shallow vale lay a freshwater lake, the Fjallavatn, a smooth sheet of silvered glass. I dropped down in order to walk along its shore. On its far side the mountains climbed up towards Arnafjall. An old hut stood by the lakeside. As I approached, a fisherman called out to me from his stool in front of it. Empty spirits bottles lay beside him on the shingle beach, and he smelled of cigarettes and cheap vodka.

'Where are you going?' he called out to me in English.

'I'm going up there,' I pointed up at the mountain, 'and over to Gásadalur.' Gásadalur was the name of the village on the other side of the Arnafjall.

'What are you thinking about! Can't you see how steep it is! Let me show you on the map.' He took the map from my hands, and shakily traced a path that I should take back up the valley towards the main road, and round towards the south of the island.

I explained that I wanted to get to the top of the mountain because I was following a route someone had taken over a thousand years before. He clearly thought I was mad, but decided to humour me. 'Oh well then,' he rolled his eyes, 'Don't say I didn't warn you. Have you been there before?'

'No,' I told him.

'Gásadalur is a strange place. There's no tunnel to get out you know. Oh, they started one but the politicians couldn't decide if they could afford it and so they've stopped digging. And it's got no harbour. They have to lift boats up and down from the water by a winch! What are you going to do when you get there?'

'My map says there's a path out of it.' I showed him the thin trace of a line up from the village to a mountain pass, and from there to the town along the beach.

'It's very steep. But maybe you can manage it. You look strong!' He slapped my shoulder and laughed. I caught another strong whiff of vodka.

'And that path is very famous,' he went on. 'The men of Gásadalur used to carry coffins over it, because there's no graveyard there. The nearest graveyard is in Bøur, here.' He pointed to the next village on the map. 'And so if they can manage to carry the dead, I suppose you can manage your rucksack.' He slapped me on the shoulder again, and I began to walk off. 'But be careful!' he called out after me. 'The weather is going to get worse. I will be safe in my little hut, but you…' He pointed up to the top of the ridge, where the summit was appearing and disappearing in the cloud. 'You will be up in the mists.'

The Fjallavatn did not end in a shore but petered out into a wide sump of a bog, filling the valley in a mattress of oily water and dirty brown moss. The ooze of the bog coalesced into a short sewer of a stream, which almost as soon as it had formed ran over the sheer cliffs of the western coast. I spent an afternoon wading in the bog, cursing its foul stink and the skuas and oystercatchers that continued to swoop over my head. When I finally reached the ridge I watched the sunset play over the western cliffs while the mud dried and cracked on my trousers, and the effort seemed worthwhile after all. Plumes of cloud reddened as they rolled in from the west, darkening the sky. The horizon was a thin stripe of sapphire and steel. On an isolated spit of land far below lay the crumbling remains of the settlement of Víkar, long since abandoned. The coast was remote and exposed. Decades before the comforts of the twentieth century had gradually rendered life there too narrow and mean and it had been abandoned. A chill crept into the air. I set up my tent, and slept.

By the next morning the light had dulled, and sullen clouds threatened to sink and dissolve the ridge entirely. The rocks were slippery in the settling mist. From the summit I saw between breaks in the cloud that Mykines did indeed lie just across a narrow strait, but it did not look lush and inviting as it had to Brendan. It looked forbidding and gloomy; a cubist tangle of basalt. I picked my way through wide fields of scree slopes towards Gásadalur. Besides the hamlet on Mykines itself it was the westernmost and most exposed village of the islands. Instead of a road it had a helipad, and I saw the yawning hole of earthworks abandoned in the mountainside. Brendan's Paradise of Birds lay just across the strait, a sulking mass of grey rock in the mist. Four or five houses clung to the side of a scooped-out valley. Fields that were a lustrous green from the heavy rains were squeezed into the scraps of land between the cliffs of Arnafjall and the cliffs of the coast. The realisation that the mountain pass was the only way out added a desperate edge of claustrophobia to the silence.

Down in the village the houses seemed abandoned. I did not see anyone. But the farms were still working, and beside one of them stood a bright new tractor that must have been flown in, or winched up from the sea. It lay next to the rusting skeletons of its two predecessors; the three standing together like a frieze from a museum of agriculture. On a bright day in summer it must feel like a world apart there, I thought, the mountains and cliffs sheltering a haven of retreat from the towns. The winters must be miserable.

Looking out across the sound towards Mykines I wondered how it would be to live in such a place, how the realities of community life had played themselves out over the centuries. On the other side of the ridge I had seen Víkar, now abandoned because of its remoteness, but perhaps Gásadalur would be saved in time by a tunnel. It seemed a paradox that initially, in opening up the villages to the outside world, the tunnels had taken people away, whereas now they seemed the best incentive for them to stay on, perhaps even to come back.

It was unlikely that Mykines would get a tunnel under the strait to connect it, and a bridge would be too exposed on this southern shore. But there was another paradox; sometimes the very remoteness of a place meant that its future was assured. I thought of St Kilda and Fair Isle, both remote islands off the coast of Scotland. By their very remoteness they are often now seen as romantic escapes, and somehow as purer or wilder places to live. Both now have long waiting lists of people who are willing to pay to go to live and work on them for a season, either to work on archaeological digs, restore old buildings, or to identify and ring birds. And though their communities could be said to be artificial (they are administered by the National Trust) they have not been abandoned. I would still wish a more sustainable future for Mykines.

*

From Gásadalur I climbed up the path towards the pass. A sign marked the place where the coffin-bearers used to rest on their way over to the graveyard at Bøur. I climbed up into clouds again, and then down into the next valley where the sky cleared and my clothes started to dry off. The graveyard was bright with spring flowers, and I stopped there to rest and pay my respects. It had seemed like a long way to carry a coffin.

*

The small Mykines ferry looked like a fishing skiff. It was tied up in Sórvagur harbour, delayed by the poor weather. Its captain was red-faced and jolly, and he was optimistic about our chances of getting there. 'Soon we leave,' he said, resting his gumboots on the gunwales of the boat and smoking his pipe. The wind was getting up.

Waiting on the boat were two teenagers on a Danish exchange programme and their hosts. One of them was a bored Australian girl with an empty expression on her freckled face. She wrapped her jacket tightly around her and muttered, 'I hate this place, it smells of fish. You just try spending a year here.' Her Faroese host winced as if he had chewed tin foil. After a year in the islands she could not pronounce the name of the village she lived in. She gorged herself on crisps and fizzy juice, and complained about the weather.

The other was a Turk. He had quick eyes, sleek styled hair and creamy olive skin. When he laughed he threw his head back with a roar. When I asked why he had come to the Faroes his arms shot into the air and he bellowed, 'The Faroes chose ME!' Although he had only been on the islands for six months he chatted to the captain fluently in Faroese. The two local boys who were their hosts had never been to Mykines. It was rare that the weather was good enough to land there, they said.

The wind seemed to calm for a while, and the captain decided to risk a crossing. We sailed west out of the fjord and past the island of Tindholmur, a series of improbable pinnacles extending in a line towards the west. 'You know there's a legend around here,' said one of the boys to me, 'that if you didn't keep your babies safe indoors the eagles would take them and fly them up there.' He looked up at the spires of rock and whistled. 'There's an old story of a woman who climbed up there to get her baby back, but its eyes had been pecked out by the time she made it.'

Passing Tindholmur it felt as if we were leaving the world where people were in charge, and entering one dominated by birds. Crossing the sound an infinity of them swarmed around the boat. Billows of seabirds wheeled between the stacks and arches of rock of Mykines which burst forth from one another at impossible angles. I counted gulls, guillemots, puffins, gannets, razorbills, terns, kittiwakes, fulmars and skuas. The easterly wind whipped against the incoming tide, and the sea boiled amongst the caves and columns of basalt. The Australian girl started to vomit up her crisps and juice. The captain held his course under the southern cliffs of Mykines and then tried to bring the ferry in closer to the mouth of the stream that ran up into the island. Men waved at us from a short pier, their boots awash as the waves broke over the concrete. The captain puffed at his pipe, and looked impatiently at the bag of mail that he was supposed to deliver to the village. A beam of light broke through the clouds and fell on the village, shining on the church spire. It lay along the banks of the small stream, which was about the width of a coracle.

After half an hour of trying to bring the ferry in alongside safely, he turned the vessel around. There was a chorus of protest from us all. But his decision was final. 'What about the mail?' I asked.

'It will have to go by helicopter,' he said. It would be over a week before he would try to get to the island again.

*

It was disappointing not to get to Brendan's Paradise of Birds, and on getting back to Sórvagur I found that the small helicopter was fully booked until well after I was scheduled to leave the islands. But I consoled myself that at least I had seen the cliffs and the birds that must have awed the Irish monks all those centuries ago, and seen the stream that Brendan had taken to be a gift from God.

*

The speaker dominated the common room of the small youth hostel. His forehead was high and domed like a spinnaker at full sail and his beard was a mat of kelp on his chest. Even his wire-framed spectacles did not detract from his uncanny resemblance to Neptune. Though he was a Dutchman he held forth in English with ease, and for an hour or two I was held in his sway.

'These Faroese,' he said, 'are not an open people. They love their country, but they do not want to share it. I find it difficult to get on with them. To them I will always be an intruder.' And then:

'They will not survive independence. Iceland did it because they left in 1948, before the revolutions of the welfare state. They had to create the new society themselves. The Faroese have Danish policemen, Danish doctors, Danish teachers all paid with Danish taxes! They can't go alone!' And:

'I like to take photographs, but they don't allow it! They are an insanely private people! I have to pretend I am pointing out something or someone to my son, and then take a picture. I don't like using my son in this way.'

His son was a mild-mannered little boy with sandy hair and a pair of binoculars slung around his neck. While his father spoke he was at the window, watching terns wheeling over the sound. The Dutchman regularly travelled back and forth across the North Atlantic – Orkney, Shetland, Iceland and Greenland – working as a tour guide and photojournalist for 'lifestyle magazines'.

'What are "lifestyle magazines?"' I asked.

'I must confess that I don't really know,' he replied, and looked out of the window where light glittered on the sea around the islands of Hestur and Koltur. 'But they pay the bills.'

He was a self-confessed lifestyle-magazine snob. 'They tried to publish the *National Geographic* in Dutch, but it was untranslatable! That view of the world, it is like bubble-gum. Oh, it is alright chewing through it at first but then you realise it is all the same!'

When I told him that I was on my way to Iceland and then to Greenland his face grew watchful. 'Be careful in Greenland… Colonialism has failed there and it's in collapse. Alcoholism, rape and murder are much more common than in Europe, and you can buy shotguns in the supermarket! The Danes are in retreat, and the Greenlanders are getting angrier about them being there.'

It was the most pessimistic view of modern Greenland I had ever heard. 'What do you think went wrong?' I asked him.

'They totally underestimated the Greenlandic mind. Their thinking is Asiatic, not European, but the Danes tried to bureaucratise them in a way alien to them, put them in high-rise flats and get them to work in Danish industries. It's been a disaster for those people.'

He sat back in his chair, closed his eyes and began to smooth his beard. 'But out on the ice-cap, or hunting with them on the sea ice with their dogs, you see the Greenlanders as they really are. They love it out there, and when they see that you love it too, then they can start to trust you. Maybe.'

＊

After leaving the Paradise of Birds Brendan had sailed west until he had found a large island that sounded, from the description of the *Navigatio*, suspiciously like Iceland. Like the Faroes, those islands still had small communities of Irishmen living on them when the Vikings arrived late in the ninth century. In the three hundred years between Brendan's voyage and the westward expansion of the Vikings it seems that the Irish monks continued to nurture those tiny island communities across the North Atlantic. Though the monks wrote little about these communities themselves, descriptions of them have survived thanks to the literacy of Charlemagne's Frankish court.

To many, Charlemagne, King of the Franks, was a glutton, a drunkard, and an illiterate oaf with an appetite for brutality. In one day's campaign in 782 he slaughtered nearly five thousand Saxons. A couple of centuries after Brendan wept on the Paradise of Birds he marched into Saxony, Lombardy and Bavaria, and spilling the blood of thousands of Europeans, united the Holy Roman Empire. But, like King Alfred the Great in Saxon England a century later, he respected book learning and longed to become more educated. At his court in Aachen he gathered together the intelligentsia of Europe, including an ambitious monk from York by the name of Alcuin.

It was Alcuin who began what became known as the Carolingian Renaissance, taking charge of the intellectual development of the court and summoning some of the greatest scholars of the age. New trails were being forged between Iona and York, Aachen and Lyon, Salzburg and Pavia. One of the men to take the long march to the seat of the empire was a monk named Dicuil, from the island of Iona. It is fitting that he should have been an Irishman.

Frankish custom decreed that on Charlemagne's death his empire should be divided between his sons, but only one of them actually managed to make it to adulthood: Louis the Pious. In 814 when Louis was crowned the Second Holy Roman Emperor Dicuil had already begun the major astronomical treatise for which he is renowned. By 825 he had completed the work, which he called *Liber De Mensura Orbis Terrae* or, 'The Book of the Measure of the Earth'. In his cell in Aachen he read all that the ancient and modern authors had to say about the edges of the world, and he was not afraid to interject his own experience and that of his contemporary Irish monks when those works seemed to him incomplete. The only author as yet to have described Iceland was Pytheas, but the fragments that came down from 'Concerning the Ocean' made no reference to the Faroe Islands. Pytheas may have missed them in fog, or it may simply be that as they were not at the edge of the earth he did not make much of them in his account.

Here is Dicuil on the subject of the Faroe Islands, well known to him as the Islands of Sheep:

> A trustworthy priest told me that he had sailed for two summer days and an intervening night in a little boat with two thwarts, and landed on one of these islands. These islands are for the most part small; nearly all are divided from one another by narrow sounds, and upon them anchorites, who proceeded from our Scotia [Ireland and western Scotland], have lived for about a hundred years. But as since the beginning of the world they had always been deserted, so are they now by reason of the Norse pirates emptied of anchorites, but full of innumerable sheep and a great number of different kinds of sea-birds. We have never found these islands spoken of in the books of authors.

*

Dicuil was a man of eminent good sense. It seemed strange to him that the Faroes had not been mentioned by any of the great authors, especially as they were so well known to him and to his fellow monks. It is with the same offhand manner that he describes visits to Iceland, which he calls Thule, as if there had never been any doubt as to the identity of that island and he did not understand what all the squabbling by the ancient critics of Pytheas had been about. He writes as if it was common for the Irish monks to travel between their home monasteries and there, even if only for a summer.

In his book he describes a visit of a group of monks to Thule in 795. They arrived at the start of February, which indicates with what ease they made the journey; even taking into account the relatively benign climate of the eighth century, February would still have been one of the stormiest months to sail in the North Atlantic.

In preparing his description of *The Measure of the Earth* it is the properties of the northerly latitude that interest him the most. What had been to the classical world unbelievable celestial wonders had become to the Carolingian Empire simply an intellectual curiosity:

> It is now the thirtieth year since some monks who dwelt upon that island [Iceland] from the Calends of February to the Calends of August told me that not only during the summer solstice but also during the days near that time, towards evening the setting sun hides itself as if behind a small hill, so that there is no darkness for even a very short time; but a man may do whatever he wishes, actually pick the lice from his shirt just as if it were by the light of the sun; and if they had been on top of the mountains the sun probably never would have hidden from their eyes.

Some authors had drawn mistaken conclusions from the work of Pytheas. It had been reported that there was continuous day on Thule for six months, and then six months of continuous night. Dicuil sought to put them right:

> During the winter solstice, and during a few days around that time, dawn occurs for only a brief time in Thule, that is

to say, when it is midday in the middle of the earth. Therefore those are lying who have written that the sea around
Thule is frozen and that there is continuous day without
night from the vernal to the autumnal equinox; and that,
vice versa, from the autumnal, to the vernal equinox there is
perpetual night.

But he took care to corroborate one part of the story of Pytheas,
one of the greatest stumbling blocks to the acceptance of his reports
by the disbelieving Mediterranean world: that just to the north of
Thule the sea had been frozen, and for that reason he could not
go on. 'Those monks who sailed there during a time of year when
naturally it would be at the coldest and landed on this island and
dwelt there always had alternate day and night after the solstice; but
they found that one day's sail from it towards the north the sea was
frozen.'

With Dicuil the first tentative steps were taken towards a systematic
exploration of the North since the voyages of the Romans. Given
more time perhaps emissaries from the Frankish Court would have
explored the Faroes and Iceland on the strength of the stories of the
Irish monks. But the history of Europe was about to take one of
its convulsive turns, and the Franks were soon to have their hands
full with other matters. Dicuil had hinted at them when he said
that the Faroes had been emptied 'by Norse pirates'. It would be
these 'Vikings' who would harass the Frankish Empire and also
undertake the next stage in the exploration of the North. It was
their story I would follow on the next stage of my own journey, in
Iceland.

The youth hostel in Miðvágur was a few kilometres from the Faroes'
little airport. It was the only place in the Faroe Islands where there
was enough flat land to build a runway, and a short one at that.

The weather systems of the North Atlantic so conspire with the landscape that it is not unusual to be stranded for weeks waiting for fogs to clear. A visitors' book in the hostel was filled with entries written by those waiting for the weather. I had thought at first the book represented a high turnover of visitors, but then I noticed that the thin volume stretched over a decade. They were all nationalities, and some seemed like modern anchorites in Brendan's tradition, in search of the sensation of being on the edge of Europe: 'I came to Føroyar to find the silence. I found silence indeed in this place. And rain, and wind. It looks as if the world around has disappeared. Jan, Belgium.'

Some were disappointed to have missed the storms that grounded the aeroplanes and blew the sheep from the cliffs: 'I have done this travel in the Faroes to see the famous September storms of the North Atlantic. The sea was quiet and the weather really sunny. But these islands are also very interesting under the sun. I shall come back. Roland, France.'

The sky was clear, the sun warm on my face. I walked to the airport, taking a detour around a lake to the south where it spilled over cliffs into the Atlantic Ocean. Waves rolled into the caves far below, squeezing tonnes of water into the rock and sending thunderous booms shuddering up through the basalt. The spray caught the wind and refracted it into rainbows which drifted away to the east on the breeze. It occurred to me that I had never before hiked to an international airport, and kicking the mud from my boots, I enjoyed the new sensation.

The plane, when it arrived, was a light aircraft with twin-propellers, and as it banked up into the sky I looked down on the Islands of Sheep. They slowly became insubstantial, clouded by the mists flowing down out of the Arctic. Through a break in them I caught a glimpse of Brendan's Bay. A golden sheen played on the water and a fishing boat ploughed a white furrow into the fields of the ocean.

Iceland
THE GREAT HEATHEN HOST

THE AEROPLANE CIRCLED the airport at Keflavík, sliding between dense layers of grey cloud. Rain streaked the window. The pilot manoeuvred to approach the runway and the landscape rose steadily through the mist. Heaps of volcanic black slag and ash slouched in succession to the horizon, gleaming in the rain.

The plane touched down. 'Velkomin heim!' said an Icelandair announcement, 'Welcome Home'. It is well over a thousand years since the languages of the Anglo-Saxons and the Norsemen diverged, and yet many of our words are still shared, still recognisable.

Reykjavík felt like a ghost town the wet afternoon I arrived; a grid of rain-splashed empty streets and squat functional buildings. The whole town was grey in the fog. I walked past a little parliament building, its size a reminder that this country, larger in area than Ireland, has a population of less than three hundred thousand. About two thirds of those people live in Reykjavík. But walking its streets on a rainy afternoon it felt provincial, and I was reminded that towns are a new phenomenon for Iceland. The soil has for centuries been too poor to allow intense farming and the population has traditionally had to disperse itself thinly. Only since the rise of the fisheries in the early twentieth century, and especially since the Second World War and independence from Denmark, have people moved to the towns in earnest.

Even though the town felt newly built, its rich history lay just beneath the surface. From the Austurvöllur square a road ran down

Iceland

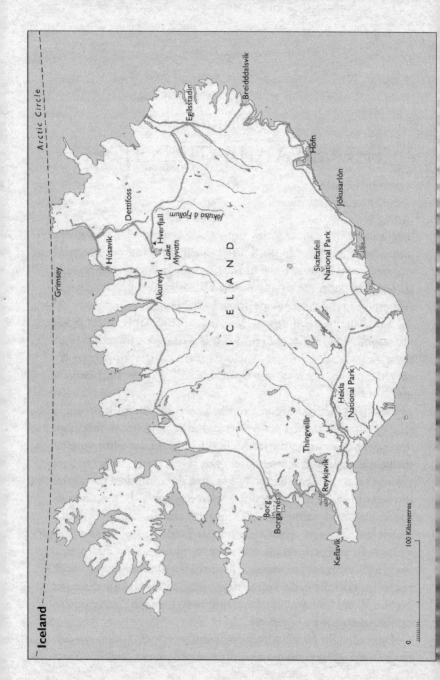

Arctic Circle

Grimsey

Húsavík
Dettifoss
Hverfjall
Lake
Myvatn
Akureyri

Jökulsá á Fjöllum

Egilsstadir
Breiddalsvik

Höfn

Jökusarlón

ICELAND

Skaftafell
National Park

Hekla
National Park

Thingvellir

Reykjavik

Borg
Borgarnes

Keflavík

0   100 Kilometres

to a broad harbour where fishing boats jostled among cargo ships from Norway, Denmark and England, just as they have done for over a thousand years. A statue of Ingólf Arnarson, Iceland's first Viking settler, puffed out his chest and clutched his shield to his side as he looked out over the bay. His homestead is thought to have been under Reykjavik's main street, and his hay-field under the Austurvöllur. The Icelanders, as Viking descendants, feel some pride that their capital rests on the lands claimed by their earliest pioneer.

I already had two threads that I wanted to gather up while I was in Iceland. I wanted to see what Pytheas must have seen when he reached his Thule, and walk in the places where Brendan had come ashore on his way to the Land of the Promise of the Saints. In addition I hoped I would be able to get a glimpse of how it felt to be an Icelander in the twenty-first century, and delve deeper into the world that grew out of the Dark Ages: the mediaeval northern Europe of which the Norsemen were kings.

*

The Norse god Óðin (or Wodan) was known variously as the Lord of the Slain, the God of Death, the Chieftain of the Asir, and the God of War. His name means 'Frenzy', and three frenzies were his: the fury of the warrior, the trance of the sorcerer, and the reverie of the poet. His legacy is celebrated every Wednesday, which means 'Wodan's day'. He had only one eye, and galloped throughout the earth on his eight-legged stallion followed by ravens and wolves that fed on the spoils of the battles he wrought. His symbol was one of the early prototypes of the swastika. His consorts were the Valkyries, 'the Choosers of the Slain,' female goddess-demons of slaughter. It was they who picked over the battlefield, killing those who would not survive their wounds and escorting them to Valhalla where they would feast, do battle, and die before being reborn every day to fight again.

Óðin's ancestry was unusual, even for a God. According to ancient Germanic legend he sprang from the sweat of a hoarfrost giant, the result of the coupling of a Man-God and a Giantess. He slew his own Creator, Ymir, and from his body created the world. As blood poured forth it formed the ocean. From Ymir's bones Óðin made the mountains, from his skull the vault of the heavens, from his hair he made the trees and plants and from his brain he made the clouds. From sparks of Muspelheim, the furnace-like world of the south, he made the sun and moon, stars and planets. The gods' realm had been Asgard, but this new world he called Midgard, or 'Middle Earth'. Like Homer's world it was a flat disc, and running around its rim was the encircling ocean.

The ancient Norse religion was called Ásatrú, 'the way of the Asir'. Throughout the ninth and tenth centuries its followers poured out of Scandinavia like a plague of rats along the rivers and coastlines of Europe intent on winning riches and conquering new lands. In 820 a fleet of them were repulsed from the mouth of the Seine. In 835 they set up their first permanent camp on the Isle of Sheppey in the Thames and in 836 they plundered Antwerp and laid the foundations of the Norse port of Dublin. When Charlemagne's son Louis the Pious died in 840 the Frankish Empire was divided between his three grandsons. The empire was weakened, and the next five years saw the Vikings sack Rouen, Hamburg, and Paris.

Within twenty years the 'Great Heathen Host' had arrived in East Anglia and swept throughout England, beating the Anglo-Saxons back onto the shores of the Channel and occupying all the lands of England outside the kingdom of Wessex. They were less successful in Moorish Spain; a raid on Seville ended in over a thousand Norse deaths. Four hundred prisoners were caught and strung up along the riverbank as a warning to the captains of the fleeing longships. The only land they did not need to shed blood over was Iceland, where their arrival merely scared away a few Irish anchorites. Throughout the last quarter of the ninth century they began to arrive on that island and settle down in increasing numbers.

The men who called themselves Vikings were from all over Scandinavia. 'Viking' was both a noun and a verb; Old Norse accounts speak of summers spent 'a-viking' among the monasteries and ports of the British Isles. The word has now become synonymous with all the mediaeval warrior peoples of Scandinavia, but even then they were formed into distinct groups. It was Danes who harried France and the eastern coast of England, while Swedes under the name of *Rus* penetrated the trade routes of the Volga and the Dnieper, giving their name to Russia and carrying furs and slaves from the forests of Eastern Europe to the Baghdad Caliphate and the Byzantine capital of Constantinople. Early in the tenth century Ibn Fadlan, an Arab ambassador to the Bulgar towns on the Volga wrote: 'I have seen the Rus as they come on their merchant journeys, and stay encamped on the Volga. I have never seen more perfect specimens, tall as date palms, blonde and ruddy.'

But it was largely the Norwegians and their Celtic slaves who settled Iceland. Many of the Icelandic sagas begin with the same story of how their migration came about: In 870 a King Harald had become the ruler of Vestfold, a small district in the south of Norway. He asked for the hand of Gyda, a noblewoman of the neighbouring district, but she refused to surrender her virginity to 'a petty king'. Enraged, Harald vowed both to unify Norway under his kingship and to leave his hair uncut until he had accomplished the deed. In a world where vows and deeds were as important as the names of fathers and grandfathers he became Harald Tangle-hair. Fifteen years later, after battles the whole length of Norway on sea and on land, he succeeded. Gyda joined his seraglio (polygamy was often practised) and he had a haircut. Afterwards the sagas report that his hair became unusually lustrous and fine, and he became known as Harald Fair-hair. All those who would not submit to his rule he executed or hounded out of the country, where they helped greatly in the drive to settle Iceland.

Adam of Bremen wrote in the eleventh century that the physical beauty and skill in war of these 'Vikings' was such that he thought them descended from the Hyperboreans themselves.

＊

I stopped for something to eat in a bar on the main street. It was dark inside, and not busy. A plastic guitar on the wall blinked yellow and pink, and a few teenagers munched hamburgers and glumly watched the rain. I ordered a beer and sat by the window, wondering whether to wait in Reykjavik for better weather or head out into the country anyway. I had read a great deal about Iceland before coming there and wondered how it was going to meet my expectations. The image of modern Reykjavík I had picked up suggested that despite the island's remoteness it had a vibrant youth culture and was enjoying a strong economy based on banking and fishing. It did not seem to have the depopulation problems that troubled the smaller isles I had visited so far. The Icelanders also seemed to be very proud of their Norse traditions, including their mediaeval sagas.

When I first returned to Europe from Africa and started to read about the history of the North I had quickly come across the sagas of the Icelanders. I had been dimly aware of them before but it was only on planning a trip to the island that I started to really take notice of them, and was surprised at how readable and exciting they were. 'Saga' has the same root as the English word 'say', and so they have the sense of being stories that come to life when spoken. Many of them chart the settlement of Iceland by various powerful Norwegian families, the blood feuds that sprang up between them, and the involvement of different Icelanders in the wars of Europe. They were first written down in the twelfth and thirteenth centuries and are rich with an attention to the details of everyday life that is missing from the literature of their European contemporaries. While Dante and Chaucer were composing epics of verse, the Icelanders hit on a literary style that would not reach the rest of Europe for another four hundred years.

The sagas introduced men and women who, unlike the explorer Greeks, imperial Romans or Irish mystics, were essentially settlers who pushed out fearlessly over horizons that previous cultures had not dared to cross. When the Norsemen loaded their ships in the harbours of Scandinavia they took their wives and children, their livestock and furniture, their ploughs and their hoes. Their approach represented a whole new phase in the history of the exploration of the North.

*

The waiter had hair like a seam of quartz, pale blonde and flecked with grey. He had tied it into little bunches with elastic bands. He put down my beer and lingered, as if waiting for me to speak.

'You're early for the tourist season,' he said, glancing at my rucksack, 'not many of the campsites are open yet.' His accent in English was stiff and nordic with a hint of cockney. It was by now mid-June. I said that I hoped the weather would be mild enough to camp outside by now.

'Well, you're in for some bad weather here in the west. I'd get out to the east if I were you, it rains a lot here in Reykjavík.' He looked down at the book I had been reading as part of my research, 'Egil's Saga'.

'You're reading *this*? Man, we had to read this stuff at school! Do you *enjoy* that stuff?'

'Some if it,' I said. He picked it up and shook his head.

'I didn't even know you could *get* this in English.'

He told me he had been brought up in Reykjavík but had gone to music college in London. For three years he had lived on Mile End Road. 'You can't get much further from Reykjavík than Mile End,' he said, and laughed. His face eased when he spoke about London; he liked the city, but had always known that he would come back to Iceland. He hinted at indecision over the choices that he had made. Gesturing at his apron and looking back at the bar behind us he said, 'There aren't too many jobs here for music graduates... but Reykjavík, it's a cool town, you know? There's always something going on.'

I had finished the beer. I put the book away and gathered up my rucksack. I thought the rain on the street outside was starting to ease.

'I'm in a band, you know,' he said as I went towards the door.

'Hey! Do you want to come along to one of our gigs? We're having a gig later tonight, you wanna flyer?'

I looked out again at the rain and turned back to face him. 'Sure,' I said.

*

Páll, the waiter in the diner, had written the club's name on a scrap of paper for me: Gaukur à Stong. It seemed more like the name of a Viking warrior than a nightclub. He had drawn a map on the back and I found it easily.

Inside a DJ was pumping out a mixture of garage music and punk. The lights were low. As my eyes adjusted I heard a shout from a table in the corner. Páll was sitting with a group of four others. The table was already covered in empty bottles and shot glasses. I waved over to them and made a gesture to ask if anyone wanted another drink, but they all shook their heads. Páll jumped up and came over, laughing. 'Don't offer to buy anyone a drink before you've seen the prices,' he yelled into my ear over the music. 'It's a bit more expensive than in the UK! Come over and meet the band, our set starts up in ten minutes'. I squeezed in between two of them on a bench. 'I'm Svein, the drummer,' said one of them, 'and this is Maria, our groupie.' She laughed.

'He wishes,' she said. 'Hi, I'm Páll's girlfriend. Pleased to meet you.' She had bright yellow hair backcombed and hairsprayed into place. It stuck straight out from her head like the petals on a sunflower.

'I found this guy in the diner reading Egil's Saga!' shouted Páll to the others. They all laughed and I tried to protest.

'It's good stuff, honest, I really like it.'

'You wouldn't like it if you had to study it in school,' shouted Maria. 'You guys probably get bored stiff with Shakespeare, well we have to do the sagas.'

'And can you read them straight without translations?' I yelled back at her.

'Yeah, unfortunately. Maybe a translation would make them a bit more bearable.'

The band went to get set up and left Maria and I to talk. She had never travelled outside Iceland, she told me. She had her own all-girl punk band and would love to get famous and tour the globe. At the moment she was biding her time working in the summers as an attendant at a camp-site and in the winters at a fish-processing factory. But her real life was in the evenings and weekends when she went out drinking and played her music.

'But mine is a common story here in Reykjavík,' she sighed. 'Sometimes it feels as if there are as many bands as there are people here!'

The band started up with a punk version of Dylan's 'Girl from the North Country'. Their other tracks were all their own, and most of them were in Icelandic. About halfway through the set the dance-floor started to fill up, and the temperature of the club to rise. 'You have to teach me better English,' Maria shouted across the music as we were dancing.

'There's nothing wrong with your English,' I shouted back.

'But it needs to be better, I need to start writing songs in English instead of Icelandic.'

'Why do you want to do that?'

'Listen to Páll singing, Icelandic doesn't work with this kind of music. English is more elastic, you can bend it more. It's the language of rock and roll, the language of the future!'

*

We stumbled out of the club at about 3 a.m. The sun was already high over the horizon. I do not remember much of the rest of the night, except that Icelandic apartments have blackout blinds against the midnight sun and that eating half a sheep's head is not good on an upset stomach. From the welcome they had given me, Reykjavík seemed like a good city after all.

*

The greatest scholar of the mediaeval Norse world was an Icelander, Snorri Sturluson. It was Snorri who first wrote down many of the sagas. He had a classical education and was familiar with the libraries and courts of Europe. His learning led him to fancy himself a genuine Hyperborean. In his *Prose Edda* of 1220, he interpreted the ancient Germanic legends of his people and wrote an alternative history of his ancestors. In this version the Asir were so called because they were originally from Asia. In a curious reversal of the Greek belief that only in the North could mankind live purely, he believed that he was descended from a pure race of Mediterraneans who were expelled by the Greeks from Troy. Aeneas had not taken the Trojans west to Italy after all, but east into Asia and from there they had fled north-west to Scandinavia. His vision of history resonates with the Greek myth of the Hyperboreans being forced to flee the centres of the earth. According to Snorri's belief, Ódin was not a divine being, he was simply the chieftain of the Trojans. After his defeat at the hands of the Greeks he had fled across the Black Sea and established his capital of Asgard near the Crimea, on the shores of the Sea of Asov. Thór, God of the Sky was really Tror, the grandson of Priam.

As the Mongol hordes of Jinghiz Khan thundered across the steppe, burning and laying waste to Central Asia, Persia, and the last scraps of the Eastern Roman Empire, Snorri sat down to his prologue. With a raven's feather, ink made of berries and on pages of calfskin he scribed an account of how his ancestors were harried out of those same lands and migrated north from the edges of Asia into Europe: 'The Asir took wives for themselves in that land, as did some of their sons, and these families became populous. As a result they spread throughout Saxony, and from thence through the Northern Regions. Their language, "Asia-manic", thus became the proper language of all the people in these lands.'

Snorri is not alone in history in describing this origin of the Germanic peoples, he was only adding his weight to an established tradition that Scandinavia was originally populated by a southern warrior people who had deliberately set out for the edge of the Earth.

In the sixth century, Procopius, the Byzantine historian and chronicler of Justinian's reign, wrote a history of the Gothic peoples called *De Bello Gothico*. He spoke of an ancient tribe called the Erilar who had migrated across the Danube into Europe from an area north of the Black Sea. Invincible in battle, they had terrorised the other European tribes and waged wars regularly out of boredom. Feeling that in the luxury of central and eastern Europe they were stagnating, one of their leaders suggested that they uproot once more and journey 'to the ends of the earth'. They travelled overland to Jutland in Denmark and from there took ships to Sweden. It is thought that this tribe fought with the Goths against the Romans in the wars of the third century AD.

In 550 Jordanes the Ostrogoth wrote of them, '[They came from] a great Island called Scandza [Scandinavia]… and burst forth like a swarm of bees from the lap of this island, and came to the lap of Europe.'

When in battle these Scandinavians were merciless, but when at home they were among the most courteous and honourable hosts of the Dark Ages. This quality was thought by Jordanes to be to do with the extreme fluctuations of the seasons in the northern parts of the world: 'In the middle of summer [Scandinavians] have continuous light for 40 days and nights; sorrow thus alternating with joy, so are they unlike others in benevolence and injury.'

'Unlike others in benevolence and injury'; it seemed to describe the Norsemen of the sagas perfectly. I had already seen how welcoming the modern Icelanders could be. I hoped they were no longer so delighted by causing injury.

*

I woke up the next morning on a sofa, and remembered the half sheep's head of the night before with a wave of nausea. No one else in the apartment was awake yet. I left a note on the kitchen table thanking the guys for the welcome they had given me, and went out to find some strong coffee.

My mind cast back over what I remembered of the evening before. Páll and his friends had drunk and partied with an abandon that was different from the parties I had been to before. I wondered if it was a function of the remoteness of Iceland, that people here lived out extremes more readily. I had seen an Icelandic film back in Edinburgh, *101 Reykjavik*, which dealt with the youth subculture in the city. Páll and Maria would have laughed at the film's polarisation of characters, but still may have recognised elements of their lives and those of their friends in it. The central character, Hlynur, is a twenty-something young man, still living with his mother and drawing unemployment benefit. He spent his weekdays sleeping and masturbating and his weekends staying out drinking continuously. 'Each weekend I drop dead,' he says in the movie. At one point he was asked what he did for a living and he replies only, 'Nothing.'

'What kind of nothing?' he is asked.

'A nothing kind of nothing.'

He is content for the excellent Icelandic welfare state to manage all of his needs. His nihilism is built up as a kind of Icelandic norm during the movie, and his approach to life is not really challenged by his mother or his friends. It is only on meeting an outsider from the south, a Spanish flamenco teacher, that his world is shocked into re-engaging with the possibilities open to him.

In a development that would seem natural only in the Nordic countries, Lola the flamenco teacher falls in love with Hlynur's mother and moves in with the two of them. On a drunken weekend with his mother away Lola and Hlynur sleep together and his world is given the jolt it needs. His life seems suddenly too shallow and his friends start to bore him. The announcement by Lola that she is pregnant with his child adds the final blow – Hlynur now has to watch his mother and his lover bring up his baby (who becomes his step-brother) in the house they all share.

101 Reykjavík is a slacker movie, but with an Icelandic twist. It was interesting that the woman to jolt Hlynur out of his stagnant life was chosen by the writer to be a southerner, and Maria had told me that in Iceland many people felt they needed more of a southern influence. Without it they were prone to melancholy, she said, especially during the long winter. Like Anna, the Icelandic woman I had met on the beaches of East Africa, ever-increasing numbers of Icelanders were leaving for several months of the year to sit out the winter months in the Mediterranean or even further south.

Hlynur's infatuation with an older woman also seemed more acceptable in Iceland than it would in much of the rest of Europe. The sagas have a multitude of strong female characters and it is not unusual in them for a young man to marry a powerful older woman. The film seemed to suggest it was a part of Icelandic culture that continued to the modern day.

*

In Reykjavík there is a saga museum dedicated to illustrating the way the Icelanders lived in the tenth and eleventh centuries. I took a walk around it in a daze, but it did not tell me anything I had not already read in the sagas themselves. As in Shetland I felt that to get a flavour of the past it would be better to get out into the countryside and see the traces of it that still lie in the landscape. It did not feel like a day for museums. As I had moved north I realised it would be progressively easier to find the routes of the individuals that I hoped to follow. In Shetland the classical descriptions were lost, and only hinted at. In the Faroes the descriptions were overlain with fantasy and religious symbolism. Now here, in Iceland, I could walk to places that were described, see them with the same names on the map and even follow particular features of the landscape.

I wanted to take a bus east to the Parliament Plains that Icelanders call Thingvellir. Icelanders claim that the Althing, the parliament that met there throughout the Middle Ages (and the name still given to the modern Icelandic parliament), was the first of its kind in Europe. It was where important decisions were made affecting the fortunes of all the powerful Icelandic families that had fled the tyranny of the King in Norway. For a couple of weeks each year the plain would fill with tents, booths and stalls. Clan-chiefs and globe-trotting Vikings would assemble to pass laws and judgement, make and break allegiances, and drink together.

The river coiled across the plain of Thingvellir like a blue ribbon cast to the wind. The flood banks it ran through shone a vivid green after the days of rainfall. This was the gathering place. Empty now, I tried to imagine the shouts and jeers, music and laughter, as the most important men in this fledgling state came here with their families over a thousand years ago and set up their tents and booths. There would have been horses and cattle, children running and playing, and hawkers shouting their wares. The air would have been filled with the smell of the beasts, roasting meat, ale, and unwashed bodies. The saga of Gunnlaug Serpent-Tongue talks of the women washing clothes down in the river here while the men fought, and sometimes died, for the right to marry one or the other of them. It was a brutal world they lived in but, beholden to no monarch, the people here lived lives in many ways more free than their European contemporaries. Together they could decide their own laws each year and review the penal code of the country. This began in the tenth century, nearly three centuries before the Magna Carta and the first Commons assembly in England. Christianity itself was adopted in Iceland in the year AD 1000 after a vote at the Althing (although Norway had recently begun a 'persuasion poli-cy' of kidnapping and ransoming the sons of the nobility to help sway the vote). It was also after a vote in 1117 that they decided to start writing the laws down instead of relying on 'Lawspeakers' to memorise them. There was fierce resistance to the idea at first. Many thought, as did Socrates before them, that reliance on books instead of memory would weaken the mind and promote vice and laziness.

Above the plain where the delegates slept, washed, and fought, stood the volcanic amphitheatre where they debated. It was as if a giant had thrust his fist up from beneath the earth's crust, tenting the thin skin of bedrock to the sky and cracking it open. Inside the rent in the earth, surrounded by walls of frozen lava which echoed and amplified sound, the men had at times debated for days on end. It is recorded that at the debate on whether to convert to Christianity one man had complained that the old gods would become unhappy with them, and had already cursed them for thinking of turning to the new faith. 'And what were the gods unhappy with when they tore these rocks and this earth,' a rationalist is recorded as replying.

Rationality was something they appeared to use only rarely, however. Decisions were swayed as much by the power a family wielded or the favours they could call upon as by a sense of justice. Like the tribal courts that still function today in many parts of the world, turning up at the Althing with twenty fighting men could help your cause as much as a sound argument.

*

In the diner in Reykjavík I had been looking through Egil's saga for clues that I could follow up now that I had arrived in Iceland. It was one of my favourites. Egil's tale bridges the gap between legend and historical events. His grandfather had been hounded out of Norway into Iceland by King Harald and his father was a *berserk* ('bear-shirt'), a shape-shifter who could fall into a mystical battle frenzy. It not only describes life in Iceland in the early years of the tenth century but also has international scope, the narrative moving between Iceland, Norway, the Slavic lands on the shores of the Baltic, and England.

At the age of three Egil was grounded because he could not handle his ale well enough. At seven he took an axe to the head of an older boy who beat him at a ball game, and his mother praised him for bravery. As a teenager he travelled to Norway and outdrank all the Vikings at the court of Eirik Blood-Axe. He then infuriated many of them by reciting better poetry than any of the court skàlds and narrowly escaped with his life. After a few years' raiding along the shores of the Baltic Sea he and his brother found themselves back in Norway, at the court of an earl who welcomed them. The men all drew straws for places at the table, and Egil found himself next to the Earl's beautiful daughter. His attempts to impress her failed, and she spoke a verse:

> What do you want my seat for?
> You have not often fed
> Wolves with warm flesh;
> I'd rather stoke my own fire.
> This autumn you did not see ravens
> Screeching over chopped bodies,
> You were not there when
> Razor-sharp blades clashed.

The most sensitive aspects of any Viking's pride were being attacked: his prowess as a warrior and his abilities as a poet. Egil was by this time skilled in both. He replied:

> I have wielded a blood-stained sword
> And howling spear; the bird
> Of carrion followed me
> When the Vikings pressed forth;
> In fury we fought battles,
> Fire swept through men's homes,
> We made bloody bodies
> Slump dead by city gates.

She was impressed. The saga reports that 'They drank together that night and got on well together.' How well they really got on is difficult to say. When the sagas were converted from an oral to a written tradition many of the literate scribes were monks. It is strongly suspected that gory as they are, the sagas were heavily censored.

It is difficult for translators to know how to approach the Old Norse poetry used in the sagas. Maria had confirmed for me that Icelanders can still read the original but the rest of us are not so lucky. The form uses kennings (a type of descriptive circumlocution) and a poetic trick known as a *drottkvaett* stanza, with eight lines of six syllables each. Alliteration, full rhyme and half rhyme are all laced with rich metaphors which were widely recognised and accepted by the intended audiences at the time but which can seem over-elaborate today. Translators inevitably have to sacrifice most of these to hold on to the sense of each line. But as a portable art form, Viking poetry was well suited to the way of life that men such as Egil led.

From the Norwegian court where he used his poetry to such good effect, Egil's story moves on to England, where he offers his services as a mercenary to Athelstan, the grandson of Alfred the Great.

The Dublin Vikings, the Britons of Strathclyde and the Scots marched down through England until they met Athelstan's army at a place known as Wen Heath. The location of this moor (possibly near Carlisle), has never been verified, though the battle that took place there was said to be the most bloody ever fought on English soil. The Anglo-Saxon Chronicle for that year, 937, is unusual in including a contemporary verse sung of the battle which illustrates how culturally similar the Anglo-Saxon and Viking worlds were at that time. The whole poem is a devastating hymn to the cruelty of war. This is an excerpt from the last few lines:

> The land of Wessex, triumphant in war.
> They left behind them, to enjoy the corpses,
> The horn-beaked raven, black of plumage,
> The white-tailed eagle, garbed in grey,
> The hungry war-hawk, and that dark beast
> The forest wolf. Never before,
> In all this island, as ancient sages
> Tell us in books, was an army put
> To greater slaughter.

✳

Five kings died there, and seven earls. The poem lingers over the ignominious retreat of 'the Northmen' and the 'hardy bands' of Scots, their numbers decimated by Athelstan's army. Egil's saga too is unusually descriptive in its account of the advance and retreat of the standard bearers through the chaos of battle, and painstakingly details the death of Egil's brother Thorolf. It is true that Athelstan was victorious, but according to the saga, only narrowly so.

The moor must have been soaked in blood. The Anglo-Saxon Chronicle hints that the battlefield was overrun with ravens, wolves and eagles that picked over the flesh of the fallen men. Egil's saga skips over such details, but the Irish Chronicles of the same era give us a description of a battlefield that leaves less to the imagination. In the mid 880s after a battle between some Danes and Norwegians on a stretch of Irish coast, some messengers from Maelsechlainn, the High King of Ireland, went to meet the victors. There were not enough stones on the field for their cooking pots and so the Danes balanced their cauldrons on piles of dead Norwegians, bracing them together with long spits so that the flames burst their bellies. The Danes defended their behaviour to the Irishmen, saying the Norwegians would have done the same to them given half the chance. The annals report that the messengers went away impressed by the Danes, who seemed more cultured than the Norwegians that they were more used to in Ireland: 'for the Danes had at least a kind of piety; they were for piety's sake capable of ceasing for a while from their eating and drinking.'

*

Athelstan's victory meant that he ruled all the lands from the Dorset coast to the river Forth. For the loss of his brother he compensated Egil with three gold arm rings weighing a mark each, and two chests full of silver. Egil returned to Iceland and married his widowed sister-in-law, as was the custom.

The saga is quiet about his next few years. He lived a quiet life as a settled landowner in Borg, visiting the Althing each year and managing his estate. In this period it includes a description of his father Skallagrim's funeral: 'Skallagrim's body was put in a ship and they rowed with it out to Digranes. Egil had a mound made on the edge of the promontory, where Skallagrim was laid to rest with his horse and weapons and tools.' It was one of the very few descriptions of a place in Iceland that might still be identifiable. In the twenty-first century there is still a settlement called Borg to the north of Reykjavík, within the commuter belt. Anna the Icelandic woman I had met in East Africa lived there, and had told me to look her up if I ever made it that far north.

*

On the bus to Borg I was the only passenger. The suburbs of Reykjavík thinned out, and the road dropped down to skirt the coastline. The low cloud had rolled in again, and sea fog clung to the shore, obscuring the water. According to the map the road ran around the littoral of Hvalfjörð – 'Whale Fjord' – but there were no whales to see. It was smothered in banks of mist. The few cars that passed were sturdy jeeps and four-wheel-drives, their headlights softened into haloes and the sound of their engines dampened by the wet air. The bus left the district of Reykjanes and entered the lands claimed over a thousand years before by Skallagrim.

The mist gradually cleared and features of the coastline emerged. Bare escarpments of coal-grey rocks rose almost immediately from the water's edge, where great piles of rubble had slid towards the sea. Between the sheer grey slopes and the tidal zone lay a viridian green strip of earth which carried the road around the edge of the mountain. Its colour stood out from the dull monotone of the rock, the sea and the sky.

The road rounded a shoulder of the mountain to a vantage point over the Borgarfjörð. A low concrete bridge crossed the strait and joined the Digranes peninsula where Skallagrim had been buried, a cold black ridge of lava soaking in sub-Arctic water. Onto its thin spine was squeezed the village of Borgarnes, and beyond it Borg.

I doubted the landscape had changed much in a thousand years. Even as a commuter town it was a backwater, an outpost on the edge of the ocean, poles apart from the courts of mediaeval Scandinavia or the battlefields of England. Yet the boy who grew up there ended up shaping the history of powerful nations like Norway, Denmark and Wessex.

*

Anna's and her husband Olafur's house was a typical suburban home, a white cube on a friendly street that seemed out of place in the landscape that lay around the town. The black cliffs to the south across the fjord seemed to glower in disapproval. Electric lighting and central heating, however appreciated by the people of Borg, jarred with their surroundings. I had the impression that the mires around the town wanted to swallow it up.

Anna had welcomed me in enthusiastically. 'Oh my God, I can't believe you made it up here!' she had shouted, 'Come in, come in!'

She showed me through to the kitchen, where fresh bread was baking and the table was set for dinner. Olafur opened a bottle of wine. 'So,' I asked. 'How was the rest of your stay in Africa?'

She had been working as an administrator for a project trying to prevent malaria transmission through the distribution of mosquito nets for children. 'And how did you get on with the project?' I asked.

'Fine, fine. It was an amazing thing to be part of. But my job and funding came to an end, the ex-pats were all pulling out. And now I'm back! My time there seems to have gone so quickly.'

'And what are you up to now?' I asked her.

'Just doing some office work for a company in Reykjavík. It pays the bills, but to be honest we're glad to be leaving. We're heading off in a few weeks' time. Olafur's got a new job, in London.'

Olafur is a scientist, and had been on a visiting scholarship while Anna was working and travelling in Africa. I asked if he was going to work with the same team.

'That's right,' he said. 'It's brilliant to get offered a contract, and there'll be so many more opportunities for Anna in London than there are here, to keep doing the kind of thing she wants to do.' Anna wanted to find more work in non-governmental organisations that work with humanitarian projects. It was a way, she hoped, of doing work she loved and felt was important while continuing to be able to live in two worlds, north and south.

'It's a pity that there aren't more chances for you guys to do the things you want to do here in Iceland,' I said.

'Well actually it's pretty common to leave in your twenties for ten, or even twenty years,' said Olafur. 'There just aren't enough people in Iceland to support the kind of science that I'm involved in, or the kind of charities that Anna wants to work in. Icelanders often leave for university in Scandinavia, the UK or the US, and then get their experience abroad before returning if they can, once they're more established. We all want to come back eventually; well, most of us. You could say we're over-educated.'

'I heard that Icelanders read more books than people in any other nation,' I said, 'maybe that's why you're so educated.'

'It could be just because we're so brainy,' Anna laughed, 'or it could be because there's nothing else to do in the winter here but read! It's either that or turn to drink!'

'So how's your trip going?' asked Olafur. 'Anna told me a bit about it. Which explorer are you following now?'

I explained that I wasn't really following an explorer, but was looking for traces of the Iceland that existed in the time of Egil's saga. I asked if they knew of any archaeological sites or monuments in the area. They smiled at the oddness of a foreigner being so interested in the sagas.

'There's something in the park in the village, we'll take you there in the morning,' said Anna. 'But you must be hungry, what have you tried of Icelandic food so far?'

'Only hamburgers and sheep heads, I'm afraid. Why, are you going to serve me some rotten shark meat?'

'Oh, so you've heard about *hákarl*?' said Olafur, with a grin. 'No sorry, a bit of an acquired taste for a foreigner. Tonight it's just mutton and potatoes.'

'That sounds fine to me,' I said, lifting my glass of wine. 'A toast, to Egil Skallagrimsson and the weird tastes of Icelanders!'

*

The next morning Anna and Olafur drove me over to the Digranes peninsula. It jutted into the fjord like a curved rib-bone, snapped out of its skin. One street ran the length of the village of Borgarnes in a gentle slope. They took me to a park with a small mound at one end. A plaque by its side suggested it was the site of Skallagrim's burial, but in truth it was unlikely to be the real location. His grave is a great loss for archaeology not only because there is such a clear description of what was buried in it in the saga, but because it was the burial place not only of Skallagrim, but also of Egil's son, Bodvar. The discovery of two skeletons inside, of an old and a young man, would have been a great boost to the credibility of the saga.

The saga says Bodvar was drowned in the fjord by a freak storm, and his body was washed up on the shore. A sculpted relief by the mound in the park showed Egil on horseback with his son draped over the saddle. The saga describes Egil as an ugly man, and the relief showed his craggy face, stony with grief. According to the saga, after placing his son in the burial mound he locked himself away in his sleeping closet, refusing to eat or drink, and claiming that he wanted to die. It was only the intervention of his daughter Thorgerd that saved him. She rode from her home to join her father, claiming that she too wanted to join him in Valhalla. Once inside his bed-closet with him she cunningly persuaded him to live in order to write an elegy for Bodvar. The poem, 'The Loss of My Sons', is included in the saga and has immortalised the grief of a father for his son.

Later the saga describes Egil's descent into a cantankerous old age, spent griping at his grandchildren and writing poems about his 'drooping, dribbling' penis, or the aches in his bones. His last act before dying was to ride out into the marshes around Borg and bury the two chests of silver King Athelstan had given him. It is not clear from the text whether he too was buried along with his father and son in the mound of Digranes, but it seems likely that he would have been.

A description of the burial rituals of the Vikings, like those that may have been performed for Skallagrim and Bodvar, has by chance survived not among the Norwegians but among their Swedish neighbours. For powerful individuals these rituals seem to have involved human sacrifice. There is evidence from Norway and the Isle of Man that the slaves of powerful Vikings sometimes followed their masters to the grave, and the Icelanders too came from Norwegian culture and were rich in slaves. Skallagrim is described in the saga as killing one of his own slaves in a rage, after she had dared to come between him and Egil while he was trying to discipline him. But no slave sacrifices have yet been found in Iceland. It could be that they did occur but authentic descriptions of burial rituals were censored out of the sagas by monks over the centuries, or it could be that in Iceland slaves were too precious to kill. We have the literacy of the Arabs to thank for the preservation of at least one eye-witness account.

Ibn Fadlan, an ambassador from the mighty Islamic empire of the Abbasids, was living on the Volga in the year 922 and described the funeral of a Swedish chieftain there. The tone of his description hovers around that of astonished amusement: the Arabs and Persians needed the slaves that the Swedes brought down out of the forests of Eastern Europe, but they never forgot that they were dealing with a barbarian culture. Many of the Norsemen were, after all, still living in huts of wood and turf while the Caliphate was revolutionising architecture with cities such as Baghdad and Córdoba.

His account is a window into a forgotten world. First of all, he says that the slave girl volunteered for the duty: 'So, when the man of whom I spoke had died, they asked his girls, 'Who will die with him?' One of them answered, 'I.' She was then committed to two girls, who were to keep watch over her… During the whole of this period, the girl gave herself over to drinking and singing, and was cheerful and gay.'

A ship was drawn ashore and lavishly decorated, and the dead man was dressed in cloth of gold and propped on pillows and quilts inside it. His skin had turned black. A dog, two horses, two oxen, a cock and a hen were slaughtered, chopped into pieces and thrown into the ship. And then the ritual developed a theme indicating the ancient inextricability among pagan faiths of the two rulers of destiny: sex and death. 'The girl who had devoted herself to death meanwhile walked to and fro, entering one after another of the tents which they had there. The occupant of each tent lay with her, saying, 'Tell your master, "I did this only for love of you."'

She was given strong drink, and was starting to stagger. Three times she was hoisted into the air to look over a ceremonial wooden frame which had been built for the funeral. Each time she reported that she saw paradise approaching.

Once inside the ship she was approached by an old woman called the Angel of Death, 'She was dark, thick-set, with a lowering countenance,' Fadlan says. What followed sounds like a sacrifice to Óðin. The girl's jewellery was stripped from her body and she was roughly dragged into a tent on the ship where her dead master was propped on his silk cushions.

> At this moment the men began to beat upon their shields with the staves, in order to drown the noise of her outcries, which might have terrified the other girls, and deterred them from seeking death with their masters in the future. Then six men followed into the tent, and each and every one had carnal companionship with her. Then they laid her down by her master's side, while two of the men seized her

by the feet, and two by the hands. The old woman known as the Angel of Death now knotted a rope around her neck, and handed the ends to two of the men to pull. Then with a broad-bladed dagger she smote her between the ribs, and drew the blade forth, while the two men strangled her with the rope till she died.

One of the dead man's kinsmen walked naked to the hull of the ship and with a burning torch set it alight.

A Swede approached Fadlan and his interpreter. 'You Arabs are stupid,' he said.

'Why?' asked the ambassador.

'Because you take the people you love and honour most and put them in the ground, where worms and insects eat them. But we burn them in the twinkling of an eye, so that they enter Paradise at that very moment.'

After lunch I said goodbye to Anna and Olafur and hitched north. The Icelandic landscape impresses with a clarity and a simplicity which turns the mind to reflections on Earth and Time. There are almost no trees, and its soil is disappearing fast. The volcanic unfolding of its geology is evident in every hillside and valley. The mountains seem hastily constructed, and are toppling down again so quickly that serrated peaks and arêtes line its horizons. The icecaps which deserted most of Europe over ten thousand years ago still groan and creak through the mountains' narrow shoulders, splintering and cracking under their own weight. There is so much *space*. The roads are raised like Dutch dykes traversing the endless flood plains formed from spring thaws and summer rains, and the farms are solitary and occasional. The Icelandic wind is relentless; it is a standing joke among Icelanders how many over-enthusiastic cyclists arrive from continental Europe only to abandon their bicycles after the first few miles. Hitch-hiking through the west of Iceland, the landscape reminded me of Patagonia: the same backdrop of snow-dusted mountains, the same ubiquity of sheep, and the same enormity of space in which to lose oneself.

The Icelandic landscape was not always so barren. When the Norsemen arrived at the end of the ninth century it was well forested with birch and willow. As each new settler claimed a new plot of land they set about burning it to clear pasture. They had been fooled into thinking that the soils of Iceland would be like the ones they knew well from Norway and Scotland, because the same sort of vegetation grew there. They had no way of knowing that without the woodland the much lighter volcanic dusts that make up Icelandic soils would quickly leach away with the rains and be blown away by the storms. Grazing sheep on the land only accelerated the decline and so, within only decades of the arrival of the Norsemen, many of the higher pastures were already on their way to becoming deserts. Lower pastures, where the ancient soil could be up to twenty metres deep, survived for centuries rather than decades, but eventually many of those too have been denuded. The winters are so cold in Iceland and the pressures on the land so great that even with the best modern farming practices the rate of soil formation occurs painfully slowly. One recent book described Iceland's landscape as, 'ecologically the most heavily damaged in Europe.'

The Icelandic government is well aware of the scale of the problem, and has been directing large amounts of its resources to finding a solution. They were the first nation in the world to set up an agency to study soil conservation, and they recently hosted a NATO conference on restoring ecologically damaged environments. The president has recently announced a strategic partnership with soil scientists at a major US university to develop new initiatives in soil conservation. Iceland aims to become carbon-neutral within 25 years, and finding plants that could reverse the leaching of its soils and sequester carbon at the same time could revolutionise agriculture, not only for its own suffering farmers, but for farmers everywhere. Their hope is that if successful, they will find the way to roll back the relentless desertification of many fragile environments all over the world.

*

One day I dropped down towards Iceland's second town, Akureyri, a fishing port in the north. It lies at the head of the Eyjafjörð, the longest slash of coastline to cut into the island, and has one of the most sheltered harbours in the land. From a sun-warmed concrete pier I counted trawlers and cargo vessels from all over the North Atlantic. The fjord was like a narrow but extravagant boulevard stretching into the north, lined by soaring mountains and traversed by ships sailing out into the Arctic. Vessels left from here to ferry to and from the island of Grimsey, the only part of Iceland which crosses the Arctic Circle.

The Arctic Circle, at 66° 33′ north, is the line of latitude along which for at least one day of the year the sun will not set, and for at least one day of the year will not rise. The Norsemen, who lived all their lives with light summers and dark winters, showed little interest in it. But for the classical world it had represented the outer fringes of the earth. I had finally caught up with the limit of Pytheas' travels.

*

Once he reached Iceland he must have skirted its shores until coming to the northern coast. It is as wild and exposed to blasts of Arctic weather now as it would have been then. Perhaps he met with a now forgotten local people when he went ashore to fetch fresh water, or maybe he met with a summer hunting party of men out of Shetland or Faroe. Perhaps his guides to Thule had travelled with him all the way from either of those groups of islands. Either way, the only direct quote from 'Concerning the Ocean' which survives today is a phrase from Geminus of Rhodes about Iceland, where he quotes Pytheas' statement that on Thule, 'the barbarians revealed to us the sleeping place of the sun.'

We need to jump between even more texts to find out what happened next. The first is back to Pliny's *Naturalis Historia* where it is written that, 'one day's sail from Thule is the frozen ocean called by some the Cronian Sea.'

It seems that Pytheas sailed north out of Iceland until he was stopped by the edge of the Arctic pack-ice, which can extend all the way to the northern coastline itself. He and his men must have been afraid. The Mediterranean was a distant memory, and they were approaching the very bounds of the world. It sounds as though instead of the edge of the earth they came to a region of thick polar fog where the motion of the waves was breaking up the edge of the pack-ice. The ship could not go on through the ice, but neither were the men able to get out and walk. It was an entirely new experience. Strabo describes the scene: '[In] those regions there was no longer either land properly so-called, or sea, or air, but a kind of substance concreted from all of these elements, resembling sea-lungs, a thing in which, he says, the earth, the sea, and all the elements are held in suspension; and this is a sort of bond to hold all together, which you can neither walk nor sail upon.'

Whatever it is that he encountered, it was said to resemble a 'sea-lung'. The word, *Pleumōn thalattios* in Greek and *Pulmico Marinos* in Latin, has had different interpretations among classical authors. Plato and Aristotle both used it to describe a kind of mollusc, but to Pliny it meant 'jellyfish'. Suddenly the metaphor comes alive; the whole surface of the sea was seen to have an opaque and gelatinous skin that seemed to pulse in a rhythm with the waves like the contractions of a colossal jellyfish. The air had changed, replaced by dense freezing fog in which the horizon itself had vanished. The men could neither sail nor walk on the substance in which they were increasingly becoming beset. All the elements: the air, the ice, and the sea, seemed to be transforming into a gelid soup.

Pytheas dropped his sails and his men took to their oars. There were no Hyperboreans after all. He turned the ship around, broke out of the ice and began the long voyage back to the Mediterranean.

Like Odysseus before him, he seemed to have come to the very edge of the world.

*

On a hillside overlooking Akureyri stood its botanical gardens. In its thin soil, shrubs, trees and flowers more at home on the shores of the Mediterranean scrabble for life on the edge of the Arctic Ocean. The trees tossed their branches in a gentle breeze, delicate yellow flowers unfurled into the sunlight. Spring comes late to Iceland, and in June the gardens still quivered with expectancy. Apart from the whisper of the leaves it was silent, but I could imagine that below the threshold of hearing lay the hum of the trees and grass, the creak and snap of cellulose dividing; the sound of summer arriving. In the gardens I met another traveller in search of a promised land.

A young woman sat on one of the benches. Her hair was clipped short and a long pleated tail, rescued from the shears, hung from what had once been her fringe. She had been dozing in the sun, but opened her eyes when I sat on the bench to admire the view. 'It's beautiful, isn't it?' she asked me. She closed her eyes and settled more comfortably into the bench. 'I love it here.'

She was a Dane from Århus, whose childhood had been spent among the communes and squats of Copenhagen's Christiania, one of the world's few successful 'anarchist' enclaves. When a crowd of idealists in the seventies claimed the sprawl of dockland warehouses as their own, the government had responded with a level of tolerance and humanity which characterises the Danish nation in modern times. 'Why not?' they said.

As a reaction to a childhood spent playing in dark warehouses and learning to deal with the demands of communal living, she had turned to the wide open spaces of the world. At age ten she had walked the streets of Kathmandu, and at age eighteen she had returned there. But she had missed the North Atlantic and had now come to Iceland on a pilgrimage to indulge the greatest love of her life: Icelandic horses. For centuries, she told me, they were the only means of travelling overland on the island and had developed a unique fifth gait to help them cope with the dangerous terrain. She had worked for two months on a ranch in the south-west and had at first enjoyed the chance to ride and to care for a whole herd of these beautiful animals. But she had been lied to by her employers. They worked her too hard, did not allow her any leave, and in the wide and empty valley she had felt increasingly trapped. One dusky night she had packed up her belongings, written a note in questionable Icelandic, and fled. Now in Akureyri she had found somewhere to rest.

Her questions came two or three at a time. 'What do you think?' she asked, 'I could start a shop here making and selling clothes.' 'Have you seen the shopping street in the town?' 'I think there will be a lot of tourists here later in the summer.' 'Do you think I could get a grant from the Icelandic government?'

I did not have any answers. Iceland has learned to defend its economy fiercely. Its people are too few, its situation too remote, and its resources too scarce to take any chances with immigrants and their business ideas. But an agreement persists with Norway and Denmark, its old colonial rulers. The citizens of those countries can still slip through the red tape more easily than other foreign nationals.

She sighed and closed her eyes once more. 'We will see. But I like it here in the North. I feel *truer* here somehow.'

*

Hitching in Iceland was usually the same routine: a smart spacious car pulled up, sometimes a people-carrier, sometimes a four-wheel drive. I ran after it dragging my rucksack, and looked expectantly into the passenger window. A smile or a nod and the door opened. Usually the driver was alone. I mentioned the name of a town, or a headland; another nod, and I climbed in. Empty roads, the radio playing frenetic Icelandic pop or a discussion programme, the language like a melody, unchanged over the centuries and to me intricate and mysterious. Always silence between myself and the driver. And then a mile or so from the agreed destination, the questions, in flawless English: Where was I from? Was it cold out at night? How long would I stay? Did I like Iceland? And always I waited until spoken to; to fill the silence with unwanted chatter would be violating it. Within the last few shared minutes we could be like old friends, reluctant to part. I have addresses of roadside acquaintances from all over the north of Europe.

I hitched a lift from Akureyri to the northern town of Húsavík. At its south end there was a fishing harbour and a small museum which paid homage to the whaling industry. They now made money advertising whale-watching tours, and I took one. For an afternoon I watched minké whales soaring through the water and Arctic terns wheeling and diving in the shelter of the bay. The open-air swimming pools lay at the other end of the town, mercifully upwind of the fishing harbour.

Despite its cold climate, Iceland luxuriates in heat. Geothermal power stations suck abundant and endless energy from the lava bubbling under its thin crust. In many of its villages there are public baths with separate magma-heated pools at three or four different temperatures. That the pools are often in the open air adds to the surrealism of the experience. Squalls of snow and banks of freezing fog roll across them while people lounge in the shallows wearing swimsuits. As I lay in the water children shrieked and splashed around me, and pensioners gossiped together in the hot tubs. My mind was cast up and out into a serene place which fills the space between the mountains. I was pleased to have made it up to the north-east corner of Iceland. There was another trail that I could pick up there.

Another of my favourite sagas was the saga of Gunnlaug Serpent-Tongue. Like Egil's saga the narrative in Iceland moves between the homesteads of the Borgarfjörd and the Parliament Plains of Thingvellir. It also has international scope, jumping between events in Norway, Sweden and England. Unlike Egil's saga the story at several points swings up to the north-east corner of Iceland. It is an empty quarter of the country, with blasted moors and an unforgiving landscape. It was the very difficulty of the terrain that had a major effect on the outcome of Gunnlaug's saga, and I wanted to see it for myself.

*

Between modern Icelanders it is common, on first meeting, to ask, 'Who are your people?' It is a way of connecting a new acquaintance into the web of friends and relations that stretches across the small Icelandic population. Even today the Icelandic phone book is arranged by first name, and each person takes as a surname the first name of his or her father or mother just as they did in the Saga Age.

The saga of Gunnlaug Serpent-Tongue begins in a similar way, establishing connections in the minds of the audience by first introducing one of the famous Egil Skallagrimsson's sons, named Thorstein. One night Thorstein Egilsson had a dream that he had a daughter who brought great unhappiness into the world. His wife was heavily pregnant at the time, and as he rode out to the Althing shortly afterwards he told her that if she was to have a daughter while he was away she was to leave it outside to die. The saga explains his behaviour: 'When the country was completely heathen, it was something of a custom for poor men with many dependants in their families to have their children exposed. Even so, it was always considered a bad thing to do.'

The baby girl was so beautiful that his wife could not bear to expose her, and so she sent her to be brought up with her sister-in-law (Thorgerd, the same woman who had rescued Egil from his suicide bid not long before). While visiting his sister's home six years later Thorstein commented on the beauty of a girl playing by the fire, and was finally told that it was his own daughter.

'I cannot blame you for this,' he said, '... I'm so pleased with this girl that I count myself very lucky to have such a beautiful child.'

He took her home to Borg with him and brought her up in his household. She was called Helga, Helga the Fair.

At the same time on the banks of the river Hvita at the head of the Borgarfjörð a young boy was growing up, the son of a great Viking named Illugi the Black. The boy was strong-willed, ambitious and argumentative, but supremely gifted with words. He was called Gunnlaug, and his skills as a poet earned him the nickname 'Serpent-Tongue'. At twelve he resolved to run away to see the world, but his father would not let him. In a fit of pique, he left his father's household and went to work for Thorstein Egilsson at Borg. He became playmates with Helga, and in time they fell in love.

When Gunnlaug was eighteen he approached his father once again and said that he wanted to travel abroad. This time Illugi agreed to let him go. As a parting gift he bought him a one half-share in a trading ship headed for Norway. Gunnlaug began to have second thoughts about leaving Helga behind but there was a lot at stake, both his father's status in the community and the significant investment he had made in the ship. He was torn between staying with the woman he loved and his thirst to see the world before settling down as a husband and landowner. Shortly before he was due to leave, Thorstein offered Gunnlaug a fine stallion as a parting gift, but he refused.

'But why don't you offer me something I will accept?' he said.

'What's that?' Thorstein asked.

'Your daughter, Helga the Fair,' Gunnlaug replied.

'That will not be arranged so swiftly,' he said, and changed the subject.

When Illugi heard that Thorstein had refused his son's proposal, it meant that the honour of his son, and by extension himself, was at stake. He rode to Borg and warned Thorstein that he counted the refusal as an affront to his family. As they argued Thorstein used his political skill to reach a compromise. He agreed to 'promise' Helga to Gunnlaug, but would not formally betrothe them. Helga would wait three years, and if Thorstein did not like the way Gunnlaug turned out after his travels, he would be free of obligation. Gunnlaug agreed, and set sail for Trondheim.

That summer and the next, probably those of 1003 and 1004, brought good winds, and Gunnlaug travelled throughout the Norse world composing his poetry. In Trondheim his insolence nearly got him killed and Earl Eirik Hakonarson swore that he would never live another eighteen years. In Dublin King Sigtrygg Silk-Beard gave him a suit of fine cloth and a fur cloak, and in Orkney Earl Sigurð Hloðvesson rewarded him with a fine broad-axe.

The King of England at this time was Ethelred II, whom history has cursed with the name of 'the Unready'. Rather than being unprepared, his name arose from his readiness to refuse advice: *un-raed* in Anglo-Saxon means 'without counsel'. In thanks for a poem Gunnlaug composed for him, Ethelred gave him a fine cloak lined with furs and decorated with an embroidered band, and a sword that saved him from a Danish *berserk* who tried to mug him on the streets of London. In gratitude Gunnlaug became his follower and spent the winter there. When he left the English court the King made him promise to come back the following year, after he had travelled to Sweden and the court of King Olaf. It was there that he met his match. Hráfn Onundarsson is described in the saga as a 'big, dashing man', and he did not take kindly to sharing the honour of being the skáld of the Swedish court. They argued, both tried to impress King Olaf, and both insulted one another's poetry in public. Although they were fellow Icelanders, by late spring they were sworn enemies.

Hráfn sailed for Iceland, and Gunnlaug returned to England to spend the winter with Ethelred once more. He had now been away for nearly three years, had won great riches, and was looking forward to returning to Iceland to marry Helga. But in the spring when he asked for leave to return, Ethelred refused.

Looking into other historical sources we can find clues why Ethelred might have been reluctant to part with a man like

Gunnlaug. The previous ten years had seen him spending ever greater amounts on *Danegeld*, or protection money, to stop the Danes harrying his shores. In November of that year, 1004, he had had enough, and instead of paying up ordered the death of every Danish man and woman in his kingdom. The massacre took place on St Brice's Day, the Danes' bathing day, and he knew that they would be unprepared. Memories of the event were still sharp enough two centuries later for this account of the massacre to be written by John of Wallingford: 'They spared neither age nor sex, destroying together with them those women of their own nation who had consented to intermix with the Danes, and the children who had sprung from that foul adultery. Some women had their breasts cut off, others were buried alive in the ground, while the children were dashed to pieces against posts and stones.'

It is a mark of the authenticity of the sagas that they are often accurate about historical events, even though they were written down as much as two hundred years after the events they describe. The mercilessness of Ethelred succeeded only in rousing the Danish armies against him with even more ferocity. He told Gunnlaug: 'Since you are my follower it is not appropriate for you to leave me when such a war threatens England.'

'That is for you to decide, my lord,' he replied, hoping that Helga would wait for him. 'But give me permission to leave next summer, if the Danes don't come.'

The following summer he managed to catch the last ship bound for Iceland. It was bound for the north-east corner of the country, a peninsula called Melrakkasletta, and so he would have a long ride through some of the roughest terrain in Iceland in order to make it back to Helga before the winter closed in.

Meanwhile Gunnlaug's rival Hráfn had heard about this most beautiful of women waiting in Iceland. The previous year he had approached Thorstein to ask for Helga's hand in marriage. He reminded Thorstein that three years had passed and Gunnlaug still had not returned.

'Yes,' said Thorstein, 'but the summer isn't gone, and he might yet come back… We'll all come back here next summer, and then we'll be able to see what seems to be the best way forward.'

Another year passed, and at the next parliament Thorstein agreed that if Gunnlaug did not return soon, Hráfn could marry Helga in the late autumn. Helga was said to be less than happy about the new arrangement.

Gunnlaug reached Iceland with fourteen days to spare before the wedding. The night before he was due to ride to Helga he fell and broke his ankle. Slowed by his injury, with ten men he started riding through the Melrakkasletta, down the Jökulsá á Fjöllum river and then turned west to cross the interior of Iceland. He had heard about the wedding plans, and knew time was running out.

✳

From Húsavík I hitched a lift across a ridge of hills and down into an alluvial plain. To the north of it sands stretched to the ocean, crossed by a delta of glacial melt water. The river was a daughter of Iceland's greatest ice-cap, the Vatnajökull, which lay off to the south beyond the horizon. Its waters meandered over the silt and swamp of the delta in fast-flowing eddies and locked up in pools, glittering amber in the evening sunlight.

We crossed the Jökulsá á Fjöllum, the river that Gunnlaug would have followed, and the road swung towards the north. Flat-topped mountains irrupted from the scrub-lands to the east, solitary and decapitated. Even on their lower slopes there were still pockets of snow. They stretched into a wide and empty peninsula, the Melrakkasletta, strewn with bogs and lava fields which reached out towards the Arctic Circle. After a few miles I asked the driver to stop and let me off. I climbed up away from the road towards the route that Gunnlaug must have taken.

It was after midnight when I stopped to pitch the tent. I had watched the sun set an hour before and it was just about to rise again. The horizon was suffused with a soft ember glow. Owls hunted around me in the half-light while the moon rose, crisp and round as a blood-orange.

After another day of walking across the moor I was looking down over the river delta of the Jökulsá á Fjöllum once again. On the other side of it lay the volcanic formation of Ásbyrgi, with scooped-out walls of cliffs standing in graceful arcs. The formations are hundreds of metres wide, gouged into the solid plateau of lava like giant hoof-prints in sand. I took a footpath that wound up past them onto the plateau through gradually thinning forests of pine and birch. The river oozed between giant plugs of basalt like liquid opal, heavy with glacial silt. Freshwater tributaries trickled in from the banks, bleeding thin streaks of clear midnight blue into it.

The path beside the river grew more difficult. Sometimes it led into the river itself, and a small signpost indicated that I should roll up my trouser-legs and wade across. Once it led directly to a rope dangling from a cliff-face and I realised that Gunnlaug, on horseback, must have taken another path. The rock was shiny and smooth where many hands had scrabbled their way to the top. Once up on the plateau the moor rolled out in an expanse of heather and scrub, and the air was thick and warm. It hummed with insects, and plovers flitted anxiously in the sky watching their nests.

It took me two days to walk from Ásbyrgi to where the river leapt into the air at the great waterfall of Dettifoss. I stopped to watch it tumbling through the gorge like molten lead, saturating the air with spray and a roar that silenced everything else. I admired it for an hour, then turned west, following Gunnlaug's route into the interior of Iceland.

*

Gunnlaug reached his father's house on the very evening before Helga and Hráfn's wedding. His father refused to let him go on down to Borg where he still had a chance of stopping the ceremony, and with his broken ankle he was a prisoner.

Helga was miserable. She assumed Gunnlaug was dead and

went through with the wedding to Hráfn, having no idea that just
a few miles away he had returned and was trapped in his father's
house. Hráfn, however, quickly heard rumours of Gunnlaug's return. Soon afterwards Helga lay in bed watching her new husband
having a bad dream. When he woke he told her that in his night-
mare he had been stabbed with a sword staining their bed with
blood. The odd metaphor he used for a sword, a 'yew of Serpent's
dew', was a direct reference to Gunnlaug with his Serpent-Tongue
and Helga realised that her husband was afraid. That could mean
only one thing: Gunnlaug must be alive. She wept bitterly that she
had been tricked, and insisted that they move back to her father's
house at Borg where she would be closer to him. It was not long
until the two lovers met up at another wedding, that of Helga's
half-sister:

> The women were sitting on the cross-bench, and Helga
> the Fair was next to the bride. She often cast her eyes in
> Gunnlaug's direction, and so it was proved that, as the say-
> ing goes, 'if a woman loves a man, her eyes won't hide it'.
> Gunnlaug was well turned out, and had on the splendid
> clothes which King Sigtrygg had given him. He seemed
> far superior to other men for many reasons, what with his
> strength, his looks and his figure.

They spoke together after the wedding, and Gunnlaug composed
poems in praise of her beauty. He told her why he had been delayed,
and gave her the English cloak given to him by Ethelred. Hráfn
threatened him, and the two men were pulled back from one another
and prevented from fighting. The married couple returned to Borg,
but Helga had made up her mind; she would never sleep with Hráfn
again now that she knew Gunnlaug was alive.

Gunnlaug and Hráfn tried to fight at the parliament the next
year but were stopped again, and the very next day a law was passed
outlawing duelling in Iceland. The two lovers met afterwards on
the riverbank at Thingvellir, and though Gunnlaug took much joy

in seeing Helga, his poem hints at the sadness he anticipates will come from their love.

> The moon of her eyelash – that valkyrie
> Adorned with linen, server of herb-surf,
> Shone hawk-sharp upon me
> Beneath her brow's bright sky;
> But that beam from the eyelid-moon
> Of the goddess of the golden torque
> Will later bring trouble to me
> And to the ring-goddess herself.

*

Hráfn seems to have felt the dishonour most keenly, living as he was with the most beautiful woman in Iceland but made unwelcome in her bed. He burst into Gunnlaug's house one day with twelve men and challenged him to a duel overseas. They would sail to Trondheim and fight there.

Once again Gunnlaug rode to Melrakkasletta. He put off leaving for as long as he possibly could, and this was the only passage he could find. It seems that he was still troubled by indecision. He was so late in leaving that he had to winter in the Orkney Islands, and by the time he reached Trondheim Hráfn had gone east again, to Sweden. With two Norwegian guides he set off in pursuit. He caught up with Hráfn by a small lake in the Swedish forests. The Norwegians guides were asked to stay out of the fight to tell the story of the battle.

The forest rang with their cries and with the sound of swords on chain-mail. Gunnlaug killed two of Hráfn's men at once, and Hráfn too fought bravely. 'In the end, all their companions fell.' Gunnlaug was fighting with the sword given to him by Ethelred, and with one stroke he cut Hráfn's leg cleanly off. Still Hráfn did not fall. He hopped backwards and dropped the severed end of his leg onto a tree stump. It was a mortal wound. His leg spurted blood on the earth, but he was composed enough to carry on a conversation:

'"Now you're past fighting," Gunnlaug said, "and I will not fight with you, a wounded man, any longer."

"It is true that things have turned against me, rather," Hráfn replied, "but I should be able to hold out all right if I could get something to drink.""

Gunnlaug went to the lake and filled his helmet with water. He handed it to Hráfn, asking him on his honour not to trick him.

> But as Hráfn reached out his left hand for it, he hacked at Gunnlaug's head with the sword in his right hand, causing a hideous wound.
>
> 'Now you have cruelly deceived me,' Gunnlaug said, 'and you have behaved in an unmanly way, since I trusted you.
>
> 'That is true,' Hráfn replied, 'and I did it because I would not have you receive the embrace of Helga the Fair.'

And so Gunnlaug killed him. The wound in his head was partially through the skull. According to the saga he was carried to a church by the Norwegian guides and was given last rites by a priest. He died three days later.

*

Helga never forgot him. After a while Thorstein found her another husband who lived out in the Westfjords. Though she did not really love him they were happy enough, and had several children. For the rest of her life, from time to time she would take out the cloak that Gunnlaug had given her and stare at it for hours.

One year there was a terrible plague going through the valleys, and Helga caught it. As her body grew weaker she asked for the cloak to be brought, and spread it out over her sick bed. Its fine furs and embroidered bands, fit for the English court, must have looked as if they came from a magical otherworld, unconnected with that poor farmhouse in a distant corner of Iceland. Thorstein's dream had proved true; the life of his daughter had brought great unhappiness into the world after all. But as she lay dying, I wonder if her last thought was that the greatest unhappiness it brought was her own. Still, despite all of her misery, the saga's message is clear: it is better to live with all the heaviness and drama of life than to have left a baby girl outside to die.

✳

The landscape of Iceland's interior is scarred and wounded, as if the skin of the earth has been torn. One of the greatest fault-lines in the crust of the planet runs through the centre of the country, and the dance of plate tectonics is never-ending there. Iceland is wrenching itself apart, getting wider by a few centimetres every year. The landscape is pock-marked with volcanoes and calderas, cracks in the rock billow forth sulphurous steam day and night, and vast plains are smothered in blackened lakes of cooling lava. A few miles from Dettifoss lay the almost unpronounceable lava-field of Leirhnjúkshraun, formed over twenty years before from an ooze of volcanic slag. The rocks were bloated and bulbous, twisted into bizarre shapes by the heat. After all those years they were still warm, and melted the soles of my boots. A volcano nearby had a crater known locally as Víti, 'hell', and the rains had gathered in it. The water was heavy with minerals and warm with geothermal heat. It had bloomed into a blue of clouded sapphire like an eye of the earth gazing out at space.

I walked all day in this wonderland. Pools of mud bubbled and slapped among mountains of pink and orange rhyolite, geysers shot forth sprays of rainbow mist and everywhere there was the sulphurous stench of the underbelly of the earth. It invaded the eyes, the mouth, the nose, and coated the body in a thin film of acid. In some places unimaginable forces had rent open the rock, and the path leapt over yawning crevasses from which clouds of steam gently drifted. The magma chambers and the mysterious workings of the planet lay just under the surface. The earth itself felt young and alive.

The landscape of the interior would have been similar when

Gunnlaug rode across it first in his bid to reach Helga in time, and then to meet his doom in Sweden. The soil erosion and deforestation caused in the early years of the Viking settlement was more pronounced in the broad dales and uplands nearer the coast than in the barren interior. The sagas speak of the central regions of Iceland as a place for ghosts and outlaws, a barren place to be afraid of. Many Icelanders are still superstitious about the 'dark heart' of the country, and I had even been warned (in all seriousness) of places to avoid camping in because they were considered haunted by trolls or ghosts. Some sagas, such as that of Grettir the Strong, have their heroes retreating in and out of the wasteland of the interior where they live as outlaws.

It is still a barren, empty place today, but there is increasing interest in its unique flora and fauna, and it is no longer considered by the urban Icelanders as so much worthless space. National parks have sprung up to conserve large parts of it and hiking trails have been marked across it.

*

I reached the village of Reykjahlið and went to the headquarters of the national parks agency. There was a ranger there with long black hair like molasses who despite being born in Iceland, spoke English with a smooth French accent. 'I used to live in Normandy,' she explained, 'but I like it better here in Iceland.'

'Why?' I asked her.

'France is a bit too busy for me. And there isn't enough space, you know, wild space. There are too many fields there. There's something in our blood, us Icelanders, that means we need more space than other people.'

She told me that genetically the people of Iceland are more similar to those of north-west Scotland than the Norwegians or Swedes. Like the people of the Faroes, their dark hair and slighter build was probably the legacy of Irish people, the slaves and wives that the Norsemen brought with them on their way west.

She put on a video for me advertising the work of the conservationists, and describing the geological formations of the area. There were a whole series of 'pseudo-craters' scattered in and around the lake and a colossal blast crater, the Hverfjall, all formed by seismic explosions of gas. Two hundred years before a lava flow had reached the village. The church was built on a little prominence which alone was spared. The locals took its survival as an act of God rather than an act of gravity.

When the video finished the ranger and I went on a walk past the church. It was supposed to be a guided tour, but it was early in the season and I was the only tourist to go. The campsite was nearby and a few tents were nestled between the neat rows of lava, each one curved like a furrow of newly ploughed earth. In Myvatn ('Midge Lake'), she pointed out divers and grebes as they fussed among the reeds. 'But sometimes I'm not so sure about the benefit of this national park,' she said, whispering as if she were preaching revolution, and spies were everywhere. 'Perhaps it would be better if we all just went back to Reykjavík and left the birds and the lake to themselves.'

'What makes you say that?' I asked.

'Look over there.' She pointed out some gulls that were circling around the rubbish bins at the camp site. 'And tell me where they should be.'

'At the sea.'

'Exactly. But they're miles from where they should be because they can feed off our rubbish. That's what I mean when I say I wonder if we do more harm than good. Maybe the guys in the old days were right to leave this place alone.'

One of her assistants approached, an Englishman who was on an exchange from the National Trust parks of the English Lake District. He was a shy man in his fifties, with short silver hair and quick eyes. She introduced us.

'Whereabout in the Lake District do you work?' I asked him, trying to make conversation.

'Eskdale,' he said.

'I've been in Eskdale quite a few times,' I told him. 'A friend of mine has a house nearby.' At this his eyes became brighter, and he chatted animatedly about the valley and the terrible problems they had had during a recent foot-and-mouth disease scare there.

'It's so beautiful there, isn't it?' he asked.

I nodded. 'Have you been a warden for the National Trust for a long time?' I asked.

'Oh no, I was a machinist in Manchester for thirty years. But I hated it. Every weekend, every holiday I was out volunteering with conservation groups,' he said. 'And eventually I just took the plunge, quit my job, and found this post in Eskdale. I took a fifty percent pay cut but now instead of commuting through Manchester I live in the most beautiful place in England and get to come on work exchanges like this!' He made a flourish with his hand, taking in the lake, the volcanic formations, the distant silhouettes of mountains against the sky. 'Oh, sometimes it's hard, when it's snowing out and I've got three miles of fencing to fix up, but I'm always sure I made the right decision.'

That night I camped between the furrows of lava that had frozen solid just before engulfing the church two centuries before. The light on the lake was very clear and delicate and I thought about the Englishman and the tough decisions he had made. I wondered what it was about wildness and open landscape that drew him. Maybe it was just to be out of doors, maybe to work independently, or maybe it was the silence.

*

I split away from Gunnlaug's journey and turned east. Walking along the road with my thumb out a Volkswagen camper with German number plates pulled up. The door in the side swung open, and a grinning woman waved me in. Once I was inside she introduced herself and her husband and son: Claudia, Carsten and little Torsten. They fed me sandwiches and tea as we bounced along the road towards the Eastfjords. They had driven in a circuit around the whole island and were now on their way to take the ferry back to Hamburg. My greetings in German were met with a frown from Carsten, and he cried enthusiastically for Torsten to practice his English. He counted it as great good fortune to come across a native English speaker in the wastes of Iceland. Torsten frowned and bit his bottom lip.

They had loved Iceland, he said, but most of all they had loved the desert interior. 'Next year,' Carsten said, 'we'll go to Namibia! This is just a trial run!'

'What is it you like so much about the desert?' I wanted to know. 'And does it matter if it's an icy one or a sandy one?'

'Oh no, that doesn't matter. And there are so many things I like,' he said. 'For instance, they are so clean! If I see a piece of litter in the desert, like an old cigarette packet, it looks so out of place there, such an insult. But in the town you wouldn't even notice it.'

'It is the silence that I love,' said Claudia. 'It's a silence that goes inside your head and when you come out of the desert it stays with you.'

'And it's simple,' said Carsten. 'There are only extremes: sunrise, sunset, hot days, cold nights, black sky, blue sky. It's so immense and unfeeling. Being in the desert is like sailing across an ocean...'

'I like the way the road gets disappeared,' said Torsten, interrupting his father in full flow. 'Under the sand or the lava.'

His father's face beamed with pride. 'Wunderbar, Torsten, but you should say, "I like the way the road can DISAPPEAR".'

'Well done,' I told him. 'I knew exactly what you meant.'

I saw what they all meant. When asked why he loved the desert, T. E. Lawrence too had said, 'Because it is so *clean*.' Perhaps that clarity and simplicity is the reason that so many prophets and mystics seem to reach deeper understandings in them. And despite the harsh indifference of the desert, people fall in love with them so readily. The deserts and the edges of the earth seem to be joined in the hearts of so many of us who live in the cities of the south. We go on making pilgrimages to them.

✳

'Car bomb,' he said by way of explanation, though I had not asked for one. 'Killed me best mate. I'm lucky to be alive.'

Where his legs would have been his thighs ended in discs of hard-wearing plastic. He swung them around and hopped off the bench. 'Want anything from inside?' he asked. I shook my head and he stepped nimbly indoors.

I was sitting in the sun at a roadside café near the village of Egilsstaðir, at the crossroads of the Eastfjords. Carsten and Claudia had dropped me off before driving on to catch their ferry. Robbie, my new friend, was going south. His hand-bike gleamed in the sun despite the hammering it had taken on the gravel tracks of the interior.

He reappeared, and in one fluid move sprang up onto the picnic bench. His arms and shoulders rippled like a gymnast's. 'Sure you don't want one of these?' he asked, tucking into a hot dog. 'You know, I used to do what you're doing, hike around, camp where I like. I've been all through the Canadian Northwest. Secret of low-impact camping is to pitch your tent in the *least likely* place.' He did not say that he would still be doing it if he could, but then he did not need to. One foggy Belfast morning he had climbed into his car, there was a flash and a deafening blast, and there had been an end to all of that.

He was hand-biking round Iceland to raise money for injured servicemen and army widows. He had competed in the Para-Olympics, and spoke at length how it was very difficult to beat the paraplegics. 'They can't feel anything, so they stick needles in themselves to get their endorphins going. Unbeatable. It's bloody cheating, if you ask me'.

Iceland so far had not been easy, not easy at all. And he was only halfway round.

An apron of grass ran down to the edge of a lake. We had left the desert behind. Children hollered and giggled among the birch trees on its banks, and beyond them the water sparkled into the distance. Its name was Lagarfljót; a long spindle of a lake that ran like a spoke from the hub of Iceland towards the coast. It was fed by another of the waters of Vatnajökull, the Jökulsá í Fljótsdal, the names so difficult for me to shape in my mouth, but which seemed to fit so well in the landscape.

'Oh well, best be off.' He grabbed hold of his bike and swung agilely into its seat. 'There aren't many roads in this bloody country, maybe I'll see you around!'

*

Blood is an excellent fertiliser. It is said in the days before Christianity came to Sweden that the grass beneath the sacrificial oak in Uppsala was verdant all year round. Every nine years there was a festival, or orgy, of death there. Nine men, and nine each of nine different species of male animal had their throats slit and were hung upon the tree. The saga of Gunnlaug Serpent-Tongue says that Gunnlaug was blessed by a priest and buried in a churchyard, but in the pagan heartland of Sweden in the first years of the eleventh century that's very unlikely. Christianity would not be accepted by the Swedes until at least a century later.

Below the twelfth-century church of Old Uppsala there lies the remains of a wooden temple. It was an evil place to the Christians of the south. Adam of Bremen wrote in his *Gesta Hammaburgensis Ecclesiæ Pontificum*, or, 'The History of the Archbishopric of Hamburg', that it was decked in gold, and inside stood a holy trinity of statues of the gods Óđin, Thór and Frey:

> Thór, they say, presides over the air, which governs the thunder
> and lightning, the winds and rains, fair weather and crops. The
> other, Wodan (that is The Furious) carries on war and imparts
> to man strength against his enemies. The third is Fricco [Frey],
> who bestows peace and pleasure on mortals; and they fashion

his likeness with an immense phallus. But Wodan they chisel armed, as our people are wont to represent Mars.

There are three ancient mounds near the site of the temple and centuries of tradition has named them after Óðin, Thór and Frey, but excavations have shown them to be royal burial mounds of the Vendel, or Wendel, period of Sweden, the fifth to the eighth century AD. The legend of Frey is about five hundred years older than the mounds, and Snorri's explanations of the entry of Frey into the Norse pantheon take us even deeper into the history of those peoples who migrated up into Scandinavia from the Black Sea.

According to the Ynglinge saga the original Scandinavian people, the Asir, had a rival tribe known as the Vanir who were as fierce as they were in battle but unusually worshipped female deities as well as masculine warrior gods. Óðin captured the chieftain of the Vanir and his two children, who were known as Frey and Freyja. Soon afterwards the two tribes joined forces. Incest was common practice among the ruling class of the time, and Frey and Freyja were lovers. Later, once he had entered the pantheon, Frey is described as marrying a giantess who emerged from the earth, their union symbolic of his power over fertility, the success of the crops and the renewal of the seasons. His sister Freyja was a wild and sexually insatiable woman who may have been Óðin's wife (who in some manuscripts is called Friggja) but was described as regularly copulating freely with elves, beasts, giants and men.

Tacitus in his *Germania* wrote of the spring fertility rituals among these early Germanic tribes. A virgin representing the Earth Goddess would be pulled between settlements in a wagon, during which time there was unbroken peace between men, 'and every object of iron is locked away'. Then she and a priest had intercourse, probably on the first furrow of a field to be blessed. The ritual persisted in a form up to historic times in Sweden, where a young girl would ride in a wagon from village to village in a cart beside a wooden image of Frey. Stallions were sacred to Frey as the ultimate expression of masculine power, and as late as the seventeenth century in Norway the outcome of stallion fights held on St Bartholomew's Day were said to be able to predict the success of the harvest.

As Wednesday belongs to Wodan, and Thursday to Thór, Friday belongs to Frey. Thank Frey that it's Friday.

Frey, Frigg, Freyja, Friggja, Fricco. All these names come from the same stem of an Old Germanic word, and are all perhaps best translated as 'fuck'.

I walked along the south-eastern shore of the Lagarfljót. The valley that it lay in was narrow, and forked at the end into two rivers which drained the lava plains to the south. Along all the riversides lay thin strips of fertile soil lined with blue-grey roads like veins linking the homesteads of this back-country of the east. The volcano of Snaefell rose between two white thighs of the southern ice-cap, and meltwater the colour of seminal fluid flowed from it into the river.

Another of my favourite sagas was set in these lands around the Eastfjords, and it would be the last I would follow here in Iceland – the saga of Hrafnkel, Frey's Goði. It describes the whole landscape that lay around me as being once sacred to Frey. It is one of the most brutal sagas in a literature that is renowned for its brutality, and is suffused throughout with the brooding power that the old pagan Gods still held over the newly Christianised Norsemen of the early mediaeval period.

In the days of Harald Fair-hair, the saga recalls, there came to the Eastfjords a man called Hallfred. He put his ship into Breiðdal, 'Broad-dale', and together with his fifteen-year-old son, built a homestead. Then he had a dream that told him to move west, across the Lagarfljót: 'That is where your luck is,' the dream told him.

His son was called Hrafnkel, and when he came of age he rode out across the land and selected a valley in which he wanted to make his home. The valley lay beneath Snaefell, and the river running through it would have been the same milky colour then as it is now. He built his house, then built a temple and made sacrifices to Frey. Hrafnkel was a goði, the closest that the pagan faith of the Icelanders ever came to having priests. In his religious duties he loved no other god more than Frey, god of fertility and sensual pleasures. He was a cruel and overbearing man who bullied his neighbours into supporting him at local assemblies. He was also given to making rash oaths. He owned a powerful and virile stallion named Freyfaxi which he claimed was sacred to Frey, and he vowed to murder any man who he found riding it.

The inevitable happened. A shepherd lost some sheep in the valley, and the only way to find them was to ride on horseback. The only horse which would consent to be ridden was Freyfaxi, and afterwards the stallion ran dripping with sweat back to its master.

Hrafnkel took an axe to the shepherd's head. A blood-feud begins, and the saga of Hrafnkel, Frey's Goði comes alive.

The shepherd had a cousin called Sam who summoned Hrafnkel to the Althing to face charges for the slaying. With seventy men Hrafnkel rode across the moors, down the valley to the east, and in seventeen days reached Thingvellir. Sam took a short-cut west past Myvatn across the wasteland of the interior as Gunnlaug had done, and managed to arrive at the assembly first. He started to gather support for his case, because Hrafnkel was a powerful man to bring charges against.

Only one man had principles enough to defend him. Thorkel Thjostarsson was his name, and he had been an elite imperial guard in Constantinople. He was not afraid of a small-time goði from the Eastfjords. Thorkel was so well thought of that when Hrafnkel arrived he was sentenced immediately to outlawry, meaning that Sam and Thorkel were entitled to all of his lands and property and could slay him with impunity if they wished.

The saga is very particular about explaining how the law of outlawry could be enforced, and in what way. It says that the sentence could not be carried out for fourteen days, and so they had to wait for their moment. Hrafnkel was still in bed the morning they arrived, as he had intended to ignore the sentence. Thorkel's training on the shores of the Bosphorus came in very handy. He bound Hrafnkel and his men, then cutting holes through the thin web of skin behind their achilles tendons he strung them together by the heels with rope and hung them from the rafters of the house. Then he held a 'confiscation court' one arrow's shot from the house in order to claim all his property according to the custom of the law.

Hrafnkel was totally humiliated. 'They took Hrafnkel and his men down and laid them in the hayfield. The blood had run into their eyes.' Although Thorkel wanted to kill them as was their right under the law, Sam gave Hrafnkel the option of being killed there and then, or of being banished out to the banks of the Lagarfljót and taking only those possessions that Sam would grant him. As he lay on the grass, blood running down his cheeks, he replied, 'Many would prefer a quick death to such a humiliation, but I will be like so many others and choose life if it is an alternative.'

Sam and Thorkel then set him free, burned his temple to Frey and pushed the horse Freyfaxi over a cliff. When Hrafnkel heard what they had done he swore that it proved what a vanity it was to believe in gods. From then on, he said, he would have nothing to do with them.

Six years passed. He and Sam would occasionally meet at public gatherings, but they never spoke of what had passed between them. Hrafnkel set up his homestead on the south-eastern shore of the lake and gradually managed to build up his household to the position he had held before.

One day Eyvind, Sam's brother, returned from overseas. He was a merchant and had been travelling for several years, among other places to the Aegean and Constantinople, 'where he gained great honour from the King of the Greeks'. On his way home he met people who told him all about the dispute, and so with his retinue changed direction towards his brother's new home.

Eyvind passed by Hrafnkel's new homestead. His shields glimmered in the sun and it was obvious to everyone that he had become a very wealthy man in his time abroad. One of Hrafnkel's servant women goaded her master, telling him that it seemed to her that people no longer lived with the same sense of honour as they had done in years gone by, allowing the kinsmen of those who had humiliated him to live. It was all too much for Hrafnkel to bear.

He gathered up a rabble of men, caught up with Eyvind and ran him through with a sword. When he returned home and told the news, the honour he obtained by the slaying meant that he grew in the esteem of the people who lived around him (either that or they were now terrified of him). He was now able to gather seventy men to his side and with them surrounded his old farm and dragged Sam from his bed. He gave him the same stark choice that he had been given on the same spot six years before.

Sam too chose to live.

The moral of the story? That it is a vanity to believe in the heathen gods? The sagas are never that straightforward.

*

The road twisted through a pass between two narrow shoulders of rock and then, gathering pace, it slid down into the wide vale of Breiddal. The valley was bounded on both sides by high mountain ridges sprinkled with snow, their summits angular and brittle, whipped into peaks like a tray of meringues. The valley was as broad as its name suggested. A river meandered across it, meeting tributaries in a sunken brocade of lace linked with shining threads of water. The sky was clear and serene, bisected by a thin streak of vapour thirty thousand feet above, a reminder that the quickest route from Europe to North America now, as in the Middle Ages, lies directly across Iceland.

At the end of the valley the little village of Breiddalsvík edged into the North Atlantic. In a shop there I asked if it was possible to buy a mountain map of the area, and was told in a tone usually reserved for tiresome three-year-olds that one bought maps in map shops.

'Where could I find a map shop?' I asked.

'Akureyri,' came the smug reply.

The weather was very clear, so I decided to climb up into the mountains anyway. The summit ridge seemed to be made entirely of gravel. Thick dry moss smothered the slope, inches thick, and came away in clods with every footfall. Climbing onto it triggered a thousand land-slides in miniature, every step forward leading to half a step back. In the shadows and hollows lay brittle remnants of the winter ice, still a virgin white, and there were no other footprints. I wondered if anyone else had been up yet this year.

I sat in the lee of the wind just over the summit. On the northern slope the evening sunlight slipped over the mountainside like honey. There was total stillness; a golden plover called to its mate hundreds of metres below, and a waterfall whispered near the valley floor.

On the way back down I found the dictionary first. It was a German-Icelandic one, rotten and torn, with mildew spreading over its pages. It could have seen two or three spring thaws before reaching its present state. A few metres on there was a plastic bottle, swollen with gas and choked with mould, its label bleached by the sun. Further on down the hillside again there was a torn cloth rucksack, and beyond it the sleeve of a ripped plastic raincoat sticking out from under a carapace of ice. My heart was beating hard as I tugged on the sleeve, wondering if I would pull out a rotten arm with it. A body could lie undiscovered for years up here, I thought.

In the end I dug out the raincoat, and was relieved to find no corpse attached to it. Above where it had fallen towered a wall of crumbling rock. I looked up to see two ravens circling me slowly. Their cries were eerie and rasping, stirring a primitive dread, as if there is a part of the human memory that still links them to death, or the carnage of the battlefield. In the Qur'an it is written that a raven told Cain the way to bury Abel's corpse, and in Irish mythology the goddess Morrígan took the form of a raven when she settled onto Cú Chulainn's dead body. They are intelligent birds which mate for life, a life which can last a century, but as they wheeled above me I remembered only how a shepherd in Scotland once told me how they will pick the eyes out of lambs to make them wander away from the flock.

It was late. The hillside was strewn with rubble the colour of rust. There was no moss there, only ancient lichens in fractal patterns and occasional tufts of dead grasses. I set up my tent but the weather was rapidly worsening and the flysheet had to be weighed down with boulders against the wind. All the time the ravens circled above, croaking. The words 'raven' and *hráfn* are cognate. From *hráfn* comes the name Hráfnkel, and it seemed to me that the ravens were trying to tell me something, perhaps reminding me of the brutal world that Hráfnkel had lived in. Listening to the wind and the croaking of the birds I was struck by how harsh this land could be, of past famines and terrible winters, of Hráfnkel strung up nearby, hung by the heels to the rafters of his own house with blood running into his eyes. The modern world seemed to lie on the valley outside my tent like a fragile veneer, as if the old world that the Vikings knew could break through again at any moment.

By five in the morning the route back down was lost in the mists, but by following the sound of water to a stream I picked my way carefully back towards the village. I tried hitching for five hours, but only three cars passed in all that time and none of them stopped. I wanted to get to the south end of the island, where the great glaciers lie directly over the volcanic fault line. Luckily a bus turned up.

We sped over wide flood deltas and the road skirted mountains high above the North Atlantic. By late morning the ocean was calm, and the weather bright and sunny. At Jokulsárlon, a lagoon that has become Iceland's favourite icon, I got off to watch icebergs calve from the Vatnajökull ice-cap. Like sculpted ships of ice they floated around, blown gently by the wind, melting slowly in the June air. Glacial ice often glows like sapphire with the softest, the most delicate, gentle blue light. It can be startling, but at the same time somehow soothing in its unearthliness. If virtue had a colour, it would be glacial blue. But some of the icebergs were a dirty grey like old snow on muddy ground, scraped from the earth by the grinding action of the glacier that created them. Arctic terns ducked and swooped between them from their nests out towards their fishing grounds. In the west and north of the country I had seen very little of the stuff that gave Iceland its name. Despite the speed at which the ice is melting and the warnings that man-made climate change is destroying the ice-caps, there in the south I would see a lot more.

Jokulsárlon is a good place from which to contemplate this warming trend. A century ago there was no lagoon, and the nearby Atlantic shoreline was under a hundred feet of glacial ice. Now the spit of ice has retreated over two miles from the sea, and every year the lagoon of meltwater gets bigger. I looked across the lake at a tongue of the mighty Vatnajökull ice-cap, the biggest in Europe, and thought how strong and eternal it looked. But appearances were deceptive; the glacier is shrinking so quickly that if it maintains the same rate of loss the whole ice-cap will be gone in less than 300 years. The effects of climate change are so immediately obvious at Jokulsárlon that it has become a rallying point for environmental activists, especially now that concern for global warming has become fashionable. *Vanity Fair* recently ran a cover by celebrity photographer Annie Leibovitz of the actor Leonardo DiCaprio posing in a down jacket and crampons there. For added appeal (and a nod to the status of polar bears as endangered by climate change) a cute polar bear cub from Berlin zoo was pasted into the photo electronically. Concern for global warming was officially 'in', and Iceland a trendy place to comment on it.

✳

The southern coast of Iceland is dominated by ice and fire; two of the greatest examples of the destructive power of the elements to be found anywhere in Europe. To the east lies the colossal ice-cap of Vatnajökull, and to the west lies the simmering volcanic complex of Mount Hekla. Mount Fuji, Erebus, Vesuvius, Popocatepetl, Hekla; Iceland's greatest volcano takes its place among the greatest of the world. Their contours as a rule are sleek but gentle, their lines more horizontal than vertical, and as portals into the hell beneath our feet they have fascinated mankind for millennia. As natural phenomena their potential for destruction ranks alongside hurricanes, floods, earthquakes and tsunami, but none of these others are so fascinating for us to watch. Volcanic eruptions are like fireworks hurled from the depths of the earth itself, a poisonous gift to the land. Through the centuries eruptions on Hekla have caused thousands of deaths from starvation by blackening the sky and blighting crops. It smothers its slopes in rivers of fire, and can belch forth ash that blows for hundreds of miles. After a single eruption of Hekla it has been known to snow black on Orkney, seven hundred miles away.

If the two energies of ice and fire combine, the destruction they can unleash is unimaginable. An eruption *under* the ice-cap can vaporise millions of tonnes of glacial ice and release a flood which washes away everything in its path. To the south of Vatnajökull great plains of silt deposits are fed by thousands of meltwater streams which lie between the glacier and the sea. Over the centuries the periodic eruptions have cleared this landscape and scoured away any permanent settlements. Concrete bridges have been snapped like eggshells by the waters, but the government goes on repairing the road. The grinding action of the glaciers reduces mountains to dust, and their sludge has settled in the coastal waters over millennia leaving long sloping shallows off the southern coast. Ships are grounded long before they reach the shore.

At first sight the glaciers seem immense, and in European

terms they are. They edge down over the fulcrum of barrier ridges in the mountains, cracking and groaning with a power that trembles beneath the surface like subterranean thunder. At Skaftafell National Park I climbed up to the confluence of two of the greatest tongues of the Vatnajökull and felt the earth shaking beneath me as the ice split around the mountain.

It would soon be time for me to leave Iceland, but I had one more trail to follow up. I wanted to travel along the south coast of the island, where ice meets fire and which St Brendan described more than three hundred years before the Vikings arrived.

*

One day after leaving the Paradise of Birds the *Navigatio* says that the monks came to the southern shores of another great island. 'The countryside was wild and dotted with slag heaps and numerous forges. "Brethren," said Brendan, "that island makes me feel uneasy. I have no desire to land nor even to go near, yet the wind is taking us straight towards it!"'

He began to pray for deliverance, but as he was doing so a man appeared on the shore, emerging from one of the forges. He looked angrily at the monks, and then rushed towards them carrying a piece of burning slag in some tongs. He threw it at them, but it flew far over their heads before striking the water, hissing with steam. More and more inhabitants of the island started to emerge, and joined in with throwing burning slag at the monks. The water simmered like stew and the sound of wailing filled the air. 'An intolerable, fetid stench emanated from the island and was still perceptible after they had lost sight of it.'

They fled out to sea. The next day a mountain appeared in the north. They thought at first that it was swathed in cloud, but as they drew closer they realised that it was actually smoke pouring out of the mountain's peak. The water was as shallow there as it is today along the south coast of Iceland, and the coracle was grounded in volcanic sand long before reaching the shore. 'When they looked back from afar, they saw the mountain, clear of clouds, vomiting forth flames sky-high and then sucking them back upon itself, so that the whole mass of rock, right down to sea-level, glowed like a pyre.'

There is no doubt that the author is describing a volcanic eruption, even down to the sulphurous stench. The lumps of slag causing the sea to boil suggests an eye-witness account of a sub-marine eruption, and would pass for an account of the formation of Surtsey, a volcanic island which emerged off the south coast of Iceland in recent times. The second event, that of witnessing flames being ejected from a mountain that glowed as if on fire could only be a description of an eruption from a volcano pouring lava out over the land.

After he had passed the coast of Iceland Brendan came upon perhaps the most astonishing phenomenon he and his monks had yet seen, to him an incontestable manifestation of the wonder of God: 'One day, when the masses were over, they noticed a column rising out of the sea... This column was covered with a most unusual canopy – so strange indeed that the coracles could pass through the openings in it... It was the colour of silver and seemed harder than marble. The column itself was of pure crystal.'

Brendan ordered the monks to ship the oars and they drifted between the pieces of the 'canopy' that floated around the iceberg. The monks were as amazed as they had been on the Paradise of Birds. Reverentially they began to push into the openings in the water, and spent a full day circumnavigating the 'column of crystal'. The water was so clear that they could see its base extending far below the surface.

To the west of Iceland the prevailing current carries icebergs from the Arctic all the way to Cape Farewell at the southern tip of Greenland. They break up into fragments as they melt, and may be accompanied by flat chunks of sea ice which float around them like a net laid upon the water. This East Greenland Current carries ice as far south as the coast of Newfoundland and beyond. It was one of these icebergs that sank the Titanic. After passing the volcano Brendan seems to have strayed into the Denmark Strait west of Iceland and into the path of the monstrous but magnificent mountains of ice which float in its waters. Unfamiliar with glaciers and unaware of processes which can calve off pieces of ice as big as whole Irish counties, Brendan and the monks were silenced in awe. 'Now let us draw through the opening, and let us inspect the wonders of God, our Maker,' he said. Brendan pushed his way through the ice towards Greenland.

∗

Like Brendan I too was leaving Iceland for Greenland. But instead of sailing over the Denmark Strait I was going to have to fly to Denmark, and from Copenhagen airport fly back out west again over the island I had just left. It seemed wrong, especially in these days of concern over our 'carbon footprints', but in planning my trip there had been no other way. I hoped that one day I would return and try it with a big enough sailing boat.

I followed a road up from the silt plains of the south towards Hekla. It wound up through blackened foothills, then passed through mountains of gold and umber. The landscape grew increasingly barren as I moved into the interior again, taking a short cut back to Reykjavík through high volcanic country. Near the lava-fields of Laugahraun plumes of steam burst from the rocks by the side of the road. Hekla was snoozing peacefully to the west. The mountains in those parts are known for their hot springs, called *laugar*, and smoking rivers coursed down the hillsides.

I stopped there for the night, and after pitching the tent climbed into one of the steaming pools near the campsite. It was my first bath since Húsavík.

The woman sitting next to me said she was a psychiatrist. It surprised me; she had none of the distracted manner that so often plagues psychiatrists, burdened every day as they are by madness and despair. In fact she was a model of serenity. 'It is important in life to be intellectually challenged,' she told me, 'but what is more important is that one has a great deal of leisure in which to think about what is important. Calm reflection is greatly underrated in our society.'

She repeated the word 'leisure', enjoying its shape, and its meaning. Though she was German, she took great joy in the English language. The word hung between us. Pearls of sweat gathered on her forehead, stringing her silver bobbed hair and adding a shine to a face already reddened by the heat of the water. Her skin was finely lined, and her expression at rest was peaceful. A smile twitched at the corners of her lips. Her bathing suit was decorated in large blue flowers. 'Why have you come to Iceland?' she asked.

'I'm travelling around the north of Europe,' I said. 'I grew up in Scotland and had never been further north. I like to walk, and I like to see the edges of places. Iceland seems to give me plenty of opportunity to do both.'

'You have made a wise choice. I come here two or three times a year,' she replied. 'There is nowhere on earth like it.'

All around us were mountains of blue and amber rhyolite, the river banks were lush with grasses, warmed by the steam of the river. There was a hint of sulphur in the air. Patches of snow still lay in the shadows nearby, while mosquitoes whirred in the heat above the water's surface. None of them were biting. Where we sat a pool had formed from the confluence of three streams. Each stream was a different temperature, and by moving around the pool it was possible to find a spot where the water was deliciously comfortable. My thighs started to burn on the rocks, and my companion and I moved further along the bank where it was cooler.

'I used to be a paediatrician,' she went on, removing her spectacles and wiping the condensation from them. 'For newborn babies. But after ten years fighting my way into a career I had to give it up. There is more to life for me than working all through the night, every night. I needed a change, I had to get out of that routine.'

I told her about the National Trust warden I had met at Myvatn lake, how he had worked for thirty years in a city before realising that he had to change.

'Thirty years is a long time,' she said. 'But he was a lucky one to realise, and to have the option to get out at all. And what about you?'

'I'm still working out what I want to do with my life, I'm afraid,' I said. 'Maybe that's another one of the reasons for my trip.'

'Aren't we all, my dear boy,' she said, sinking down into the water so that only her face was dry. 'Aren't we all.'

*

From the air, Denmark and Sweden look like old friends. Both roll back from the sea in tessellated patchworks of gold and green, and their coasts smile at one another across a narrow strait. The strait is crossed by a bridge now, linking by road two nations whose place in history has been governed by their mastery of the sea.

The aeroplane banked over Helsingør, Hamlet's 'Elsinor', and then over the thin umbilical cord of a bridge connecting Copenhagen to Swedish Malmö. Cargo ships and supertankers punctuated the sheen of the water, drifting south to the Baltic and north into the Kattegat, and from there out into the North Sea. From twenty thousand feet the waves and ships, towns and motorways were silent.

After the spacious austerity of Iceland, walking in Copenhagen was an assault on the senses. Summer had arrived. Turks and Eastern Europeans sold mock designer sunglasses on the streets and canal fronts, and wealthy tourists drank caffé latte and watched street performers in the sunshine. I passed through Christiania in search of a rebellious counter culture but found only tattooed, burned-out men selling hash cakes, and teenagers glancing into window reflections to adjust their dreadlocks. There were wide streets, shady parks, rivers of bicycles, and a glut of magnificent palaces. The city has not lost the shine of grandeur it picked up in its golden age, the fifteenth to the seventeenth centuries. In those days Denmark governed Norway, Iceland, Greenland, at times most of Sweden and parts of Finland, and mortgaged Shetland and Orkney to the Scots. Now it governs only the Faroes and Greenland, and both are agitating for independence.

In the afternoon I walked out to the Danish Polar Institute, lost among the dockside warehouses of the canal district. It was closed, but through the window I saw some of the Institute's collection of Inuit ethnographic sculptures. The sculptor had emphasised low foreheads, wide cheekbones, and jutting orbital ridges. They seemed stripped of any nobility and turned into caricatures of their physiognomy, so different from that of the Europeans. Through another window I could see the alluring spines of the books in the library: *Land under the Pole Star*, *Ultima Thule*, *Tales and Traditions of the Eskimo*.

The tarmac on the pavement was soft in the heat. I sat by the canal to drink a beer in the evening light. An old Inuit man passed between the people collecting empty bottles and picking up cans which when returned could earn a few pennies each. Two drowned rats floated down the canal past my feet, bloated with gas, their bellies pointing at the sky. It felt a long way from the 'cleanliness' that Carsten had sought in the desert of Iceland.

My journey through the histories of the North had taken me up to the eleventh century. It was good in a way that I had found myself having to return to Denmark, because it was events in that century in Denmark and England that would shape the history of northern Europe for many centuries to come. In modern political and economic life Denmark and England often seem to have little in common, but they share a common history and in many ways a common people. They are cousins, but have been more like blood brothers.

Here is the saga of Gunnlaug Serpent-Tongue on the closeness that the Norse and the Anglo-Saxon cultures maintained to one another, even five hundred years after the Angles and Saxons sailed west out of Denmark and northern Germany. 'In those days [the year 1000], the language in England was the same as that spoken in Norway and Denmark, but there was a change of language when William the Bastard conquered England. Since William was of French descent, the French language was used in England from then on.'

In over five hundred years the Anglo-Saxons had changed their language so little that the Icelanders could still understand them. In less than two hundred years the language of the Danes who settled Normandy had become unrecognisable. But whatever the Frankish Empire had done to them, however their language had become overwhelmed and bastardised by Latin, the Normans were still Danes.

Danes conquering Danes. Denmark has a lot to answer for.

*

To follow those events that took place in the eleventh century I took a train out to Roskilde, the principal seat of power of the mediaeval kings of Denmark. There was a rock festival playing that weekend and the trains were packed with the same teenagers that had posed and preened in Christiania. An English ticket tout hawked on the underpass while the crowds shoved past him, carrying crates of beer on their shoulders or dragging them behind themselves on ropes. Down in the town centre itself the streets were quiet.

The cathedral, Roskilde Domkirke, was a monument to death and immortality. Its corners were busy with marble and granite. Semi-clad female statues wept over sarcophagi and ancient tombs gathered dust in rooms briefly glimpsed beneath the floor. Reflected in every nave and chapel was the legacy of contact with the Baltic east and Slavic culture – you could think yourself in Riga or Kraków. Assembled there were the graves of the Danish and Norwegian royalty through the last few centuries.

Down at the harbour there was the legacy of an older race of Sea-Kings. Sometime in the middle of the eleventh century five Viking ships were scuttled in the Roskilde Fjord. They were valuable, and so there must have been a great threat to the city at the time. The ships were filled with rocks, sailed out of the harbour and then sunk. The fjord is wide and shallow and the ships blocked the only navigable channel at the time, protecting the seat of power and by chance leaving a magnificent monument to Viking ship-building preserved in the mud. In 1962 an enclosure was built around them, the water pumped out, and piece by piece the sodden wood was lifted to the surface and painstakingly restored. The reconstructions that were created are the best insight that we have into the trading and cargo vessels of the Norsemen. Analysis of the timber of the five ships has shown they were made as far apart as Ireland and the Baltic. Four of them were coastal ships, for raiding, ferrying or small-time trading. Only one of them was built to make deep-sea voyages, a vessel known as a *knörr*. There have been plenty of finds of Viking longships associated with burials, but the knörr was the deep-sea vessel that was used for the voyage across the ocean to Iceland and Greenland. Until the find at Roskilde none had ever been found.

I walked around the knörr, a ship that sailed the North Atlantic and may itself have pushed through the ice-fields of the Denmark Strait to Greenland. It was small, only sixteen metres long, but its lines were voluptuous, deep and full-breasted as a swan. Its pine and oak timbers were the colour of roast coffee beans, rich and finely grained, stained by the millennium they had lain in the silt. Built in about 1030, the ship would have had two small decks, fore and aft, with an open hold in the centre that could take over twenty tonnes. It would have been packed with furs, grain, livestock, even chained-up polar bears – a white bear was the greatest gift the Norse Greenlanders could present to any European monarch. It was rigged with a single square sail and would have performed very badly into the wind. But running before the wind it could do over ten knots, and with an easterly it could have sailed from Denmark to Greenland in under two weeks.

Outside it was a beautiful summer's day. The water of the fjord was placid. Hammer blows rang from a workshop by the museum, where replica ships were being built using the same materials and technology that were available to the Vikings. Instead of sawing planks for the hull, tree trunks were shivered apart using wedges to split the grain. Working with the grain of the wood gave the planks twice the strength and flexibility at a fraction of the weight. In a storm their ships must have twisted and rolled with the waves like living beings. The sagas tell that a particularly famous or successful boat would adopt a life of its own. Its keel would be restored and reused and a new boat could be rebuilt around it, thus imparting some of its magical properties into the new vessel. There is a legend that Leif Eiriksson's knörr, the one he used on his voyage to North America, had a keel that came from another famous boat that had sailed far into the west. Leif's nickname was Heppni, meaning, 'the Lucky'. Perhaps he thought his luck was down to his choice of keel.

I sat on the edge of the jetty looking out into the bay. A replica of a Norse warship cruised towards the jetty. Its sail was fully rigged, but I could hear the splutter of an outboard motor being pulled. From beyond the forest surrounding the town the repetitive thud of the rock concert drifted over to join the blows of the craftsmen's hammers. I could not make out any of the music, but a distant roar of applause filtered through the air. In one of the boats moored to the jetty a couple sat holding one another and looking out to sea. I tried to imagine the scene a thousand years before when the raiders arrived here on their way to ransack the richest town in Denmark. When their longships knocked into the scuttled boats I wondered if the army managed to get away, foiled, or if they were showered with arrows and their ships burned to the waterline.

It is impossible to know for sure, but the outcome of that day may have had far-reaching implications across the North Sea in England. It was King Harald of Norway's army that was attacking Roskilde during the 1050s, the same man whose armies were defeated by England's at the battle of Stamford Bridge in 1066. If he had had more ships to launch his invasion, and therefore more men at Stamford Bridge, it could have been the Norwegians rather than the Normans who triumphed over Saxon England.

To understand the roots of the Norman success we have to understand events that happened and decisions that were taken decades before.

*

Ethelred the Unready did not achieve much with all the Danegeld he paid out, despite the help of men like Gunnlaug Serpent-Tongue. He had to capitulate in the end to Knút of Denmark (known to history classrooms as the hubristic King Canute who ordered the tide to turn back). When Knút conquered London in 1016 he married Emma of Normandy, Ethelred's widow, and for twenty years ruled over a joint kingdom of England and Denmark. He defeated King Olaf 'the Saint' of Norway too, and so for a brief time ruled a Kingdom unifying Denmark, England and Norway. Two thousand miles away at the centre of the Byzantine Empire the heir to the throne of Norway plotted his revenge.

Harald Sigurdsson was a giant of a man, standing nearly seven feet tall. Adam of Bremen called him 'the Thunderbolt of the North' and as an elite imperial guard in Constantinople his ruthlessness had him promoted to the highest ranks. He campaigned for Byzantium against the Arabs on the banks of the Euphrates, the Normans in Sicily, and the Bulghars in Thessalonica. When Emperor Michael the Fifth was deposed, it was Harald who gouged out his eyes with his thumbs. Harald massed enormous wealth and stored it in the Rus (Swedish) town of Kiev, and in 1042 escaped Constantinople. He was on his way to Norway to reclaim his kingdom.

Knút had died in 1035. His bones still lie under the arches of Winchester Cathedral. Two of his sons squabbled over the kingdom, but by 1042 both were dead. Their successors decided that they had enough on their plates with governing Denmark, leaving Edward the Confessor free to reign. He shifted the capital from Winchester to London, and was the last Anglo-Saxon King of England.

Meanwhile Harald had returned to Norway, recovered his kingdom and somehow earned the nick-name Harðráða, meaning 'hard ruler'. He was a fierce warrior and his armies must have been a terrifying sight: his battle standard was called 'the land-waster' and he had images of the Raven of Death embroidered on it. Through the 1050s he was raiding in Denmark, but though fearsome, his armies were suffering losses that might later prove decisive.

Edward the Confessor was an Anglo-Saxon, but his power rested on the shoulders of the Danes. His most powerful earl, Harold Godwinsson, was the grandson of a Danish raider who had conquered English lands in the early years of Knút. His earldom stretched from Cornwall to Kent, the most powerful noble in England, and with Edward ageing fast and still childless, he was the man most likely to rule in Edward's place.

On 5 January 1066, Edward died. Godwinsson succeeded to the throne, but as he was not a clear blood heir the ravens of Northern Europe gathered. William the Bastard, Duke of Normandy, claimed Edward had promised the Kingdom to him. He summoned all the mercenaries of Europe to his side and started constructing landing craft to carry a great army over the sleeve of water separating him from England. In Norway Harald Harðráða too prepared his armies. After his raids in Denmark he still had some three hundred ships to sail across the North Sea.

By the beginning of September that year the Norwegians had landed on the Northumbrian coast. While all English eyes had been trained on the threat from the south he was joined by re-inforcements from Scotland and Orkney and began to close on London from the north. On Wednesday 20 September he took York, but suffered heavy casualties. Some swift messengers must have survived the battle because only five days later Godwinsson's troops had marched north to meet him at a place near York called Stamford Bridge.

Some sources suggest that Harald Harðráða mistakenly thought Harold Godwinsson would surrender the throne, and had not properly prepared for battle. The saga of King Harald describes what happened next.

> The weather was exceptionally fine, with warm sunshine; so the troops left their armour behind and went ashore with only their shields, helmets and spears, and girt with swords. A number of them also had bows and arrows. They were all feeling very carefree.
>
> But as they approached the town they saw a large force riding to meet them. They could see the cloud of dust raised by the horses' hooves, and below it the gleam of handsome shields and white coats of mail… the closer the army came, the greater it grew, and their glittering weapons sparkled like a field of broken ice.

Godwinsson's English army broke over them like a wave, and Harald Harðráða was shot through the throat by an arrow. His Norwegian armies were caught unawares and unarmoured, and were utterly defeated.

As the battle raged, William was preparing to sail from Normandy. He probably had no idea that Harald Harðráða had sailed with an army from Norway. King Harald's saga reports that as he rode from his court in Normandy his wife ran out to say goodbye. From the back of his horse he kicked her in the chest with his heel, driving his spurs into her and killing her instantly. 'William was exceptionally tall and strong,' King Harald's saga explains, 'and a fine horseman. He was an outstanding warrior, but very cruel.' Three days later he landed in England.

As Godwinsson rode south from his victory he heard the news. He spent only a week gathering forces in London, and his haste was his downfall. When he faced William's army on a field near Hastings it was only nineteen days since the Battle of Stamford Bridge. In just three weeks he had marched his men nearly 400 miles from London to York and back again, and 50 miles from London into Sussex. They were exhausted. The Battle of Hastings was the pitiful last gasp of a Saxon England facing insurmountable odds.

On Christmas Day in 1066 William the Bastard, now known as 'the Conqueror', was crowned in the new abbey that had just been built at Westminster. The Viking Age was over, their heathen world had become Christian. It was a decisive moment of the Middle Ages, and of the history of all northern Europe. But somewhere far away across the broad river of ocean, a corner of the old society survived. There were still promised lands to discover.

Greenland
THE WILD WEST

✳

ICE WAS SPRINKLED on the ocean like chalk crumbled over a mirror. From thirty thousand feet the monstrous icebergs were inconsequential, snapped off and drifting free from the glaciers which eased themselves through the corridors of mountains lining the coast.

The eastern coast of Greenland mocks attempts at description; it is sublime. The largest ice-cap in the world outside Antarctica flows out into the Atlantic under the pressure of its own unimaginable weight. The mountains that struggle out of the ice are dwarfed by it like pebbles in a mill-race, but from below they would have been seen to soar to over three thousand metres. Most of them are unclimbed and many are unnamed. The name given to these islands of rock in a sea of ice is *nunatak*, an Inuit word, reminding the West that Inuit peoples mastered these landscapes long before Europeans ever did.

The late evening sun was lowering, casting shadows from the peaks that stretched for kilometres across the ice in jagged silhouettes. The glaciers coiled and flowed between them in whorls. The same icebergs which had awed and inspired Brendan one and a half millennia before lolled together in clusters on the edge of the ocean.

The aeroplane left the coast behind and rose over the dome of the ice-cap. The ice progressively submerged even the highest mountains, leaving only an immense expanse of unblemished snow. Something in witnessing such rare beauty seems to excite

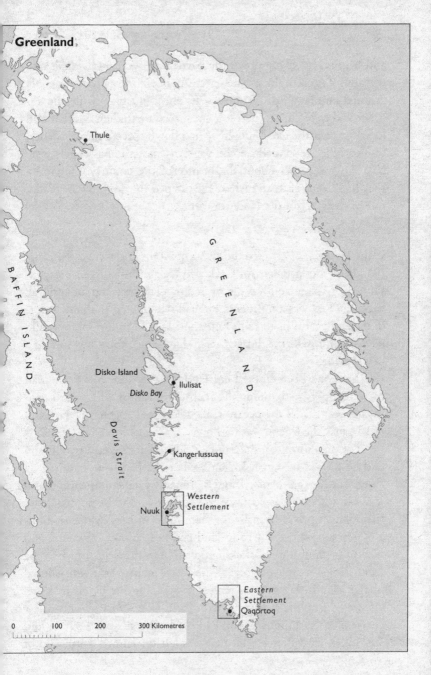

Greenland

Thule

BAFFIN ISLAND

G R E E N L A N D

Disko Island

Ilulisat

Disko Bay

Davis Strait

Kangerlussuaq

Western
Settlement

Nuuk

Eastern
Settlement

Qaqortoq

0   100   200   300 Kilometres

and inspire, knocking down the barriers between individuals and revealing a need to share experience. All down the aeroplane people grinned and laughed, swapped seats and binoculars with one another and called upon total strangers to come to their window and look out over the ice. Though we had flown three hours in silence, by the time we landed on the western coast the passengers were chattering together about the beauty of the country, the stories they had heard of it, and where they hoped to travel in Greenland, one of the last frontier lands on earth.

If Shetland was discovered through a quest for knowledge, the Faroe Islands on a pilgrimage for God, and Iceland in a drive for expansion, then Greenland was discovered in a last-gasp bid for survival. Eirik the Red was a murderer. He had slaughtered so many people in Iceland that if he did not find another land to live in, he would be killed himself. He did not really have any choice but to find a new world.

There had been clues about lands to the west. Since Brendan there had persisted among the Irish the tradition of a great island to the west across the ocean. Called Tir-na-n-Ingen, or 'the Land of Virgins', the legend was reinforced by the stories of St Brendan's Land of the Promise of the Saints. An Icelander called Are Mársson said he drifted to 'Great Ireland', where he had been baptised by chiefs in white garments. Though probably total fantasy, this island was said to be six days' sail west of Iceland and to be populated by Irishmen who had been living there for centuries. More credibly, a Norseman on his way to Iceland had been blown off course and seen some barren rocks sticking up through the fields of ice to the west. Eirik was not put off by the bleak picture that was painted of the islands, being no stranger to scraping his living in harsh circumstances. He had come to Iceland from Norway only a few years before as a fugitive, and had eked out a life on the poor and ice-ridden land that was all that was left unclaimed at the end of the tenth century. The murders he had committed there had been partly in self-defence, and so he was sentenced only to 'minor outlawry'. If he managed to stay alive for three years outside Iceland he would be safe to return.

He found the ice-clogged seas and the stony islands to the west of Iceland but continued on, rounding a cape in the south and then up the western coast of a new land where he found towering mountains backed by ice-caps, and a coastline slashed with deep and lush fjords. It was colder than Iceland, but further south and so enjoyed shorter winters and a less capricious climate. Out at the mouths of the fjords, banks of fog and mist rolled down over the ice-fields, but deep inside the valleys the summers were warm and the skies were clear. There were caribou and seals to hunt and green pasture for sheep and cattle. For a man used to the barrens of Iceland it was a rich country.

After three years exploring the coastline he had found two areas that seemed verdant enough to support the Norsemen's grazing economy. He called the whole place 'Greenland' and sailed for Iceland to rejoin his family and persuade others to join him in his New World.

In his absence Iceland had fallen on hard times. The soil was continuing to leach away, there had been another famine, and people gathered to hear about any opportunity to start anew. Contemporary accounts describe those lean years at the end of the tenth century: 'There was a winter of great calamity in the heathendom in Iceland… Men ate ravens and foxes, and much ill fit to eat was eaten, while some had old folk and infants slain and cast over the cliffs. Then many men starved to death, while some took to stealing.'

Twenty-five knörrs, carrying between six hundred and a thousand emigrants, were loaded up and sailed for Greenland in the spring of 986. Times in Iceland must have been desperate. Only fourteen made it, the others being driven back or wrecked. Eleven ship-loads settled around the southern tip of the new land where Eirik had first come ashore, and the area was named the Østerbygd

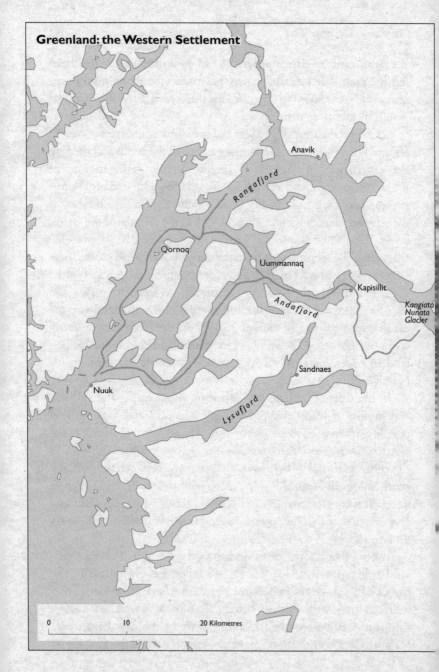

Greenland: the Western Settlement

Anavik

Rangafjord

Qornoq

Uummannaq

Kapisillit

Andafjord

Kangiatá
Nunata
Glacier

Sandnaes

Nuuk

Lysufjord

0   10   20 Kilometres

or 'the Eastern Settlement'. Three more adventurous chieftains continued on with their ships to the second area Eirik had found which lay further to the north. Its landscape was wilder, bleaker, more exposed and when settled it became the remotest outpost of European civilisation. Lying seven hundred kilometres further to the north and the west of the Østerbygd, it was called Vesterbygd or 'the Western Settlement'.

*

Santa Claus was bleached by the twenty-four hour sunlight. He announced the passengers' arrival in Greenland in Danish and English. The poster he was printed on was torn and ageing, the legacy of a tourism venture that was past its best. He looked out of place and out of season among the bare screes and scrublands of the fjord. Depending on your point of view the snows were either a few kilometres in towards the ice-cap or a few months away. Herds of caribou grazed on the far hillside in the midnight sunlight, and clouds of biting flies billowed like smoke around the heads of the runway workers. The air was very clear. Kangerlussuaq, or Søndre Strømfjord in colonial terms, is the gathering point of Greenland; all flights in and out of the country go through it. It lies about halfway down the western coast, tucked in close to the ice-cap, and was originally built as a military base. The Americans helped defend the North Atlantic from there while Denmark was occupied by Germany. They liked Greenland, and afterwards tried to buy it. Denmark refused, but in gratitude the Americans were allowed a concession: Thule Airbase, up at 77° north and only a few hundred kilometres from the North Pole.

At the turn of the twenty-first century Thule was still permanently staffed, and armed, by the Americans. Their determination to stay there is understandable; as occupiers they are only following an ancient Imperial tradition. Since the time of Pytheas the word *Thule* has been a symbol of the ultimate north, and the control of it has long been held to be the highest honour by those seeking domination in world affairs. In his *Georgics* Virgil wrote in praise of Caesar Augustus, 'whether you come as a god of the wide sea, and sailors pay reverence to your divine presence alone, farthest Thule obeys you.' Charles V of Spain too, when he sent his fleets to build an Empire in the New World had banners made declaring '*tibi serviat Ultima Thule*', or 'Let Farthest Thule Obey You'.

Pytheas' lost book has evidently inspired the empire-builders of the world right up to the modern day. The Americans look like they are there to stay. There are other permanent settlements in the world farther north than Thule Airbase in Greenland, but none of the others have nuclear weapons. The Greenlanders want them out. The Danes allow them to stay. It is another tension in their currently unhappy relationship.

There had been a strike at Kangerlussuaq among the baggage handlers. Greenland's population is so small and its communications so dependent on this one airport that a handful of men had held the country to ransom. Danish scout groups and tired businessmen slept on their suitcases in the small cafeteria. A smiling Greenlander reassured a bunch of yelling women that flights would soon be resumed. Outside on the terrace a few bored individuals sat leaking cigarette smoke and idly swatting mosquitoes. Children played on the swings, excited by the light and the lateness and the novelty of the place. I bought a plastic cup of coffee, sat down on my rucksack and waited.

*

'Oldest rocks in the world,' he said.

I was eavesdropping. The speaker was a tall and well-built man in his thirties with a black tangle of hair and a jaw bristling with benign self-assurance. His chequered shirt made him look like a Canadian lumberjack.

'Sorry, could I ask what was that you said?' I asked.

He turned round. 'Round here are the oldest rocks in the world

– well, further south, down around Nuuk. That's where we're heading, my wife and I. And you?'

'I'm going to Nuuk too,' I said.

'We're going off to camp for a couple of months up near the ice-cap, get some samples.' They were geologists, he said, from St John's in Newfoundland. They had a commission to collect samples from two different sites in the fjord system inland from Nuuk. Nuuk, the capital of Greenland, has a population of 14,000 and is the largest settlement in the country. The Danes, he told me, were trying to find mineral wealth in Greenland, some economic return for the hundreds of millions of kroner they pay annually to prop up the Greenlanders' economy. 'That's where we come in,' he grinned, revealing ivory rows of perfect teeth.

As recently as 1933 Norway was still laying claim to being Greenland's colonial master. Iceland, the Faroes and Greenland had all originally been Norwegian colonies, and even Eirik the Red's descendents had shown loyalty to the Norwegian throne when it suited them. But by 1387 the Norwegian, Swedish and Danish crowns had all merged in the familiar mediaeval drama of political marriages and untimely deaths. By 1450 a treaty had been ratified swearing the three countries', 'lasting, eternal and inviolable union.' Before recent independence Norway had spent the five hundred years since as an appendage of either Denmark or Sweden. When it wrested itself from Swedish control for the second time at the turn of the twentieth century, it found that it had lost all of its dependencies in the process. An attempt was made to occupy the eastern coast of Greenland, but in 1933 the International Court in the Hague deemed it unlawful. Denmark were the owners, Norway the squatters.

'I guess Denmark's hoping that if the Greenlanders find enough wealth to support themselves, they'll show some gratitude to the Danes for supporting them all this time,' he said. 'But it is a gamble. Some Greenlanders are pretty pissed off with the Danes.'

He told me that the delays were a common occurrence here and that in Greenland the local airline, Grønlandsfly, is nicknamed by the locals '*Imigafly*', best translated as 'Maybe Airways.' As soon as he said it there was an announcement: the flight to Nuuk would leave shortly. We gathered up our bags and ran out across the tarmac to the small aircraft. People who had been waiting to fly north for two days groaned and turned back to sleep. When the plane took off the sun, having never set, was already beginning to climb into the north-eastern sky.

Eirik the Red and his followers were emigrants. They were men and women who were unafraid, who had a vision of a better future, who were willing to work hard and who knew no other life than one of risk. Within a decade the new settlements were thriving. It *was* a rich country. The Norsemen had never seen such a profusion of seals, whales and game, and further north there were walrus, narwhal, beluga, and the greatest quarry of all: the polar bear. They grew wealthy on trade in these rare commodities. Walrus tusk was a precious alternative to elephant ivory, European access to which was blocked at that time by the Islamic Caliphate. Narwhal tusk passed off as unicorn horn was a cure for all forms of pestilence, and polar bear furs were in demand for the hearths of the European super-rich.

To begin with, it was a good land to settle in, but the momentum of the migrants carried them on further across the ocean.

There are two sagas which describe the discovery of North America by the Greenlanders. One is called *Grænlendinga saga*, 'The Saga of the Greenlanders', and the other is *Eiríks saga rauða*, 'The Saga of Eirik the Red'. Eirik's saga is more detailed but apparently less reliable, and seems to have been a later work more concerned with Christianising the legends of the Greenlanders. But it is surprising how much they agree.

It seems that Leif Eiriksson and then his family members did travel to a new land which lay to the south west of Greenland. He found grapes growing there which could be used to make wine, and so he called it 'Vínland'. In that country in the middle of winter there were still several hours of warm sunshine per day indicating just how far south it must have been. The Norsemen did not count in hours, but used vague terms indicating the position of the sun as it wheeled through the sky. This means that the latitude of Vínland is unknown, and various scholars and historians have placed it in Labrador, Virginia, and almost everywhere on the eastern American seaboard in between. Wild berries similar to 'grapes' grew on trees, but not vines as far north as Maine in mediaeval times, and it is in Maine at an old Indian archaeological site that the astonishing find of a Norse coin minted in the 1070s has been made.

Leif did not stay in the new land after he found it; he had other things to do. He was a follower of the Norwegian king, a trader, and by some accounts, a man who had a woman in every port (he is known to have left a Hebridean noblewoman pregnant on his way from Greenland to Norway one summer). It was not for him to settle a land on the edge of the earth. Leif's brother tried to go to Vínland after him but failed, then died back on his own farm in the Western Settlement in Greenland. His widow Gudrid then re-married, to an Icelander, and together they decided to make a third settlement attempt. It is this emigration by Gudrid and her new husband, Thorfinn Karlsefni (meaning 'the stuff a man is made of') that occupies most of the detail of the two sagas. As Gunnlaug Serpent-Tongue paced the streets of London, three ships and a hundred and forty people sailed west out of Greenland to start again in another New World.

*

Mist flowed down the Davis Strait out of the Arctic; dense and viscous, it clung to the sea and the earth. It had a ponderous weight, edging like dry ice smoke through the fjords which cut inland. With infinite patience it toppled over high mountains passes to fill the valleys that lay protected and sheltered nearer the ice-cap.

Crimson and lilac light leached out of the northern horizon across the mountains. The fog was like a sea, waves of it lapped against the slopes, and it was drenched with the same soft pastel shades as the sky.

The aeroplane flew west first, to the settlement of Sisimiut. The staff of the airline were used to the effect this landscape had on new visitors. The hostess smiled indulgently as passengers hopped from one side of the plane to the other, marvelling at the light and the scenery. The pilot made an open invitation for passengers to go up to the cockpit and look out over the mountains. The landscape was astonishing not only for its beauty, but its enormity and emptiness. Glaciers dripped into majestic fjords which could have swallowed whole cities.

There are no roads outside the settlements in Greenland, all communications are by sea or air. Most settlements number only a few hundred people, and each has a small landing strip or heli-pad. They cluster around their harbours all down the western coast in the Scandinavian style, their buildings bright daubs of blue, yellow and red, vivid against the leaden shoreline and the pale backdrop of the ice-cap.

Sisimiut was a toy town, a splash of colour by the sea. It is less than two hundred miles from there to Baffin Island in Canada, and it may have been from the top of its mountains that a Norse Greenlander on a hunting trip first caught sight of the New World. Now it is a busy little port with a population of about five thousand – not very many in European terms, but in Greenland large enough to make it the country's second city. After landing there to unload some cargo the pilot turned south, following the liminal zone where mist banks of the Arctic roiled against the last mountains of Europe. Greenland is technically part of the American continental plate, but as a Danish outpost many of its ways are resolutely European.

The peaks of Baffin Island to the west lay obscured by the haze over the Davis Strait. Though the sun was rising into the morning, the speed at which we flew south caused it to set over the northern horizon behind us, and the colours on the landscape kaleidoscoped through pastel shades into the richer textures of oils. The horizon rose to meet us and the plane dropped onto the short landing strip of Nuuk, the modern town at the heart of the Norsemen's Western Settlement.

*

Was Vínland the same country that Brendan had called the Land of the Promise of the Saints? Though I had been following 'explorers' on my journey, there is a point of view which maintains there is really no such thing as discovery. There has always been and will always be someone who got there first. When Eirik the Red arrived in Greenland he found some scattered ruins, stone tools and the remains of skin boats. The Norse annals mention this without curiosity; the Vikings took it for granted that they were never the first in any of their lands. It is likely that the remains were of the Dorset Eskimo culture, which began to disappear from the area around the ninth century. The Dorset people, named for Cape Dorset on Baffin Island (where one of the most illuminating archaeological sites of this culture was found), were the predecessors of the Inuit who still live in Greenland today. Inuit legend describes them as 'gentle giants,' a tall people who were scared off when the more ferocious Inuit began their incursions from what is now western Canada. But the Dorset possessed an inferior technology even to the Inuit, and were not able to tan their skin boats. Those boats would not have lasted long before rotting in the wet climate. But there is another possibility – the Irish again. Oak-tanned Irish boats would have lasted a lot longer in the freeze-thaw cycles of Greenland's seasons, and it is known that the Irish monks had the technology and skills to reach and survive there.

According to the *Navigatio*, when Brendan eventually managed to reach his Land of the Promise of the Saints it was only because the Irish Procurator of the Faroe Islands consented, after the seventh

Easter they spent on his islands, to join them as a pilot. He boarded Brendan's coracle and they sailed for forty days until they came to a region of darkness which was said to 'swirl round that island you have been seeking'. The description is reminiscent of the notorious fog banks off the coast of Newfoundland. On the other side of the banks they found an open country laden with precious gems and fruit trees. There they met another man who, astonishingly, spoke to them in Irish: 'After many more years have rolled by, this island will be revealed to your successors at the time when the Christians will be undergoing persecution,' he said.

The passage describing the island for which they have been searching all this time is remarkably short, a couple of paragraphs, almost as if it was included as an afterthought. In the monks' tradition it was the *pilgrimage* which was of importance, not the attainment of their goal. Not long after finding the Promised Land they set sail for Ireland again, which was reached easily as would be expected from the prevailing currents across the North Atlantic. Brendan's community in Galway was 'rapturous with joy' at his return. After describing the wonders of his voyage he lay back in the arms of his monks and gave his soul up to God.

But the hints of Irish voyages persist long after Brendan was in his grave. When Thorfinn Karlsefni and Gudrid set sail from the Eastern Settlement they took with them two Irish guides that Leif had brought as a gift from the Norwegian court. It could be that the Irish were at that time still making voyages across the Atlantic and were useful to the Norsemen as pilots. They also took a huntsman called Thorhall, 'who had a wide knowledge of the uninhabited regions,' and a woman called Freydis, an illegitimate daughter of Eirik the Red renowned for her bad temper and ferocity.

The substance of the following account is taken largely from the more detailed saga of Eirik the Red. In company they sailed up to the Western Settlement, where most expeditions began and where they would be likely to pick up more men who knew the 'uninhabited regions' well. From there they sailed north to an archipelago

known as the 'Bear Islands', probably in Disko Bay up at 70° of latitude. After those islands they sailed west, and then a northerly wind
took them to a barren land of flat stones which they called Helluland ('stone-slab land'). This was almost certainly Baffin Island.
After two more days' sailing to the south they reached a forested
land with many animals which they called Markland ('forest land'),
almost certainly the forested slopes of Labrador. Further south still
they came to a wild region with long golden beaches that stretched
for tens of miles, which they called Furðustrandir ('marvel strands').
The description in the saga points to the beaches of Nova Scotia,
and the two Irish guides were sent off to explore the land from there.
They hauled their ships up onto its beaches and decided to winter
nearby.

Though the summer at that latitude was warm, the winter was
still very harsh and the emigrants were unprepared for it. To survive
they were forced to eat a dead whale washed up on the strands and
afterwards they all became ill. Mutiny threatened the expedition
and the group divided; Thorhall sailed north and west, probably
into the Gulf of St Lawrence, to seek Vínland. On his way there
storms caught him and he drifted with the currents all the way to
Ireland, where the saga tells us he and his crew were beaten and
enslaved.

Thorfinn Karlsefni and Gudrid, glad to be rid of him, continued
south 'for a long time,' until they found a land where fields grew
with self-sown wheat, halibut flopped on the beaches and grapes
grew in the hills. For the Norsemen it really was a promised land;
they were astonished to find that they did not even need to build
winter stables for their animals. A son was born to Gudrid that
winter, called Snorri, the first European born in North America.
The colony seemed perfect in almost every way.

But a shadow darkened their first summer. The ships had only
been beached for two weeks before natives, whom the Norsemen
referred to with the derogatory term *skrælings*, paddled past them in
skin boats. They had 'large eyes and wide cheekbones,' and stared

at the Norsemen in wonder. Their appearance was held to be a
bad omen of things to come. Next spring they appeared again in
greater numbers, this time to trade. They paid handsomely in furs
for pieces of red woollen cloth, which they tied around their heads.
They showed greater interest in the iron and the weapons of the
Greenlanders, but Karlsefni forbade that they be sold them.

The colony lasted only three more weeks. The Native Americans
reappeared as a war party in greater numbers shrieking, firing cata-
pults and throwing stone tomahawks. The Norsemen tried to fight
them off but were hopelessly outnumbered. They ran for a cliff wall
where they could not be surrounded, but Freydis was heavily pregnant and could not keep up with the others. Yelling curses after her
men she picked up the sword of a slain Greenlander who lay with
a stone hatchet in the back of his head, and turned round to face
the natives. She bellowed at them, pulled her breasts from her shift
and slapped them with the sword. They must have been surprised
to see a woman stand and face them, and fled.

The colonisation of the New World was over. Karlsefni and
Gudrid packed up their ship and sailed for Greenland.

The *skrælings* of the era would have been the Micmacs of New
Brunswick, the Beothuk of Newfoundland, or the Montaignai of
Southern Labrador. The astonishing find of an eleventh-century
Norse coin in Maine does not presuppose a permanent settlement
by Norsemen of that era, and it may even have been traded between many different native groups before finding its way there. A
hole had been punched through it and so it is likely to have been
used as a pendant. We know, however, that the Greenlanders did
continue to sail to the New World as a matter of course for many
centuries, because as late as 1347 the Icelandic annals mentions
a ship sailing from Greenland to Markland before being storm-
driven to Iceland. It does not treat the idea of a Markland voyage
itself as being unusual, and it is unlikely that the huntsmen of the
Western Settlement, which was poor in wood, would have ignored
such rich pickings so close to their homesteads.

There has only been one unequivocal find proving that the Norsemen lived in North America. In the village of L'Anse aux Meadows, on the north-eastern tip of Newfoundland, a Norse way-station has been uncovered. It is a settlement on an exposed headland easily identifiable from the sea. The site has now been verified to include a Norse smithy, a sauna and a longhouse, and to hold in its bogs a wealth of Norse artefacts such as spindle whorls and oil lamps. In its middens traces of butternuts have been uncovered, which must have been brought back from an expedition much further to the south. As a settlement the place seems never to have been designed for long-term use, but may have been a 'safe port' from which ships could thrust south on short trips to gather wood and to hunt along the coasts of Maine, New Jersey and Virginia while still being able to retreat from *skræling* attack.

The attempt to settle the New World lasted less than three years. It would be another five centuries before European culture would return to overwhelm it with gunpowder and disease. For Europe, throughout that time, the furthest settled land across the ocean would be Greenland, and the furthest outpost the Western Settlement.

In a late-night bar themed like a cowboy saloon I met a modern-day emigrant of the Western Settlement. He wore a casual leather jacket, a heavy gold chain, and the epicanthic folds of his eyes gave him an expression of perpetual merriment. His hair was styled to perfection and gleamed like a raven's plumage. He told me he had once been a hairdresser. He had also been a policeman in Denmark. His name was Aqaluq, and now he had landed a high-ranking job in Nuuk he had come back to Greenland to stay.

It was after midnight. Outside, on the main street of the town, children played football in the dusky light.

'I was ready to come back,' he said, his eyes glinting in the half-light. 'Denmark is a good country but Greenland is my home.'

His friend returned from the bar carrying three bottles of Danish lager. He too had lived overseas for many years, working the cod and shrimp ships that weathered the heavy seas of the North Atlantic. Together we took a mental stroll around the harbours of Lerwick, Oslo and Leith.

A young man staggered to our table. His eyes were slow and heavy, and he was very drunk. After looking at each of us he turned towards me, obviously the foreigner, and said in slurred English:

'You like Greenland?'

'Yes, very much.'

'It is a great country. It is wonderful. Beautiful. And we are GREENLANDIC!' he said, with pride. I nodded.

'NOT Eskimos!' he added.

'I wouldn't dream of calling you that,' I said.

'But some people do,' he replied. He steadied himself by gripping the table with both hands. 'I have worked in Europe and in America, and people there have called me that.'

'Well I can tell you that to me you will always be a Greenlander,' I said.

'You can say "Inuit", I'll allow you! It is better than Eskimo, but still wrong.' He struggled to balance himself. 'There are Canadian Inuit too. THIS is MY country!'

Emotion overwhelmed him. He lurched away from the table. Aqaluq smiled apologetically. Across the dance-floor a fight broke out. Two men took a couple of swings at one another before being bundled out of a hidden exit onto the street by two bouncers that I had not noticed. They lay on the pavement outside, blinking in the midnight sunlight. It did feel like the Wild West.

*

Within fifty years of the settlement's foundation the new land was the talk of all northern Europe, not for its riches, but its dangers.

The *Meregarto*, an Old German poem from the middle of the eleventh century, describes the horrors of the journey west through the ice:

> There is a clotted sea in the western ocean
> When the strong wind drives ships upon that course,
> Then the skilled seamen have no defence against it,
> But they must go into the very bosom of the sea.
> Alas! Alas!
> They never come out again
> If God will not deliver them, they must rot there.

The Archbishopric of Trondheim had not yet been established, and the country was thought of as lying within the Archbishopric of Hamburg. For at least the first century of the settlement the Greenlanders did not care who their Archbishop was; if they were Christian at that early stage it was only with the thinnest veneer. The pagan traditions were still built into the foundations of the Norse world, and if they were rooted in Iceland, then they were rooted even more firmly in this frontier country settled by the defiantly pagan Eirik the Red. When Adam of Bremen wrote his 'History of the Archbishopric of Hamburg' in 1070 he did not know much about this new country in the west which was supposedly under the aegis of Hamburg, but he knew that it was a wild and dangerous land. Concerning it he wrote, 'The people there are blue-green from the salt water; and from this the region takes its name. They live in a similar fashion to the Icelanders, except that they are more cruel and trouble seafarers by predatory attacks. To them also, as is reported, Christianity has lately been wafted.'

Greenland of the eleventh and twelfth century was the Wild West of Europe. To the youth of the day it was a fabled land filled with wonder and sorcery where men could win great wealth in the hunting fields of the north, but both getting there and living there involved significant risks. A few scattered descriptions of trading voyages of the era have survived, and they always depict it as a lawless place for those in search of adventure, a place in which young men could prove themselves and win renown. In *Ólafs Saga Helga* the hero Thorarin is told that if he has not yet been to Greenland, then it is high time that a traveller like him made his way there. In the saga of Ref the Sly the hero is hounded out of Iceland but builds himself a fortress deep in the fjords of northern Greenland where he lives protected by his skills in the black arts (and his residence in Greenland is all the more appropriate for that). One of the more reliable references concerns a simple trading mission.

In 'The Tale of Audun from the Westfjords' an Icelander sells everything he owns in order to sail to the Western Settlement and buy a polar bear cub. From other sources we know that this must have been a common enough thing to do (Iceland already had specific laws about the responsibilities of polar bear owners towards any damages their animals caused). Audun planned to give his bear to King Svein Ulfsson of Denmark, but the only ship available took him instead to Norway where Harald Hardráda offered to buy it for double what he had paid. The tale is set about 1061, and at the time Harald must have been starting to think of sailing for England. It would not be long before he took an arrow through the throat at the Battle of Stamford Bridge.

Audun refused to give the bear to anyone but King Svein, and Harald graciously allowed him to take it to his enemy, at Roskilde. When King Svein eventually received it he was so impressed with Audun that he rewarded him handsomely, giving him gold, clothes, money and a ship laden with goods worth many times what he had paid for the bear. So the gamble had paid off. Audun returned to Iceland a very wealthy man.

Greenland's fame grew in the minds of those men who were determined to make their mark.

*

Cambridge University Library manages to combine the phallic thrust of a grain silo with the heavy brick presence of a power station. Outside it the river Cam slips by in a soundless tunnel of green. Inside there are grand reading rooms with ceilings in the sky where they say almost any book ever written in English can be requested and read on desks bound in leather. There are narrow warrens of stacks which ramify and proliferate up staircases and down corridors in an endless labyrinth of books. It is a bibliophile's paradise.

On a spring morning before leaving for Shetland I had gone to the reading room and ordered a facsimile manuscript of the *Konungs Skuggsja* or 'The King's Mirror', a thirteenth-century work which set out to distinguish fact from fantasy among the stories that swirled thick as polar fog out of mediaeval Greenland. In the stacks I also found a 1911 first edition of Fridtjof Nansen's epic labour of love *In Northern Mists*, a history of the early exploration of the Arctic.

Any history of the North and of its exploration would be incomplete without Fridtjof Nansen. In his character was concentrated all the hunger of mankind to push out beyond the horizons of the known world. He was perhaps the greatest polar explorer the world has ever seen, but he was also a scholar. He represented for me the archetype of so many men I had followed in my journey.

After a brief training in Anatomy he was the first to demonstrate that brain cells were discrete units. His private work on board polar vessels earned him a professorship in Oceanography. He was the first man to ski across Greenland's ice-cap, and he wrote an academic book about the Inuit he met in Nuuk. In his vessel *Fram* he drifted closer to the North Pole than any man had before him and made a daring but unsuccessful bid to ski to it. Later in his career he became a champion of Norwegian nationalism and made a significant contribution to Norway's eventual separation from Sweden. After independence he became Norway's first ambassador to London and later earned a Nobel Peace Prize for humanitarian works. An eccentric, an autodidact, and a visionary, he was prone to rages and paralysing fits of depression. He stands as one of the greatest men of the nineteenth and twentieth century. I sat down in the thick church silence of the library and read what he had to say about the *Konungs Skuggsja*. He had included several translations from the work:

> Few are the people in that land, for little of it is thawed so much as to be habitable… But when you ask what they live on in that country, since they have no corn, then [you must know] that men live on more things than bread alone. Thus it is said that there is good pasture and great and good homesteads in Greenland; for people there have much cattle and sheep, and there is much making of butter and cheese. The people live much on this, and also on flesh and all kinds of game, the flesh of reindeer, whale, seal and bear; on this they maintain themselves in that country.

'The King's Mirror' describes the dangers of Greenland's ice-fields, how ships were often wrecked on their way to and from its settlements, and how wayfarers were often stranded there for many years because of the paucity of vessels that successfully made the voyage. But it also offers an explanation of why men would willingly subject themselves to such risk:

> If you wish to know what men seek in this land, or why men journey thither in so great danger of their lives, then it is the threefold nature of man which draws him thither. One part of him is emulation and desire of fame, for it is man's nature to go where there is likelihood of great danger, and to make himself famous thereby. Another part is the desire of knowledge, for it is man's nature to wish to know and see those parts of which he has heard, and to find out whether they are as it was told him or not. The third part is the desire of gain, seeing that men seek after riches in every place where they learn that profit is to be had, even though there be great danger in it.

The desire for fame, knowledge, and riches. The passage read like an explanation of the complex character of Nansen himself.

✳

It was undoubtedly the biggest post box I have ever seen. It was a gleaming wall of redness, standing thirty feet high and towering over the old town harbour, a monument to a new mythology. Every year letters arrive in Greenland from all over the world addressed to Santa Claus, and in a small office below the colossal post box they are answered. I looked through some of them and saw postmarks from England, Greece, Poland and France, but most were written by the little boys and girls of Denmark.

On the post office walls were old sepia photographs of Europeans in formal nineteenth-century dress, arm in arm with pretty smiling Greenlandic girls wearing sealskins. For two and a half centuries colonial Nuuk was known as Godthåb, 'Good Hope', and generations of Danish administrators have married and made their lives there. It is said that there is no longer a pure-blooded Greenlander left in the whole country, but it is unfair and inaccurate to blame the Danes for that. Traditional culture among Arctic peoples has rarely been burdened by the moral and sexual reservations of Europeans, and in the colonial era the Danes were not the only Europeans to take advantage of the ease with which the Greenlandic and Canadian Inuit had always shared their wives and husbands. Scottish and Dutch whalers too spent winters trapped by the ice, and what may be seen as exploitation by uptight Europeans is even now regarded by the Greenlanders as bygones and irrelevancies. As Greenlanders they are all Inuit, which means only 'the people', and they are all part of modern Greenland.

✳

Another evening, I was drinking in a different bar. The dancefloor heaved with drunken people of all ages jumping up and down to the music. It was an anonymous nightclub on a Tuesday night, but the atmosphere was more like that of a raucous family wedding.

On the stage a solitary musician played guitar and synthesiser, rolling out seventies rock classics in well-practiced succession. Everyone knew all the words. Later on he sat down with me, obviously a fellow foreigner, to talk.

He was Bulgarian, he said, and lived here six months of the year every year. Nowhere else in Europe could he earn as much for playing music as he did in Greenland. Again and again as we spoke a clutch of girls pulled on his sleeve and asked him to come and dance with them, but he shook them off. One of them had bruises all the way up her arms and was more persistent than the others, breaking into our conversation: 'Look at my bruises, he beat me up, so now I can do what I like,' she said, 'come on and dance with me.' He shooed her away and asked me how long I would be in Nuuk. Sweat dripped from his black curls onto the bar.

He had a Greenlandic girlfriend, he said, but she would not come with him to Europe. He knew that he could not settle in Nuuk – a tiny capital on the edge of the ocean – and he had recently come to a conclusion. He loved the shores of the Black Sea more than he loved her. Later on in the autumn he would go home to stay.

The first song of his next set was in Greenlandic, and the pitch of the crowd approached hysteria.

'He speaks Greenlandic! He speaks Greenlandic!' A woman at the bar gazed up at him, her eyes syrupy with booze, then tugged on my arm. 'Come and dance with me!'

'Is it like this in this bar every night?' I asked her, getting up.

'Of course!' she shouted back, 'how else should it be…?'

Later that evening I heard an explanation for the Greenlanders' irrepressible capacity to celebrate: 'In Greenland we've always had times of hunger and times of plenty. And now the Danes are here we've got plenty, and when you have plenty, you party!'

'What about your hangovers in the morning, don't you have to work?' I asked.

'Hangovers? They don't last long until you get to party again. Hey, how long are you in town?'

'I'm leaving tomorrow,' I said, ' I'm going up towards the ice-cap.'

'So you'd better live it up here while you can! Come on, come and dance with me!'

*

At midnight the bar closed and everyone was ushered out into the street. I stood in the drizzle trying to get my bearings for the way back to my hotel. A girl walked up to me and asked if I wanted to come back to her apartment to sleep.

*

The modern harbour lay in a cove behind the town. In its shop there were shotguns for sale alongside the racks of fishing tackle. Wooden walkways and staircases had been built over the bare out-crops of rock which lay between the road and the water's edge. Pontoons lined with small motor-boats were slung to the side of the wharf, bobbing up and down with the motion of the waves. There are very few cars in Nuuk, but a lot of boats. I was looking for a particular charter boat, and after looking into nearly all of them I came upon someone to ask for directions. He was standing in a pool of petrol, casually smoking a cigarette.

He showed me the way to the right boat, and I climbed aboard. The captain was Faroese. He was tall and straight, wore a beard and a cap, and as we set off up the fjord his eyes searched the water ceaselessly for ice. Thirty years before he had got fed up with the tight, insular community of his home town of Miðvágur and run away to Greenland. He made a living ferrying children between church summer camps deep in the fjords. Bibles and hymn sheets were strewn around the inside of the cockpit. He did not ever want to live in the Faroe Islands again, he said, though some of his children had moved back there. He liked living in Nuuk, but he liked it better in the north where there was more ice.

I told him I had been in Miðvágur a couple of months before.

'I wondered if I'd see any *grind* there,' I said, 'but there weren't any hunts the whole time I was in the Faroes.'

'All this media pressure about the *grind* is a good thing,' he announced. 'Now if there have been a lot of whales killed, people think twice about starting another hunt. They never used to do that.'

A humpback whale surfaced and dived by the side of the boat, and his face cracked into a grin.

'Look! Look! Did you see it?' Like the ferrymen I had met in Shetland, he turned the boat to follow the whale for a while, for my benefit. 'Watch! It will surface again!'

The muzzle of the whale broke the surface, pushing a bow wave before it as it curved gracefully out of the water. It blew, and a cloud of vapour like a think-bubble hung in the air before gently dissipating.

'It is waiting for us!' he cried.

Its back arched like a smooth black wheel, glistening as it rolled its bulk through the water, big as an island. Its tiny dorsal fin appeared, and then its tail rose into the air and waved once before slapping down on the surface in a leviathan parting gesture. We watched in silence.

'Yes,' he said finally, 'I think it is a good thing that the Faroese people don't kill so many whales any more.'

✳

The Greenland sagas are steeped in the pagan world. It is as if the monastic scribes of Iceland knew what a frontier land it was, and as they sanitised the Icelanders' oral traditions they allowed those of Greenlanders to stand, perhaps as a warning of the perils that would face those who travelled there. Even when the Greenlanders did finally adopt Christianity their pagan rituals continued. For example, underneath the chancel of the thirteenth-century cathedral of the Eastern Settlement a row of walrus skulls has been uncovered, laid out neatly as an offering for success in the hunts of the north.

The Norse Greenlanders were so isolated that they had developed a distinct artform for the relaying of their legends, called Greenlandish verse-speech, and their sagas feel and sound different from those of the Icelanders. They were a people who lived dwarfed by a landscape they knew they could never subdue. The brooding power of it found its way into their art as it so totally governed their lives. Many of the pagan references in the two main sagas revolve around Gudrid, the beautiful and forthright wife of Thorfinn Karlsefni. Three events stand out.

*

Near the beginning of the saga of Eirik the Red the listener is introduced to a seeress called Thorbjorg who lives in the Eastern Settlement. She spends her winters travelling throughout the settlement making predictions for the coming year. She is held in high esteem and wears the finest clothes of the day, set with jewels and lined with white catskin. The saga says that on entering the house she is given porridge made with kid's milk and a platter of the hearts of all the types of animals the farm has to offer. She is then asked for help in chanting songs to summon the spirits. Gudrid stepped forward:

"'I have neither magical powers nor the gift of prophecy, but in Iceland, my foster-mother taught me chants she called ward songs."

Thorbjorg answered: "Then you know more than I expected."

Gudrid said, "These are the sort of actions in which I intend to take no part, because I am a Christian woman."'

Her principles did not last for long. The others persuaded her it could be for the benefit of all to hear what the spirits have in store for them, and so she agreed to sing the chant: 'Gudrid spoke the chant so well and beautifully that people there said they had never heard anyone recite in a fairer voice.'

The spirits were pleased with her. The seeress reassured her that a light would shine on all of her descendents and she would live a long and happy life.

*

In the saga of the Greenlanders we hear a different version of the incursion of the *skrælings* into the settlement of Vínland than the one described in the saga of Eirik the Red. In this version, Karlsefni built a strong wooden palisade around his farm to protect Gudrid and his baby son from the natives. When one of them tried to steal some iron he was attacked and killed by one of Karlsefni's slaves. At that exact moment a woman appeared in front of Gudrid:

'She was pale and had eyes so large that eyes of such size have never been seen in a human head. She came to where Gudrid was sitting and spoke: "What is your name?" she said.

"My name is Gudrid, and what is yours?"

"My name is Gudrid," the other woman said.'

The ominous echoing apparition then disappeared, and was taken as yet another sign that the settlement's days were numbered. They stayed for one more winter, but it was clear to them that they would not be able to live in such a land under the threat of sorcery and violence. In the spring they sailed for Greenland.

The two Greenland sagas agree on one more event in the life of Gudrid: the death of her first husband. It happened one winter in the Western Settlement, most likely at Sandnæs on the banks of the Lysufjord. In both sagas he dies from a contagion that is sweeping through the settlement, and during his wake comes back to life briefly to speak to Gudrid and warn her of what the future holds for her. He complains bitterly about the heathen ways of the Greenlanders, and asks that his body be taken back to the Eastern Settlement where there is a patch of consecrated ground in which he can be buried. The saga author explains his anxiety: it was common in those days to bury men in unconsecrated ground with a pole driven through their chests. When a priest came by (which could be many years later) the pole would be removed and a few drops of holy water poured down into the grave.

*

In later life Gudrid's gifts in the black arts translated into a remarkable piety. After leaving Vínland she and Karlsefni moved back to Iceland and established one of the greatest Icelandic dynasties of the Middle Ages. Tradition holds that it is Karlsefni's account of the Vínland settlement that was formally laid down by scribes in the saga of the Greenlanders. When he died Gudrid made a pilgrimage to Rome, and on her return had a church built in the north of Iceland where she lived as an anchoress for the rest of her life. Through her sons by Karlsefni she was the grandmother and great-grandmother of three bishops of Iceland.

In the Saga Age there was still no bishop in Greenland, but there were occasional itinerant priests. Eirik branded them all 'hypocrites' and showed anger to anyone who would bring them to his country on their ships. But the tide was turning, the old generation was dying away and Greenland relied on trade with a Christian Europe. By the dawn of the twelfth century, a hundred years after the Vínland voyages, the last heathens were dying out. The first roving bishops began to make the long voyage across the ocean.

*

Further into the fjord from Nuuk there were no more whales. The waters of the fjord were squeezed between shoulders of mountains, channelled by walls of the oldest rocks in the world. Their slopes rose vertically from the water's edge, their smooth faces of granite mottled by patches of stunted scrub and scored by the passage of long-gone glaciers. Snow lay in streaks on the mountainsides like powder gathered in withered skin. I could not see any pasture-land in sight, and I marvelled at Eirik's persistence in exploring this country, to carry on and find the few verdant slopes further in towards the ice-cap. The mountains were sheer and angular, and their peaks and spires were echoed in the formations of the ice drifting by. Each of the icebergs was like a masterpiece in alabaster, but they all glowed with the same delicate blue light. Every so often one of them toppled and rolled, righting itself towards a new centre of gravity as the salt water melted it from below.

The captain dropped me off at the settlement on the small island of Qornoq, a cluster of brightly-gabled wooden houses and a rusting old fishing station. I wanted to find a Norse farm ruin said to be there, and I hoped to find a boat that would take me deeper into the fjord. Further to the north the Godthåbfjord continued through the corridors of the mountains in a broad arc, called by the Norse the Rangafjord, or 'the curved'. At its furthest convexity lay the settlement of Anavík where the best preserved ruins of the Western Settlement were to be found. It also had one of only three churches that were built in the area by the Norsemen. I wanted to try to visit all three of the churches, the best surviving remnants of the lost Norse community there.

Modern Qornoq was both a fishing camp and a holiday village for the people of Nuuk. Greenlandic flags fluttered from its windows, outnumbering Danish flags by ten to one. The mountains of the surrounding islands soared around it. Rusting cans and broken glass lay in the grass by the village incinerator and children ran barefoot between the houses, squealing in pleasure and shooting water pistols in the heat. They represented every stage of inter-racial union, from dark Asiatic to blonde European, all shouting happily to one another in Greenlandic. It is a beautiful, halting language of percussive consonants and brief, functional vowels, and as much communication passes with facial expressions as with words. The houses were arranged around the solitary water tap fed by glacial meltwater. The people sat on their verandas playing cards, swatting flies and waving to me as I passed.

There are no roads in the smaller settlements in Greenland, only snaking paths through the scrub between the houses, converging as they approach the jetties. The walled remains of the old Norse farm lay on the far side of the island. I climbed over to it and walked around the abandoned home-field, but there was little to see. Over a small hill there was another bay facing north, and there I set up my tent. The fjord cod passed by in small shoals so slowly and so near to the shore that I quickly caught one, and as the sky dimmed towards midnight, cooked it over a fire made with Canadian driftwood.

To the north the Rangafjord was choked with ice. The Greenlanders have two names for icebergs, depending on their size: *illullia* for the large ones and *siqut* for the small. A double 'l' sound is made by setting the tongue on the roof of the mouth and blowing air out through the cheeks in a soft exhalation. *Illullia* sounds like the splash and roll of ice falling into salt water.

The tidal rip forced the ice into collisions which groaned like crumpling metal. The *illullia* moved ponderously through the fields of *siqut*; being larger they were subjected to deeper currents and their broad faces caught the wind like sails. Sitting there in the moonlight was like watching an ever-changing range of snowy mountains, or like travelling through mythical highlands of pearl and crystal without having to move at all.

If the men and women of the Western Settlement were pioneers, so were their churchmen. Three quarters of a millennium separated them from the Christianity Brendan knew, as it separates our era from theirs, but the first bishops and priests of Greenland lived far closer to Brendan's world in terms of its unknowns and dangers than we live to the uncertainties of the twelfth and thirteenth centuries. Like Brendan they were seamen and travellers accustomed to hardship and risk; unlike Brendan they were mired in the corruption of late mediaeval Roman Catholicism. It was normal for bishops and priests to bribe those in power, smuggle goods and extort funds in order to maintain their positions in church and secular society. It was also not uncommon to keep faith in the old pagan ways.

The first bishop of Greenland was an Icelander, called Eirik. He arrived in the country in 1112 and seems to have ruled his bishopric from Sandnæs in the Western Settlement. It sounds as if he was a wanderer at heart, volunteering to come into the Wild West and then gravitating to its remotest outpost. After nine years there the Western Settlement was not wild enough; the Icelandic annals say that in 1121 '*Eirik Grænlandinga byskup leitade Vínlands*', or 'Bishop Eirik of Greenland went in search of Vínland'. He became the first churchman since Brendan to sail for the New World. Brendan, though, had returned home. Bishop Eirik did not.

After a couple of years it must have been clear that he was not coming back. The church was holding ever greater sway in the economic life of those days, and to be respected as an economically viable trading state Greenland needed a replacement bishop.

His name was Arnald, and he was a humble, hardy, and practical man. According to 'The Story of Einar Sokkason' he could turn his hand to anything and preferred to travel in disguise without the obvious vestments and trappings of a bishop. Despite his hardiness he apparently railed against the decision to send him to the ends of the earth: perhaps he had his eye on a more profitable see. First of all he complained that he was not suited to such an appointment, then that he would have to leave his friends and family, and then that the Greenlanders were known to be such difficult people to work with. It seems that the Norse Greenlanders were winning themselves a famous reputation.

Arnald was Bishop of Greenland for 28 years. Four more bishops came and went, each of whom served for a decade or two until the 1240s, when there were decades when no one would make the voyage west over the ocean. Piracy in Scottish and Irish waters was in ascendancy, and much of Europe was slipping into anarchy. These were the decades when Snorri Sturluson was writing his sagas, Iceland was riven by civil war, and the nobility of England demanded the Magna Carta from the lawless King John.

In 1262 Iceland voluntarily gave up its status as a republic. It was no longer viable to live as an independent trading nation in that climate of larceny and privateering. They needed regular trading ships from Norway, and in return for taxes and allegiance to the king they were promised at least six vessels a year. If Iceland was rarely visited in these years, then the situation must have been much worse for Greenland.

In 1274 the Council of Lyon decreed that all Christians must pay six years of extra tithes in order to help finance the Crusades. In response the Archbishop of Trondheim sent tax collectors, but no replacement bishop, to Greenland. The letters between the Archbishop and the Vatican make illuminating reading; Popes were dying off so fast that three were involved in trying to collect these Greenland tithes: John XXI, Nicholas III and Martin IV.

A few years short of the fourteenth century a new bishop, called Thord, was sent from Norway to Greenland. King Eirik 'the Priest-hater' was on the Norwegian throne, and was busy earning his epithet. The neglected backwater across the ocean seemed like a good place to wait for the King to die. The community of Greenland was rejuvenated. The church of Anavík was built.

*

No one would take me to Anavík. There was too much ice in the fjord. Instead I picked up a lift to the nearby island of Uummannaq where I met a group of volunteers who were restoring an old Moravian mission station.

The Moravian brothers were one of the first Protestant movements, being founded in the eastern part of what is now the Czech Republic over a hundred years before Luther nailed his 95 arguments against the papacy to a church door in Wittenberg. Outspoken against what they saw as the corruption of Rome, by the early eighteenth century the Moravians had founded a model Christian community in Saxony based on the values of generosity, communal living, and prayer, and from where they sent missionaries out all over the world. The Greenland Mission was just one of over thirty mission settlements, and was one of their first international enterprises. It was the brainchild of one Count Zinzendorf, who had been very taken by a group of abducted Greenlanders that he had been shown at the court of the King Christian VI of Denmark. He considered it of the highest priority to send missionaries at once, to work on the salvation of their pagan souls.

The mission to Greenland began in 1733, but it was not until 1861 that the station on Uummannaq island was established. The brothers and sisters of the Moravian mission had established a school and a church which had lasted for forty years, until missionary zeal back in Saxony began to wane and funding for the stations in Greenland began to dry up at the turn of the twentieth century. It was this church and school that the volunteers on the island had come to help restore.

As well as ten Greenlandic tradesmen, there were ten young people from countries all over Europe. They were an eclectic bunch, including an engineer from Ghent, a landscape gardener from Braunschweig and a violinist studying at the Conservatoire in Amsterdam. They invited me to stay and work with them, and we all lived together in tents by the shore. There were no streams on the island and so for fresh water we melted small pieces of glacial ice that washed up on the beach. In the mornings after work we swam in the fjord or went fishing for cod. In the afternoons we lay in the grass reading, or carving pieces of caribou antler and Canadian driftwood. None of the volunteers wanted to leave. After a couple of weeks there neither did I.

The scenery around the island was as magnificent as that around Qornoq. To the east it was dominated by a mountain called Pisigssarfik, 'the Archer's Mountain,' a sheer face of granite over a thousand metres high. Later, back in the national library of Nuuk, I found an explanation of its name in a volume of Henry (Hinrich) Rink's *Tales and Traditions of the Eskimo*.

The legend goes that in the days of the Western Settlement there lived a young Norseman and a young Inuit who were the best of friends. They had grown up together, and spoke one another's languages. As they grew older both became great archers, and they regularly challenged one another to contests of skill and bravery. One day they agreed to settle once and for all which of them was the greater hunter. They spread an animal hide out on the beach below Pisigssarfik and climbed to its summit. The skin was a tiny brown smudge on the beach far below them. The Norseman shot, and missed. The Inuit shot, hit the target, and then, inexplicably, tossed the Norseman over the cliff.

There are quite a few legends among the Inuit about the Norse Greenlanders, whom they called *Qavdlunât*. Surprisingly there are as many about their friendship as there are about their battles. At least at the beginning of their encounters there seems to have been a friendly distance maintained between them most of the time. They rarely came into competition; the Norsemen lived deep in the fjords and the Inuit lived out at the coast among the fogs and the sea-ice. One Icelandic source even describes a Norseman, Bjorn Jorsalafare, adopting two Inuit children after they were orphaned near the Eastern Settlement (his name hints at how well travelled some Greenlanders were – Jorsalafare means 'Jerusalem-farer', the Norse name for a Crusader). The Thule Inuit culture was migrating out of the High Arctic down the western coast of Greenland in the same centuries that the Norse were settling the land. They were both new immigrants. At least in the early centuries of the settlements they seemed to believe the land could support them all.

During the nights on Uummannaq thick polar fog poured in from the Davis Strait, filling the fjords by morning. The waves sighed against the icebergs which lined the shore like sentinels, suspended between the grey of the water and the grey of the mist. It rendered them insubstantial and ghostly, but each of them was capable of sinking a ship. Every so often one would roll, rumbling with a bass thunder like the roar of a distant avalanche. The dense layer of mist was less than a hundred metres thick, and from the summit of Uummannaq the mountains were seen to stand in the sunlight, their ankles lapped by the ebbing sea of fog. As the heat gathered through each morning it melted away.

On a day where the sky was clear and the air stood idle I went out in the boat with some of the Greenlanders to check their nets. The sun was warm on our backs and shoulders, and shirtless we hauled in the cod nets that had been set the day before. Out on the water there was respite from the biting flies which plagued the shores on still days. One of the Greenlanders, a carpenter called Ole, knew that I was interested in seeing traces of the Norsemen and from the boat he pointed out the site of the second of the three churches of the Western Settlement. It was not far from the foot of the sheer face of Pisigssarfik, and we motored over in the boat to take a look. There was little to see there now. The site had been settled by the Inuit after the Norse community died out, and had wiped away most traces of it. Standing on the thin earth I thought about the strata of Norse burials that must be preserved in the permafrost below me.

We stopped at a tiny island called Qeqertánguaq, out in the middle of the fjord. I had read that a Norseman had carved graffiti into one of the rocks there over eight hundred years before. The island was a bare knuckle of leaden stone, a marker post lying at the confluence of five fjords, and could have been used as a guard post. We searched the whole island but could not find the chiselled runes. Whole centuries of Norse occupation in these valleys seemed to have disappeared without trace.

*

Another of the Greenlanders out with us that day, Marius, possessed an extraordinary reverence for life and for death. The first day I met him he took a matchbox from his shirt pocket, holding his breath with wonder, and showed me a dead bumble bee he kept inside it. He liked to carry it around because of its intricate beauty, and he liked to know it was there close to his skin. But he hated the flies of Nuuk. He grew up in Angmagssalik, one of the few scattered settlements on the rugged eastern coast where there are only seals, bears, and ice. At eighteen he had gone to Denmark to learn his trade of carpentry, but working to the clock chafed him and he had longed to be back hunting on the sea-ice in Greenland. As a journeyman he had returned home, bought 37 huskies with his savings, and took to the wilderness again. His girlfriend used to prepare the skins of the seals he killed. Sometimes when out on the endless plains of ice he would stumble on the tracks of a polar bear. The dogs would follow in a frenzy of fear and excitement, and when they found the bear they would surround it, barking and nipping at its heels until Marius could get close enough to take a shot.

His face was as round as the full moon. In a fortnight I never once saw it unsmiling. The wealth of facial expressions used among the Greenlanders reached a new level of richness wrapped in his eyes and mouth. There was a whole world of protocol involved that I was just beginning to understand. One of the most expressive gestures I learned was to arch and sustain both eyebrows as high as possible, while keeping the rest of the face almost neutral, with the hint of a smile. It seemed to mean 'I am no threat to you. You do not seem to be a threat to me. Let us speak freely,' and was used both to initiate conversation and to encourage a reluctant speaker.

His eyebrows lifted, and mine followed to encourage him. He told me that a few years ago his circumstances had changed. He had been forced to move out west to Nuuk and take up his tools again. He missed the barren rocks and ice of the east. In the north the landscape was similar, and he had heard he could make good money as a halibut fisherman up there. The hunting was poor around Nuuk, he said, and next year he would move again, this time to the rich hunting fields of the north, where in a way he would be going home. Back to the bare mountains and the sea-ice, to the seals and the bears.

*

For the Norse Greenlanders the hunting fields of the north were a wonder-land, a pristine wilderness where they could win wealth and renown. The lands north of the Western Settlement were called the Norðrsetr, 'the northern camps', and the Icelandic annals say that every man of influence in Greenland had a ship that sailed there each spring.

Traces of the Norse hunting expeditions have been found right up to 80° and far into the Canadian archipelagos. Nests of stone for eider duck like those used in Norway have been found on the shores of the Kane Basin in the High Arctic, and on the desolate coasts of Baffin and Ellesmere Islands there are dual cairns, structures which have never been built by the Inuit. A Norse hunting hut of stone still stands on the Nuussuaq peninsula north of Disko, and Inuit archaeological sites nearby show signs of close contact between the two peoples there: pieces of woollen cloth, chain mail, iron shears, and pieces of barrels coopered in the Norse way. Several wooden and ivory figures of the Norsemen carved by Inuit craftsmen have been found down the Greenlandic and Canadian Arctic coasts; one of them is so detailed that you can even see a little cross hanging on the doll's chest. For centuries it seems these two peoples hunted the same lands with a degree of tolerance and respect. Fighting, after all, got in the way of hunting.

The most astonishing find of all was in 1824 on a small island north of Disko, made not by archaeologists but by an Inuit hunter. Near a cairn he found a stone carved in runes, which has now been dated to the early part of the fourteenth century. It was only partially complete and said,

> Ellikr.sikvaths:son:r ok baanne:tortar-son:
> ok enrithi:osson :laukardak.in :
> fyrir.gakndag vardate.ok rydu:

('Erling Sighvatsson and Bjarni Thordarson and Eindridi Oddson on the Saturday before Rogation Day piled these cairns and...')

Veiled in the message is a proud boast. Rogation day is a spring festival. Erling, Bjarni and Eindridi were great hunters, and they did not need to wait for summer to travel in the North. By leaving the stone they wanted everybody who came after them to know it.

*

Sometimes the most fascinating personalities of history are the ones least is known about. But plenty is known about Geraldus Mercator. He was a Flemish cartographer, christened Gerhard Kremer at the dawn of the sixteenth century; the age when the first Renaissance *mappamundi* were being penned in the libraries of Milan, Louvain and Lisbon. He coined the term 'atlas' and was the first to place magnetic bearings on maps. His revolutionary approach to the problem of representing a spherical structure on a flat piece of paper was to project it onto a cylinder first. His invention, the Mercator Projection, is still widely used today. Mercator's world maps were visionary leaps forward in Europe's understanding of the world, but when it came to the northern regions his information was a little more sketchy. In 1569 he drew a map of the northern parts of the world from 70° to the Pole. Most of it is fantasy, but he does place Greenland in its correct orientation to Lapland, and where he surrounds the Pole with four great islands he joins one of them by a very narrow strait to Greenland at its most northern part. Where did he get his information from? The Norse Greenlanders were thought to be the only European people who knew those regions, and they did not even have a word for 'map'.

Recent research has shown that Mercator's information about the North was unlikely to have come from the Norsemen. Amazingly, it seems that it came from a peripatetic friar from Oxford who had travelled in Greenland over two centuries before. Very little is known about this friar, but his journey has fascinated navigators and cartographers for centuries. He wrote a book describing it entitled *Inventio Fortunatae* or 'Fortunate Discoveries,' a name to resonate with tales of the 'Fortunate Isles' classical Europe believed lay far across the ocean. The book has been lost, but references to it are common in letters between men of the fifteenth and sixteenth centuries who were at that time squabbling between themselves over rights to the new lands in the west. In 1497 John Day wrote about it to Christopher Columbus, and Las Casas mentions it in his *Historia de las Indias*. In 1492 the Nuremburg cartographer Martin Behaim referred to it as his source when he wrote on the globe he had made that at the North Pole, 'there is a high mountain of magnetic stone'.

Mercator had not read the book. His information about it came from an even more obscure source: an account by a Dutch globetrotter written in the late fourteenth century. The Dutchman, Jacobus Cnoyen, claimed both to have read the book and to have met in Bergen eight men who had recently arrived from Greenland, and who claimed to have met the friar there. Even more obscurely, Cnoyen's report survives only in notes that the English mathematician John Dee took from a letter Mercator had sent him. Those notes are now in the British Library in London for all to read.

> But in the year 1364 eight of these men came to Norway, to the King, and among them two priests, of whom one had an astrolabe... The priest who had the astrolabe told the King of Norway that in the year 1360 there had come to the islands a Minorite from Oxford, who was a good astronomer. He parted company with the others who had come to the islands, and voyaged further, through the whole of the northern parts, and had written of all notable matters in a book with he called in Latin *Inventio Fortunatae*.

The Minorite friar had travelled to Greenland on an English ship. The rest of the crew had stayed in the Eastern Settlement, presumably trading, while the friar travelled into the north. That the Greenlanders were trading with England in the fourteenth century is remarkable enough, but that a friar from Oxford used their trading vessel to get there before travelling independently throughout the northern regions forces a reassessment of assumptions about the supposed 'isolation' of the Greenlanders.

In the far north the friar described a ring of high mountains around the North Pole, which was made of lodestone. The mountains were arranged on four separate islands which were divided by great channels. On one of the islands he met a group of pygmy people whose description fits the Inuit. It sounds as if he made it all the way to the Kane Basin, where his 'four islands' would have been Baffin, Devon, Ellesmere, and a peninsula of Greenland.

It is not known who this astronomer was. Richard Hakluyt, the polymathic writer, priest, diplomat and champion of Elizabethan expansionism, thought that he was the mathematician-monk Nicholas of Lynn, but Nicholas was a Carmelite, not a Minorite, and there are no records of him having journeyed in the north.

On his return to England the Minorite presented his book to his king, who at that time was Edward III. The friar apparently took part in five more voyages, 'on royal business', but of which there is no surviving record. It is unlikely now that it will ever be known who he was or what he was doing there. Like St Brendan or Bishop Eirik before him he stands in history more as an explorer than as a man of God, a fearless and undaunted pioneer.

*

'Watch out for the Qivitoq when you go up there,' the skipper said to me.

'The what?' I asked.

'The Qivitoq. There's one who lives in those mountains.'

Qivitoqs are half-man, half-spirit beings. They haunt the icefields and the mountains of Greenland living as hermits, causing mischief to people who displease them by travelling through their lands. Usually they are said to have been old men who got fed up with their families and so renounced the settlements for the wilderness. Like the elderly Hindus who have become *sannyasi* they leave home and go to live at peace far from the distractions and irritations of village life. A couple of years before, an old man from the village of Kapisillit had gone missing while out hunting. No one had been able to find his body and so it was generally assumed that he had decided to become a Qivitoq.

The boat pulled up to the Kapisillit jetty. A thin isthmus of land stretched between two mountains, separating the Andafjord from the ice-filled end of the Rangafjord on the far side. Beyond it the mountain peaks caught on banks of grey cloud, tearing them open and spilling rainwater over the fjord. Above them the clouds were silver and white, reflecting not the dull grey of the granite or the water but the sucrose purity of the ice-cap.

Kapisillit was the furthest satellite of Nuuk. Its name means 'the place of salmon', because the fish course up its river to their spawning grounds high in the hills. The broad green valleys behind it lead step-wise over a high plateau to the ice-cap, and they are lined with Norse ruins. A glacial corridor of hidden and silent lakes connects the village to the third and last remaining church I wanted to try to visit, the bishop's seat at the main Norse settlement at Sandnæs.

It was raining. In the bay a Greenlander in a wet suit was paddling around in his kayak. Again and again he capsized himself only to pop up out of the water like a cork. When he realised he had an audience he stayed underwater to show off a little, and for my benefit grasped his paddle across the hull of his kayak and paddled along upside down. Sledge-dogs are useless around Nuuk; the sea-ice does not come that far south and so the people there have always hunted from kayaks instead. They are the acknowledged masters of the art.

The mist and drizzle lay heavy and dull in the air. I put on my waterproofs and hiked into the heartland of the Western Settlement. I looked out for the Qivitoq, but in five days did not see him.

*

For the first couple of hours of the hike I climbed up through thickets of dwarf birch and then onto a rolling heathland finely lined by caribou tracks. The lake valley was like a silver offertory plate, circled by the green velvet folds of the mountains.

Not far above Kapisillit the Norsemen had changed the course of the river so that the fish were easier to catch. Where it emptied into a small lake the bank was lined with stones, forcing the water into one swift channel where the fish would concentrate to feed. I saw that the river bank was much straighter than would reasonably be expected, and it was easy to cast out from it into the swifter currents where the salmon and char would lie. Standing on the banks that the Norsemen had built and using clumsy spinners I pulled three fat char out of the water in quick succession. I ate them poached in their own river water and garnished with cloudberries.

Further up the valley lay the lake of Igdlorssuit, which means 'the great house'. In among the dense scrub which coated the hillsides was the Norse ruin which gave the lake its name. The local Inuit have a tradition that a Norse boat lies submerged there, and it was said that until the beginning of the twentieth century part of it could still be seen when the water level was low. There was no sign of it now; its surface lay smooth as polished armour.

There was a delicious silence in the valley, a noiselessness made richer by the occasional croaking calls of ptarmigan, or the footfalls of caribou as they wandered by. In the late evening the sky began to clear, but a sheet of cloud remained, draped over the hilltops like a drying canvas. As the sun set in the north it glowed orange, crimson, then lilac. A half moon rose to hover beneath it, reflected in the lake.

*

How did they live in this landscape of rock, ice and stunted scrub? Towards the end of the Middle Ages the Norse Greenlanders of the Western Settlement had been living there for centuries, and they no more considered themselves Norwegian than modern U.S. citizens of Boston consider themselves English, or William the Bastard considered himself Danish. They were extraordinarily well adapted to the harshness of the climate and the demands of squeezing sustenance from the land. They were strong and capable; the grooves and ridges on their bones show that they were very muscular, and tall by mediaeval standards. Archaeological findings suggest that they lived more like the Inuit than their countrymen in the warmer, richer and more fertile Eastern Settlement. Analysis of bones in their middens have shown that they hunted and ate far more caribou too. At the beginning they kept sheep, goats, pigs, horses and cattle, though the cattle had to be stabled with hay supplies for six months of the year and the pigs and goats were later abandoned as too damaging to the soil and vegetation. They ate certain seaweeds such as the dulse that the Irish monks relied on, chickweed too, and numerous kinds of berries.

Their houses were low and sprawling, some with over twenty rooms, but all the rooms lay under the same roof and their walls of stone and turf were built several feet thick for insulation in the winter. The byre for the cattle was always sited towards the centre of the house in order to heat it from within. In the spring their animals would be so emaciated that they would need to be carried out to pasture.

At the Western Settlement the people are thought to have been good fishermen, using nets to catch the cod that still teem in shoals throughout the fjords of the Vesterbygd, but it seems that what they excelled at was hunting. All of them were accomplished seal hunters; even the middens of homesteads high in the mountains are rich in the bones of seals. They could become wealthy through trading walrus ivory, narwhal horns, eiderdown and seal blubber. The pelts of Arctic foxes and polar bears were in high demand across Europe, as were those of the martens, lynx and black bears that could be hunted across the Davis Strait in the forests of Labrador. One of the greatest captures they could make was of a white gyrfalcon, which they trapped using tethered ptarmigans as bait. Gyrfalcons were sought after by the emerging European nobility, white ones particularly so. They were just as valued by the noblemen of the

Islamic Empires: in 1396 the Duke of Burgundy ransomed his son from the Saracens for twelve Greenland falcons. The other main dealers of falcons in mediaeval Europe were the Scots, and it seems that there was communication between the two countries in the fourteenth century.

The Scots spent much of the fourteenth century embroiled in wars with the English. In its early years Edward II took a break from the Hundred Years War with France to occupy Stirling Castle, and in 1314 an attempt to relieve his besieged men there saw the defeat of his armies by Robert the Bruce at Bannockburn. Robert spent many of the following years warring with English armies in Ireland, and it seems he and his countrymen were no strangers to voyaging both there and all around the North Atlantic. The Icelanders had rules about what to do with the property of slain Scotsmen, and among the bones excavated near Sandnæs have been found those of a large Scots deerhound of the type owned only by the very wealthy nobility of the day. A few miles to the south a small silver badge has been unearthed, inscribed with the crest of the Campbell clan.

In Scotland for over three hundred years, the name Campbell has unfortunately been associated with their massacre of the MacDonalds of Glencoe. In that situation they were employed as travelling mercenaries, and it may be that it did not represent a new role for them. In the fourteenth century they were known less for their seafaring than for their cattle-rustling skills and propensity to father illegitimate children. It is impossible to tell whether the badge was left by a Campbell living in the Western Settlement or whether it was brought home by a sea-faring Norseman, but it is yet another link in the chain joining Greenland to the British Isles towards the close of the Middle Ages.

*

I climbed higher and higher out of the valley, weaving along thin caribou tracks up onto the plateau. Antlers lay strewn across the moor, sun-bleached and ghostly white. They were beautiful and intricate, like stunted trees of ivory, but the broken ones leaked an unwholesome stink of rotting marrow and I left them all where they had fallen. On the plateau interlacing networks of silent mirrored lakes lay banked by slopes of rubble. On top of each peak a small cairn stood. Helge Ingstad, discoverer of the Norse settlement at L'Anse aux Meadows, wrote that they were piled by the Norsemen to guide them between homesteads when the mist fell onto the high passes.

After a couple of days I reached the top. The ice-cap shone twenty kilometres to the east, a smooth line of opal under a topaz-blue sky. That night I camped by the ruins of an inland Norse farm. It lay hidden in a tangle of dwarf birch and rowan. The Norsemen's animals used to keep the trees down (thus accelerating the soil erosion), but by that time they had been gone for six centuries. Once through the thicket the stones of the house lay in a clearing, carpeted with soft yielding turf, kept short and neat by the caribou. The walls were four feet high in places, and three or four feet wide. I could still walk along the passages between the byre, the living room and the hay store. Somewhere in the tumble of moss-covered stones there would likely have been a sauna, but it was impossible to identify. The Sandnæs sauna was found still intact, complete with ship's beams for benches and a child's toy boat on the floor. The whole homestead lay circled by two arms of a stream, which fell into the lake now called Tungmeragdlip Tasserssua. Its Norse name is lost. At least two more farms lay on its shores to the west, where it reached a brim of rock hanging over what the Norse called the Lysufjord of Sandnæs.

In the morning I sat in the passage-house looking out over the lake; the view its Norse owners enjoyed for centuries. I wondered how many trips into the northern wilds had begun and ended there, how many tales they told of polar bear hunts, of the Inuit of the far north, and of the mountains and glaciers of the Canadian islands. They would have sat there and discussed rumours of events in far-off Europe, demands for new taxes to be paid to an archbishop they had never heard of in a country they had never visited. More close to home would be rumours of events in the Eastern Settlement, weddings and funerals, and of trading ships that had arrived there that might yet come up the coast.

The water was calm, an unbroken sheen leading all the way to that final church of the Western Settlement. To go along its shores through the dense forests of birch and rowan was unthinkable. I could not get there from this valley, I would need to approach from a different pass, and that would mean returning another year. I turned east and walked instead towards the ice-cap.

The way to the ice-cap ran across a gently sloping plateau. There were no paths, only interweaving caribou tracks running in dusty hollows between the boulders and the scrub. A series of glacial tarns brimmed over into one another, leading down towards the ice-packed end of the Rangafjord. In the distance on the mountainside lay the sites of two more Norse farms. Excavations there had shown that the grazing land around them was once excellent. When the Norsemen first arrived here the ice-cap must have stopped much further inland, the fjord would have been navigable and the hill-sides would have been lush and fertile. Now the fjord was blocked with ice and the earth looked cursed and dead; a lunar landscape.

I reached the edge of the ice. It eased down into the fjord in two glacial tongues. The bergs calving from them dragged against the fjord bottom, grating and rumbling as if the earth itself were torn apart by the ice. The pieces of ice were so closely packed that it would have been possible, though suicidal, to run across their tops to the glacier at the far side. It would have been impossible for the Greenlanders to farm in this valley if there had been as much ice then as now.

Paradoxically, the sudden increase in ice in recent years has been reported due to the *warming* of the Arctic. A NASA scientist called Eric Rignot, together with Pannir Kanagaratnam of Kansas University, has been studying the glaciers of Greenland and found a worrying trend: rising air temperature in the Arctic (estimated at 3°C over the last twenty years) has caused meltwater to run into the glacier beds and in effect act as a lubricant. The glaciers are sliding off the ice-cap faster than ever before. They estimate that the amount of ice dumped by Greenland's glaciers into the Atlantic has doubled in the last ten years. All this excess ice is melting faster and faster as the oceans themselves heat up, leading to the changes in flow around the Faroe Islands that could reverse the Gulf Stream. And sea-level, currently rising at about 2mm per year, is also expected to rise exponentially until a new equilibrium is reached.

Questions buzzed through my mind: What will this new equilibrium look like? When sea-level goes on rising what will happen to countries like Holland, a quarter of which is below sea-level, or Bangladesh, which is fast becoming a swamp? More importantly, how should we and the governments that represent us balance the desire for economic growth and consumer lifestyles with the need to address this issue, and address it quickly? I thought of my own journey, how many air miles I had flown to reach Iceland and Greenland, in order to have the luxury of observing these changes first-hand. Like many others I felt guilty about the lifestyle I had chosen, the air miles that I flew, but did not have any answers and could not decide whether to radically alter the choices that I made.

I sat by the larger and closer of the two glaciers. The Inuit named it Kangiata Nunáta. The ice had carved the mountain behind me into a vertical wall. Rubble lay on top of bergs at the edge of the fjord, tumbled from the loose fractured cliffs above. The glacier looked sullen and forbidding. In 1888 it had been the scene of the greatest geographical achievement since Stanley found the source of the Nile: Nansen's crossing of the Greenlandic ice-cap.

Haughty, mercurial and almost unbelievably arrogant, Fridtjof Nansen had set off from the eastern coast of Greenland on skis forty-one days before. He had dragged himself and five men across one of the greatest unexplored expanses of the planet. He was just twenty-six years old, having been awarded his PhD for outstanding research into the structure of brain cells only four days before embarking on the expedition.

The expedition had been beset by difficulties, and had nearly failed before it even started. Nansen had been denied funding, his ship had been blocked by ice, and he drifted on small whaling boats too far to the south after setting out from the sealing boat that had brought him from Iceland. One of his men had been injured, he had been given the wrong food, and they undertook the whole crossing in a state of semi-starvation. But he did it; on 24 September 1888 he skied down the Kangiata Nunáta glacier and into the valley just behind me. In his book *Across Greenland on Skis* he described the feeling: 'Words cannot describe what it meant just to feel earth and rock underfoot, the sense of well-being that rippled through us when we felt the heather give under our soles, and to smell the wonderful scent of grass and moss.'

When he got there he found, as I had, that the hillsides were impassable and he could not walk across the mountaintops to Nuuk. Not being the sort of man to become disheartened and being a little more resourceful than myself he cut saplings from a thicket, lashed them into a hull and covered them with a tarpaulin. He made oars by stretching canvas over forks of wood. With one of his companions he climbed into this leaky boat and rowed towards Nuuk. The improvised vessel could not make headway into the wind, and it took them six days to row the hundred kilometres. Just south of Nuuk he pulled the boat up onto the foreshore. By chance the Danish governor was walking by, and called out to them in English:

'Are you Englishmen?'

To which I could safely reply in good Norwegian: 'No, we are Norwegian.'

'May I ask your name?'

'My name is Nansen, and we have come from the ice-cap.'

'Ah, I thought as much. May I congratulate you on your doctor's degree.'

The four others were still stranded at the head of the fjord, and so two Inuit hunters were dispatched to tell the men that Nansen had got through, and would come to collect them soon. The two men were supreme kayakers, and made the journey in less than two days. They were both from the island of Uummannaq, where they lived beside the old Moravian mission station that I had helped restore.

The various delays he had suffered meant that Nansen missed the last boat of the year for Copenhagen. Instead he spent the next seven months with the Greenlanders of Nuuk, learning how to paddle a kayak and how to hunt their way. It was the skills of the Inuit that he would need for his next undertaking: a bid for the North Pole.

*

From the ice-cap I turned back towards Kapisillit. The path meandered back along different routes through valleys guarded by more long-abandoned ruins. There were no other people to stop me on the path, only inquisitive caribou that ran off when I came too close.

The Norsemen left the Western Settlement in about 1400. No one knows why they left, and none of those people ever kept any written records. Their grave crosses become crude and desultory as the fourteenth century drew to a close and the ratio of bones in their middens became increasingly dominated by those of seals. Maybe the caribou left them, and they were forced to take to the sea entirely. Maybe the worsening climate killed off their livestock, as seemed to have happened in the stony ice-locked pastures of the Rangafjord that has become so impassable today. Maybe the Inuit grew hostile and harried them out of the lands as they had been harried out of Vínland. Maybe they emigrated to Vínland and the ship, 'bound for Markland,' which drifted into Iceland in 1347 was an emigrant vessel. One archaeologist has found suggestions in the soil layers that there may have been years where plagues of grubs decimated the foliage on the hillsides. Maybe there was an epidemic. In a grave at Sandnæs a whole family has been found buried together, man and wife and their two small children, their bones huddled together against the chill of the permafrost.

The last recorded events of the Western Settlement do not give us much more of a clue. In 1308 a letter had arrived for Bishop Thord. Eirik 'the Priest-hater' had been dead for nine years, and there was a new see for him in Norway if he wanted it. He left the country he had lived in for twenty years and sailed east. At the beginning at least the new bishop had continued trying to collect the crusading tithes and Peter's pence from the Greenlanders. It took him several years, but eventually a tonne of walrus ivory arrived in Bergen to pay the last several years' worth of church taxes. (The Vatican saw hardly any of the money – the King of Norway was bankrupt and was pawning large tracts of his lands in Sweden to help finance his doomed wars against the Russians). It was the last of the Greenlanders' wealth that Norway or the church ever saw.

When at last they realised it was over a decade since they had received any tithes from Greenland, they dispatched an *officialis* of the archbishop called Ivar Bardarson to find out what had happened to their supply of walrus and narwhal ivory. On arriving back in Bergen twenty years later empty-handed Bardarson described the end of the Western Settlement. His account has confused scholars of Greenlandic history for over a century. 'In the Vesterbygd stands a large church, named Stensnes [Sandnæs] Church. That church was for a time the cathedral and bishop's seat. Now the Skrælings have destroyed all of the Western Settlement; there are left some horses, goats, cattle, and sheep, all feral, and no people either Christian or heathen.'

From archaeological sources it is known that the Western Settlement was in communication with the Eastern right up to the end, at the *close* of the fourteenth century. When Bardarson arrived there were still a few decades of the settlement left, and so his report makes no sense. It may be that he arrived very soon after a large confrontation between the Inuit and the Norsemen that had left all of the latter dead, but there is no archaeological evidence to back this theory up. It may be that he invented the whole story to explain his failure to produce any taxes from the people of the settlement, who had become his friends after twenty years, or it may be that the people of Sandnæs knew he was coming and were in hiding in other homesteads inland. They knew he had come for only one reason: taxes. In support of this explanation is the fact that he found cattle still grazing by the settlement that could not have survived even a single winter out of their byres.

Either way, the church did not get any of their money, and in less than half a century all the people of the Western Settlement were gone.

*

A few miles short of the village I passed two hunters. They were sitting by a big cow caribou that they had shot, chewing on grass stems. I asked if they were going to manage to carry it to Kapisillit and they laughed. One of them stood up, took out his knife and set to work on the carcass. He slit it down the belly and pulled out its entrails, then cracked its rib cage and did the same to its heart and lungs. He severed its spine, cut off its head, and in one fluid turn scored a line around each of its legs at the hocks and snapped them over his knee. He pulled a black bin-liner from his pocket, tossed the cuts of meat inside, then licked his fingers clean. The whole process took less than five minutes.

Outside the Kapisillit shop a sign declared that the drinking of alcoholic beverages was forbidden. It was Monday afternoon, and the supply boat from Nuuk had just come in. I picked my way up the stairs over the drunken men and women swigging from bottles of Danish lager. Inside I asked them if they knew where I could get a wash, and they directed me to the Seaman's Mission. It was

housed in a sunflower-yellow building by the shore, where for a few
kroner you could have a shower, wash your clothes, and meet all
sorts of people. It was in the laundry room there that I met another
Greenlandic nationalist.

As a girl she had lived in the village of Kangeq, a few miles
to the west of Nuuk, out among the galaxy of islands which are
sprinkled along that part of the western coast. One day in 1972 the
Danes had arrived and forced her and her family from their homes.
It was part of another push by Copenhagen to 'civilise' the Green-
landers, the scene being repeated in settlements all over the country.
They were all to be relocated to newly built apartment blocks in
Nuuk. Later on, she said, the authorities built a tourist hotel at
Kangeq, and furnished it with the property of the evicted people.
Waiters and chambermaids served Danes in rooms decorated with
the memories of their own lives.

'Could you go back now?' I asked.

'No, I don't think you can go back. Now we have made other
lives. We never should have been forced to leave.'

I said that similar things had been done in the name of the British Empire, and we moved on to talk about the relative merits of
the Danes and the British as colonial masters.

'Maybe the Danes aren't that bad,' she said, 'not when I think
of the British, the Dutch, the Spanish, the French. On the whole
we in Greenland have had it quite easy. But there are seven thousand of them here! That's how many Danes live in Greenland!
Twelve percent of our population! And if we go to find work in
Denmark they moan about "foreigners" when less than five per
cent of their population are immigrants! Did you know there are
just nine thousand Greenlanders living in Denmark, 0.2 per cent
of *their* population! And yes, there are some "bad" Greenlanders
living in Denmark, of course, but they are few.'

She told me about the re-education programmes of the 1960s
Danish government, now the shame of the current administration.
Like the Stolen Generation in Australia, Inuit children were taken

and educated in Denmark in order to return and serve as 'role models' for their own people. They were returned to a society they did not understand and a people whose language they no longer spoke, far from the Lutheran boarding schools they had come to accept as home. Most of them have never recovered, caught as they were in the most formative years of their lives between two cultures, disaffected and rejected by both.

'Did you see the drunks here outside the shop?' She looked carefully at me as if to gauge my reaction.

'I saw one or two,' I said.

'It sometimes creates a bad impression on visitors to Greenland, seeing our people like that. But you must understand, it is just that if our people are alcoholic, they don't hide away like the Danes, they don't mind anyone knowing about their vices and their problems.'

I said that northern peoples, including those living in Scotland, all had their share of alcoholism.

'Yes, but that's not what people see when they come here. I promise you, most Greenlanders are happy!'

*

I liked Kapisillit. As well as the alcoholics that hung around the shop there were a lot of young people there who were not drunk, and who seemed very happy in their magnificent surroundings. That evening I passed several groups of them walking together in the tracks between the houses, laughing in the evening twilight.

On the boat back to Nuuk was a Danish veterinarian who had been to Kapisillit to examine abattoir facilities for the culling of caribou. He clung to the gunwales with white knuckles and said that he did not like boats or water. He did not like Greenland either, and was having second thoughts about his three-year contract. Though the weather was mild, he wore two jackets and wrapped a scarf tightly around his neck. Grey strands of hair poked out from under his woolly hat, waving in the breeze. He looked very worried.

'I don't know if I can stay here,' he said, 'I don't understand these people.'

Caribou, however, he could understand. He thought that the abattoir was perfect. Next year it would be fully operational.

'Too many hunters out there shooting off their rifles, no control on the numbers. And they wonder why the population goes up and down,' he said. There were hunting licenses, he added, issued to control the numbers slaughtered, but to many Greenlanders the concept of paying the government for the right to shoot caribou was like taxing the air. No one owned the caribou. They belonged to everybody.

The engine started up and drowned out any further conversation. We slipped down the fjord passing more abandoned homefields, the small enclosed patches of land that immediately surround the traditional Norse homestead. In order to produce the best crops and fodder, these patches had been more intensively fertilised than the rest, and though they had lain fallow for 600 years the grass growing on them was still recognisably greener. On every foreshore lay unexcavated passage houses, any of which could hold the key to understanding what it was that made the Norsemen leave.

*

Bubonic plague is up to ninety-five per cent fatal. It kills so quickly that it only rarely reaches islands that lie across oceans. The crews of contaminated ships would often be dead before they reached port.

In the mid-fourteenth century much of northern Europe was wiped out by epidemics of *Yersinia Pestis*, the Black Death. Norway was very badly hit, and for a year no ships left its harbours for the west. Norwegians licked their wounds for a few decades; they had more than enough problems of their own without worrying about sending trading ships to Iceland or Greenland.

One March morning in 1378, two thousand kilometres away from Trondheim, Pope Gregory XI breathed his last. The fuse was lit to a bomb that would shake the foundations of the Roman

Catholic Church and of Europe. The Roman cardinals had had enough of French popes living in Avignon, and so they voted for an outsider, Urban VI, who though ruthless and ill-counselled, was at least an Italian. His election was a disaster. Urban started stripping the cardinals of their powers and demanding reform. The frightened cardinals fled the Vatican and re-grouped, declaring Urban's election null and void. The Great Schism began, with a Pope in Avignon and a Pope in Rome, each claiming divine authority. The reputation of the Church plummeted, and for the first time European rulers could exercise secular control on the church; each Pope had to try to curry favour for the support of each monarch.

It was a horrendous mess. Most of the information about these years has only been uncovered through letters of indulgence written by the church to the nobility. In 1401 Margrethe, now Empress of a united Denmark, Sweden and Norway, paid so much money to Boniface IX (a Roman pope) that she was declared exempt by God from all fast days, as were any of her guests. Only a few years later her son, Eirik of Pomerania, switched allegiances to the Avignon papacy, while England under Henry V stayed with Rome. In this chaos England started to supply bishops to Iceland, ignoring Trondheim.

The Great Schism ended after thirty-nine years with the election of Martin V, but the damage to the church was irreparable. Catholicism had exactly one century to go before Luther demanded the reform of the rotten and corrupt mediaeval Church.

The Greenlandic form of paganised Catholicism carried on regardless. They did not have an Inquisition there, but it seems that they did not need one. One of the very few reports of the era was that in 1407 the folk of the Eastern Settlement burned a man for sleeping with the wife of a trader from Iceland. He had used the black arts, it was said, to find his way into her bed. Maybe he was a devil, or perhaps they were in love. Shortly afterwards the woman 'lost her wits' and died.

By 1402-04 the plague had finally made it to Iceland. The

Empress of all Scandinavia was refusing to give trading vessels licenses to sail to the north-western dependencies. Those who did so were breaking the law, and were the exception rather than the rule. But the archaeological finds in the Eastern Settlement show that the last Greenlanders of the fifteenth century were still wealthy and still trading successfully. The question is: with whom?

It is known that Basque whalers were sailing in those waters at that time, but the most likely candidates are the English, and possibly the Dutch.

*

'I was arrested by a Scotswoman last month,' she said. 'She was nice, real nice. You guys have great police.'

She was a Dutch environmental activist. She was a bit young, a bit silly, and trying a little bit too hard to impress. She told me that she had been on the *Rainbow Warrior* when it was sunk in the Pacific. Greenpeace were in Nuuk, and their ship *Arctic Sunrise* was dwarfed among the shrimp trawlers and cargo giants of the harbour. It was on its way up to Thule Airbase where they had planned an action to protest against the 'Star Wars' satellite defence system and the Americans' nuclear presence. She told me in a confiding tone that they had a helicopter in the ship's hold.

'What are you going to do with the helicopter?' I asked.

'I could tell you, but then I'd have to kill you,' she replied, with a smile. The Americans knew they were coming, and had already shut down all the ship's satellite links to the media and the outside world.

All around the harbour there were Greenlanders protesting about the presence of the ship. Greenpeace had once launched a campaign against the practise of killing baby seals by clubbing them on the head. The practise was a Canadian one, but the campaign never made that clear. The Greenlandic sealing industry had been destroyed, and many hunters had lost their livelihoods. There was an Englishwoman from the Amsterdam office fielding

questions from a group of angry Greenlanders. She looked nervous, and very much out of her depth. A young man walked up to
the group and stood at the edge of the crowd. His daughter stood
at his side, a girl of six or seven years, and pulled at his sleeve. With
a concern for littering which I had rarely seen in Greenland she
handed him the wrapper of a sweetie she had been eating and he
put it carefully into his pocket. Turning to the Englishwoman he
stepped forward. He spoke English beautifully and his voice was
soft and calm and filled with patience. The others in the crowd
became quiet to listen to him.

'Greenland and Greenpeace have been enemies since this whole
sealing fiasco,' he began, 'and Greenland has lost a lot of trade
because of your organisation's poorly researched scaremongering
campaign, but that's now in the past. What we have to do is make
sure that it doesn't happen again.'

The Englishwoman stammered, denying that they had ever
campaigned against Greenland. He waved her comments aside.
'That's as may be, but you have no presence here, we are wholly
outside your organisation, and you are wholly outside us. We need
to work together so that maybe two and two make five.'

He spoke of nuclear waste from Russia drifting into Greenland
along routes used for millennia by Siberian driftwood, of pluto-
nium scattered by the B52 aeroplane which crashed on its way to
Thule Airbase, of polar bears on the east coast found mutated into
hermaphrodites by toxins in the environment. 'You need an office
here,' he said.

'But you have only 50,000 people in Greenland, how can we
fund a whole office?'

'You are only seeing problems,' he said. 'What we need are some
solutions.'

It was a grand day out. Young trendy Greenlanders in mirrored
sunglasses and mothers with crying children mingled with the protesting hunters on deck. On the bridge I spoke to the ship's third
engineer. He was a French topiarist who worked for Greenpeace

whenever they gave him a call. 'It's a good life,' he said. 'After this we're off to the Amazon, to protest about logging.' He leaned back on the rail, smoking his cigarette. 'You should get involved.'

*

Beaten, bound, dumped in the hold of a ship, stripped, chained, whipped, then marched barefoot to market. Throughout the early fifteenth century Icelandic boys and girls were sold as slaves in the market towns of England.

The centres of the slavery were Hull, Bristol and Lynn. On 29 August 1429 the annals of Lynn record that eleven Icelandic children went on sale, but there were many more whose sales are unrecorded. Only the church kept records, and those were often unreliable. Working out the activities of the sailors of Bristol, Lynn and Hull is a lot more difficult.

The plague had killed off a third of Iceland's population. The remaining population were already supplying most of England's cod, or 'stockfish', and after the plague they lost the manpower to control the trade successfully. At the same time the English were developing faster and better ships; they could run out to Iceland and back with fish for market easily in a season, and they quickly took advantage of the weakened Icelanders. The English had also been burned out of Bergen by the German Hansa merchants at the end of the fourteenth century, and so a brigand's agreement was reached. The Hansa could take the eastern seas, while they took the west. On their way to Iceland the men of Bristol sailed out around Ireland, to avoid the Scottish pirates. It would be odd if they were *not* blown to Greenland on occasion, and that they sailed with Icelandic slaves as pilots makes it certain that they knew of the existence of the Greenlanders. It is likely that the slaving ships made it to the remote settlements of Greenland too. In 1415 Eirik of Pomerania wrote to his brother in law, Henry V, to complain about the damage that the English were doing, 'in Iceland and adjoining islands.' His plea made no difference, the men of Hull and Lynn continued to burn villages and enslave peasants all along Iceland's northern coast. In 1432 he wrote again, demanding compensation for the stolen slaves and that they be returned to Iceland. Laws were even passed in Iceland forbidding the sale of children to foreigners, but still the trade continued. The Icelanders came from a different world, far from the cosmopolitan stench of the English sea-ports. In England they were despised for their poverty and ignorance, but were fast becoming part of the national fabric. William Shakespeare voiced a common enough jibe of the era in Henry V: 'Pish for thee, Iceland dog. Thou prick-eared cur of Iceland.'

By the second half of the century Denmark no longer had any power over its colonies west over the ocean. The bishops of Iceland were Englishmen, and the country was essentially occupied, destitute and powerless. Scandinavian naval power was in decline. In 1469 the King of Denmark lost Orkney and Shetland (mortgaged for a dowry), and in 1471 he lost Sweden. He was determined not to lose Iceland as well. He employed a Hansa pirate to take sea-command of Icelandic waters, but Richard III of England only requested that from now on the Bristol ships sail there in convoy and try to enslave as many Hansa as they could on the way. In the resulting mêlée the Norse Greenlanders were forgotten. A century later they were all gone.

Kirsten Seaver, a Norwegian academic living in California, thinks she knows what happened to them. Her book *The Frozen Echo* cuts a clear spotlight of historical argument through the mists obscuring the closing years of the Middle Ages.

Frozen in the shallowest layers of the Eastern Settlement are testaments to the last days of the colony that had lasted five hundred years: a cross of English pewter, a woollen coat in the English style, a tall Burgundian cap, highly fashionable on the continent at the time and also in the British sea-ports. She provides evidence that the Bristol pirates and fishermen (there was no distinction) already knew of the Newfoundland cod banks by 1430. The end of the Western Settlement and the Greenlanders' increasing isolation from both the Scandinavian church and its monarchs must have forced them to forge new trade relations, at a time when they were most vulnerable.

In 1492 the Genoese were moving to Spain where there were new prospects for skilled mariners and cartographers. Queen Isabella sat in the Alhambra, and the Moors and Jews had all been slain or forced out of Al-Andalus. One of the Genoese who had made the move was Christopher Columbus. He knew the North Atlantic well, had sailed around Iceland and had spent time in the black-trade harbours and taverns of Galway which at the time was one of the money-laundering capitals of the high seas. It was to Galway that mariners went to trade their illicit cargoes, and in Galway that one could meet men who thought nothing of sailing to the Isle of Brasil, the name given to the shadowy and largely unexplored North American seaboard. Another Genoese, Maggiolo by name, drew a map in 1511 where he called Greenland 'the Land of the English'. Five years later he drew another one and wrote on it concerning Greenland: 'Terranova de pescaria inventa de laboradore de re de anglitera tera frigida.' ('New land of fishing discovered by the Labrador for the King of England. Cold Country.')

So it is certain that the English knew Greenland and its people well throughout the fifteenth century. Denmark had forgotten them, and Iceland was paralysed. They can only have been trading with the English, and possibly some wayward Dutch Hansa. So why did the settlement which was still prospering in the middle of the century die out within fifty years? Jared Diamond, in his book *Collapse*, explains his view that several factors were responsible, including Greenland's marginal status for pasture, the cooling of the global climate, a lack of adaptability among the Greenland Norse, the increasing hostility of the Inuit, and the slavish obedience of the people to an elite ruling class of chiefs and bishops. He believes all these factors forced their society to an impasse where it finally descended into civil conflict and collapse. On the contrary Seaver thinks that most of them emigrated to establish settlements

on Newfoundland, either of their own free will or as slaves to process the fish for the English. Another possibility is that when the
Bristol pirates realised how abandoned and exposed they were, they
burned the Norsemens' settlements and carried them off in slavery back to Europe and the Mediterranean. Many of the ruins of
the last decades of the Eastern Settlement show signs of being destroyed by fire. By 1500 most of the homesteads were abandoned.
There is a solitary report from the year 1540 of a wind-blown Icelandic captain coming upon a dead Norseman lying on a beach in
Greenland. Gone were the rich fashions of the English sea-ports
– the man was poorly dressed in skins lashed with sinew. The report
adds, with pitiful pathos, that the man's iron knife was bent and
worn away to a thin sliver.

In Rome Leo X appointed another Greenland bishop, but never
considered for a moment whether there were any parishioners left for
him to oversee. The church was hopelessly out of touch both with
the new Geography and with its people. Europe stood at the brink
of the Reformation. The Middle Ages were over, the New World had
been found.

*

The fish market was quiet, with most of the fishermen protesting
down at the harbour. A few traders had stayed on, swatting flies
from the seal carcasses and the rows of livers which glistened by
their sides. There were tables of cod, salmon and char, and an as-
sortment of bizarre, alien-looking Arctic fish. A slight breeze was
just enough to keep the stink away.

Down behind the market I found the museum, and inside it the
Greenland Archaeological Institute. I wanted to find someone who
could tell me more about the ruins of the Western Settlement. An
archivist came to the desk, and together we pored over the maps of
known archaeological sites. I pointed out areas where I had found
ruins that were not marked, and he noted them down without
surprise, asking me to send him photographs. They were only

beginning to tap into the richness of the Norse sites in the area, he said.

'Have you been to Qeqertánguaq?' I asked him.

'Yes. Why do you ask?'

'Because I searched and searched for the runes that are supposed to be marked there, but couldn't find them.'

'Good.'

'Where are they?' I asked.

'I'm not going to tell you,' he said.

'Why not?'

'It's the only Norse artefact we have that is fixed on an unmovable object. The last thing we need is amateurs like you wandering around messing everything up.'

'What do the runes say?' I asked as politely as I could manage, given that he was quite happy to take down details of the other sites that an amateur such as myself had found. 'Are you allowed to tell me that?'

'It's a male name,' he said, looking down at his maps. 'Just a male name.'

*

An exhibition of photographs of ice and snow sculpture was showing at the Katuaq, the cultural centre of Greenland. It is a voluptuous building, with walls of wooden panelling running in a series of magnificent curves, stacked on a plinth of concrete pillars and overshadowing a glass façade. In one sculpture a callipygous giantess lay back on her elbows while a fish swam up between her thighs. In another, a sculpture shaped like a bottle of imported Danish lager was spilling over the ground. A tiny figure clambered on the edge of it, using it for support.

In the main square outside, the people were queuing to collect their welfare benefit. The drinking had already begun, and the weekend was still two days away.

*

Time was, and always had been. But one day, without explanation or the need of one, a man sprang out of the ground. He shook himself free of earth, looked around at his world, and saw it filled with mountains, ice, seals, and caribou. On the side of a hillock he started to dig, and soon he uncovered the first wife. Together their offspring became the *Inuit*, 'the people'. They lived well from the land, and when their time came to die they went on another journey. Those that had lived a righteous life, had worked hard and hunted well, underwent a great trial: for five days they would slide into the bowels of the earth down a great rock, and their skins would be torn and bloodied. Deep under the earth where they were bound dwelled the god Tornarsuk and his mother. If they survived the descent there they would live with him in a perpetual summer where caribou and seals were found boiling in great cauldrons over ever-blazing fires.

The lazy people, the poor hunters and the witches, did not go to that world. Instead they ascended into the sky where there was only void, and no animals to hunt. There they would be besieged by ravens that would become entangled in their hair, and they would be condemned to dance with the other lost souls in the limbo of the aurora borealis. This is the way it was forever.

One day, the legend continues, a woman gave birth to a litter of pups. These pups were called *Kablunats*; they could not speak properly and so they were loaded into an old shoe and sent out to sea. Years later they returned, all grown up and with hairy faces like the puppies they had been, and these were the White Men. They were carried by boats curved both at the bow and stern, just like the shoes they had left in, and they still spoke their strange and incomprehensible language. And that is why the White Men always come from the sea.

There were different kinds of *Kablunats*. Some were called *Qardilkaq*, which means 'ones who wear big trousers', and these were the Dutch. There were others who were more to be feared, who it was rumoured brought fire and death to the coasts. They were less to be trusted. They were called *Tuluit*, which now means only 'Englishmen', but the name follows no ordinary Inuit language rules. A legend still survives among the Inuit that it was they who killed off the *Qavdlunât*, the Norse Greenlanders.

✳

The Danish colony of Godthåb was founded two centuries after the last Norsemen were gone, by a Norwegian missionary called Hans Egede. He had been sent by the Danish crown to find his lost countrymen, who it was assumed having been abandoned for so long must have reverted to their pagan ways. So much knowledge had been lost that Egede was convinced that the name 'Eastern Settlement' meant that they must have lived on the eastern coast. For the twenty-five years he lived in Greenland he searched for them, and died back at home still expecting that one day they would be found. When he returned to Denmark his son, Poul Egede, took over the mission. It was to Poul that the tales of the *Tuluit* were told; he was keen to hear anything which might cast light on the fate of the Norsemen who had been his father's Holy Grail.

By the middle of the eighteenth century the Danish missionaries were joined by the German Moravian Brothers. It was their leader, a Dutchman called David Crantz, who wrote down many of the legends of the Inuit. Both men, Egede and Crantz, spoke nothing but praise of the Greenlanders. Though their prime motive, to convert the beliefs and the customs of the Inuit, would now be considered suspect, they loved both the people and the landscape they had come to settle in. They were the doves of the colonial age. Poul Egede said that only some great disaster could have befallen the Norsemen to make them leave such a paradise. Here is his father on the glacial scenery of the Western Settlement, in an eighteenth-century translation:

> [Of the ice] the Sea is almost choak'd with it, some flat and large Fields of Ice, or Bay-ice, as they call it, and some huge and prodigious mountains, of an astonishing Bigness, lying

as deep under Water as they soar high in the Air... Nor does their Figure and Shape alone surprize, but also their Diversity of Colours pleases the Sight: for some are like white Crystal. Others blue as Sapphires; and others again green as Emeralds.

Helge Ingstad also believed that the Norsemen could only have been forced out of the land, and that they ended their days as slaves or indentured labourers on the coasts of New World. In precisely those years that the Greenlanders seemed to disappear the first voyages from England to settle the 'New Found Land' began. They were led not by an Englishman, but by an Italian.

Like the Genoese and the Portuguese, the Venetians were great mariners of this age. At the close of the fifteenth century one of them was trailing the palaces of Europe trying to find support for a voyage of discovery to the West. In the court of Henry VII he succeeded. Johan Caboto Montecalunya, also known as John Cabot, 'discovered' the Newfoundland cod banks in 1498. The Basques and the men of Bristol had known them for decades, but they had been acting illegally; Cabot brought the New World the respectability of church and state. On the shores of Newfoundland he planted three banners belonging to the Vatican, St Mark of Venice and Henry VII of England. A century later Richard Hakluyt copied out into his famous journals some notes that he had read in an old chronicle for the year 1502:

Three men were brought to the king, having been captured on the new-found island which I spoke of earlier in the time of William Purchas when he was mayor. They were clad in the skins of animals and they ate raw meat, and their speech was such that none could understand them, while in their manners they were like wild beasts. The king kept them for a time, and when I saw them in Westminster Palace two years later they were dressed in the English fashion, nor could I distinguish them from Englishmen until I was told who they were.

They cannot have been North American natives, or they would hardly have been indistinguishable from Englishmen. Native American high cheekbones and skin colouration would have remained a novelty worthy of comment in the court. Ingstad thought that they were Norse Greenlanders, living in Newfoundland either as emigrants harried out of Greenland to the New World or forcibly settled as slaves by the men of Bristol.

*

They were waiting for me with coffee and ice cream. In Blok P, one of the graffiti-strewn housing projects built in the 1970s, I sat in the apartment Maria and Jukku shared with Jukku's daughter Sarah and talked about the future of Greenland. I had met Maria in a Danish-owned shop where she was employed, she said, to be 'the Greenlandic girl for the tourists.' To my delight she invited me round to her home for the evening. We were speaking about nationalism, and language.

'I know, I know, there are so few of us, of course we have to speak other languages,' Jukku said. 'But I don't want to have to learn two.'

I told him Faroese people had told me the same thing, they wanted only Faroese and English in school, and to forget about Danish altogether. 'Can't you be taught in Greenlandic?' I asked.

'We still have to speak Danish,' Maria said, 'or we can't get an education. But in the world outside Greenland and Denmark it is English that we need.'

'But I like Denmark,' said Jukku. He was an electrician, trained in Copenhagen. He grew up in Qaqortoq, the modern village at the centre of what had once been the Eastern Settlement, but he liked it better here in Nuuk. There was more to do in the evenings, he said, and in winter you could ski in the mountains. Together the two of them were the new generation of Greenlanders. Fiercely nationalist but international in their perspective.

'I am glad, very glad, that I am Greenlandic, but the world is much bigger than Greenland. I think I want to live in Denmark for a while,' Jukku said.

I nodded, wanting to hear more. But Maria stopped him short. 'You're so Danish!' she shouted in English, laughing and sticking out her tongue at him. Language is one way we build an identity, and the Greenlanders are gaining confidence in theirs.

I told them about my experience with the archivist and my interest in archaeology, and they insisted on taking me down to see the ruins of the old Moravian mission at the sea-front. We assembled at the door to get dressed for going out, and while Jukku helped Sarah get her jacket on Maria showed me some traditional *kamik* boots she had made from thin and supple sealskin. 'Are you going to put them on?' I asked.

'I know they look thin,' she said, 'but these are much too warm to wear in the summer.' They were red on the outside and traced with embroidery in bright colours. She told me that despite living in modern apartment blocks, many of the older Inuit traditions were kept alive.

We drove down to the sea-front to the site of the old mission. The graves in Greenland are shallow because of the thin soil and the permafrost. Skulls, phalanges and tarsal bones lay scattered across the grass, where children played with them on sunny afternoons. The wind whipped the waves into spouts; it was as if the whole bay plumed with the spray of blowing whales. A few drunks sagged in the hollows of the ground after a day's drinking. To the new generation the drunkenness of their elders is like an ongoing bereavement.

'But it will stop eventually,' said Jukku with a sigh. 'Take those hunters today, protesting about the sealing. They did not even know Greenpeace were here about Thule Airbase! Eventually they'll all be gone, and there will be a new Greenland.'

Jukku's vision was of a new technological economy, with one of the last true wildernesses left on earth at their own back door, theirs to enjoy, and to share.

*

I had to go. My flight for Copenhagen was leaving that very evening. Maria and Jukku took me to the airport. From there I would fly to Oslo, and connect with a flight to Tromsø in the far north of Norwegian Lapland. There I hoped to take a ship to the High Arctic archipelago of Svalbard.

With more regret than I had felt in any of the other departures I had made on my journey so far I waved goodbye to them, and to Greenland.

*

On 11 July 1576, Martin Frobisher, Yorkshireman, orphan, mariner of Africa, one-time prisoner of the Portuguese, affirmed buccaneer and darling of the court of Queen Elizabeth, caught sight of Greenland while in search of the North-West Passage to Cathay. He was Captain-General of the *Gabriel* and its companion, the *Michael*. When the two ships were caught in a storm they only narrowly survived; four men were lost and they drifted apart. On recovery the *Michael* found itself alone on the sea and sailed for England to report the loss of the *Gabriel* with all hands. Frobisher meanwhile had actually survived and continued on, 'knowing that the sea at length must needs have an ending, that some land should have a beginning that way.'

He did find land, which was later named Meta Incognita by Queen Elizabeth herself and which was the same country that had once been called Helluland and would later be called Baffin Island. Frobisher thought it to be a peninsula of Asia. On its shores his men found old Norse camps and tried to re-smelt the poor blooms of bog-iron that the Norsemen had left behind centuries before. They also met some Inuit who bartered seal and bearskins with them in exchange for iron, and then they sailed for England. They took a small lump of black mica which would be identified incorrectly as containing gold, but which would secure them funding for a second voyage. The next time the Inuit they met were unfriendly and showered them with arrows. When

Frobisher's men shot back, the Inuit leapt from the rocks to their deaths instead of giving themselves up. Frobisher claimed this was evidence of their barbarity, and that if they had surrendered they would have been well looked after. Perhaps the Inuit understood better than he what hospitality meant; the Captain General captured an old woman and a nursing mother from their number: 'The old wretch, whom divers of our Saylers supposed to be eyther a devil, or a witch, had her buskins plucked off, to see if she were cloven footed, and for her ougly hew and deformity we let her goe: the yong woman and the child we brought away.'

On his third voyage in 1578, the year Drake rounded Cape Horn in the *Golden Hind*, Frobisher sighted Greenland again and this time named it West England. He declared that he was the first Christian to set foot on its soil. In the tents of some Inuit who he had frightened away he found boxes of ship's nails and planks of pinewood, 'whereby it appeareth, that they have trade with some civill people.' That these others might have been Christians did not seem to have occurred to him, never mind that Bristol men had been sailing there for well over a century and Greenland had had resident bishops in the past. The weather was uncommonly severe that summer, and his men were weakened by storms and freezing winds from the north. Frobisher limped back to England to be lauded for his 'discoveries' for England in the polar seas. When the black mica was found to be worthless he was ridiculed and pilloried, but later proved himself again as vice-admiral in Drake's fleet to the West Indies. In 1588 he served against the Spanish Armada, and was knighted by Queen Elizabeth. On a land assault near Brest he was slightly wounded and according to John Aubrey (the gossipy social commentator who was one of his contemporaries), he died following the attentions of a ham-fisted barber surgeon.

While Frobisher sacked and looted in Latin America and Meta Incognita was a distant memory, the greatest mariner and navigator of his age was off the coast of Greenland, finding the proof of his later assertion that the continent of America was indeed an island. John Davis invented the back-staff, a quadrant that would revolutionise navigation, and he was a scholar and author of two major geographical and navigational treatises. In stark contrast to the pirate Frobisher he was a devout man of God, a tireless explorer, a seeker after truth and a restless nomad. After three voyages in search of the North-West Passage he would sail through the Magellan Straits, discover the Falkland Islands, and pilot for the Zeelanders in the East Indies. On finding Greenland he called it, 'the Land of Desolation'. In the summer of 1585 he was standing on its shore as a group of Inuit approached in their kayaks. The following account was written up by one of Davis' men, a man called Janes, in Hakluyt's, *The Principal Navigations Voyages Traffiques and Discoveries of the English Nation*.

Rather than shooting at the Greenlanders as Frobisher had done, Davis, 'caused our Musicians to play, ourselves dauncing, and making many signes of friendship.' One Greenlander beat his breast repeatedly and pointed to the sun, and so the Englishmen copied him. This action along with the playing of music and dancing seemed to reassure the Greenlanders, who remained peaceful.

On the second voyage they again made friends with the Inuit. Davis wrote that, 'I was desirous to have our men leape with them, which was done, but our men did overleape them.' They spent hours in this way, playing music, dancing and challenging the Inuit to games. They did not kill any of them, or carry them off as curiosities.

In 1593 Davis returned from the South Seas to find that his wife had left him for a 'sleek paramour'. Instead of rejoining family life he sat down and for the next two years composed his two masterpieces. In them he drew heavily on his experiences in the Strait that would bear his name. In his *Hydrographical Description of the Earth* he spoke of how the abundance of light in Greenland was good for the soul. 'How blessed then may we thinke this nation to be: for they are in perpetuall light, and never knowe what darkness meaneth,' he wrote. He had calculated that even in winter, the light from the full moon and the curvature of the earth gave the Green-landers more light than any other country he knew of.

The Inuit impressed themselves upon him greatly; so kindly was he received by them and in such contrast to his reception in other parts of the world that in his second book, *The Seaman's Secrets*, he compared the Inuit with the Indians he had encountered in Patagonia.

> In the frozen zone I discovered a coast which I named Deso-lation at the first viewe thereof, supposing it by the loath-some shape to bee wast and desolate, but when I came to anker within the harbours thereof the people presently came unto me without feare, offering such poore things as they had to exchange for yron nailes and such like, but the Cani-bals of America flye the presence of men, shewing them-selves in nothing to differ from brute beastes.

Davis was sure that there was a way through the archipelagos of Canada to China, but after three voyages he never found it. He wrote to Sir Francis Walsingham, secretary to Queen Elizabeth, that, 'the north-west passage is nothing doubtfull… voyd of yce, the ayre tolerable and the waters very depe.' The English would persist in their delusion of a commercially navigable North-West Passage for another three centuries. While Davis and his successors searched the straits and inlets of the Canadian Arctic, others were trying to push through the Siberian ice to find a North-Eastern passage to China. They did not know it yet, but they were on the verge of discovering a whole new archipelago, the last Hyperborean land.

Svalbard
MERCHANT ADVENTURERS

THE DINING ROOM of the cruise ship *Nordstjernen* was empty. The wind outside was gusting force nine and the vessel rolled and pitched like a log on a cataract. The waitress was unconcerned, effortlessly shifting her angle to the floor as she walked. Soup had been taken off the lunch menu.

The previous evening we had sailed north out of the calm fjords that lace between the western archipelagos of Norwegian Lapland, and into the Barents Sea. The other passengers must have been nursing their sea-sickness down below, but after a diet in Greenland of porridge and raw, dried seal-meat, I could not resist the feast of fresh fruit, shrimps and eggs that had been spread out for breakfast. I spent the morning out on deck settling my stomach, watching gulls trailing the stern and looking out over the waves which rolled in from the west, tall as houses.

This was travelling in style, I thought. No more airport departure calls, no more abrupt, disorientating arrivals. I had been obliged to fly since the Faroe Islands, but from now until the end of my journey I would travel by sea or by land.

To the west lay the Norwegian Sea, stretching out towards the eastern coast of Greenland eight hundred miles away. To the east across another six hundred miles of ocean lay the Siberian archipelago of Novaya Zemlya, and beyond it a jagged waste of ice-clogged headlands extending all the way to Alaska. Novaya Zemlya is rarely visited now. Its shores are soaked in the canker of Soviet nuclear testing, but it was once held to be the

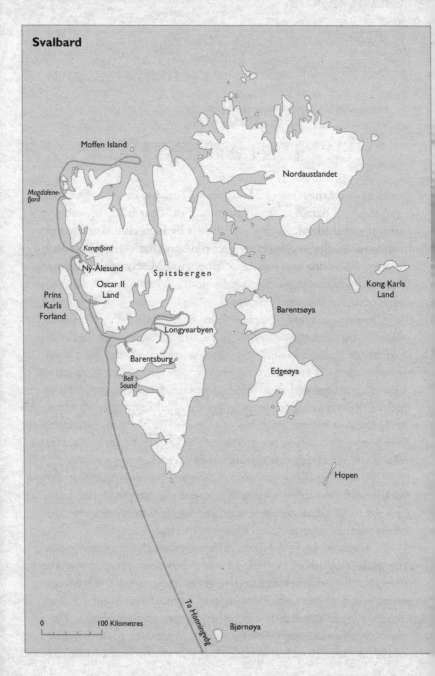

Svalbard

Moffen Island

Magdalene-fjord

Nordaustlandet

Kongsfjord

Ny-Ålesund

Spitsbergen

Kong Karls Land

Oscar II Land

Prins Karls Forland

Barentsøya

Longyearbyen

Barentsburg

Edgeøya

Bell Sound

Hopen

0   100 Kilometres

To Honningvåg

Bjørnøya

gateway to Asia and the only obstacle in the North-East Passage to China.

Flocks of little auks and guillemots, the birds which are to the ecosystems of the north what penguins are to the south, joined the ship and flew in a great river of bodies ducking and skirting the waves. The dull rocky coast of an island appeared through the mist, its stacks billowing with fulmars and kittiwakes. It was like being back off the coast of Mykines, the Paradise of Birds, but this island was no paradise. It was Bjørnøya, or 'Bear Island'; a mostly flat table of land surrounded on all sides by high cliffs, barren and torn into needles and caves by the cold seas that churned around it. Two mountains dominated its silhouette: Miseryfjellet, 'Mount Misery,' to the east, and Antarcticfjellet, 'Mount Antarctica,' to the south. The island's only inhabitants were a few homesick Norwegians who lived year-round in a meteorological station there. There was nothing else on the island, just birds, and the ruins of old coal mines. The second mate told me that the mines had been abandoned eighty years before because of low coal prices and the regularity with which the shafts collapsed, entombing the miners. It did not seem like a good place to die.

*

In May of 1553 on the eve of the Elizabethan Age, as Ivan the Terrible, the first Czar, crushed the last remnants of the sprawling Mongol Empire, three English ships sailed down the Thames and into the North Sea in an attempt to expand theirs. They were bound for China, by way of a north-east passage around Asia. The Captain General was Sir Hugh Willoughby, a courtier who knew nothing of navigation. To compensate for his ignorance the navigator and mariner Richard Chancellor was appointed second-in-command, captaining a separate ship. They were funded by a venerable society of the City of London, led by Sebastian Cabot, the son of John Cabot of Newfoundland fame, and known as, 'The Mysterie and Companie of the Marchants Adventurers for the Discoverie of

Regions, Dominions, Islands, and Places Unknowen.' In the society's optimism the two ships were fitted out with lead sheathing to protect them against the wormy waters of the East Indies.

Off the west coast of Norwegian Lapland they encountered a great storm and were blown apart. Willoughby ran aground near present-day Murmansk where he and his crew all died of scurvy. Chancellor put in at the castle of Vardø on the coast of Finnmark, the northernmost district of Lapland, where he met some Scottish merchants. The Scots knew the Lapland seas well and tried to persuade him that the idea of reaching China along the Siberian coast was preposterous, but Chancellor was resolute.

After refitting his ship he sailed out of Vardø, unknowingly passing by the place where his captain general lay dead or dying, and down into the White Sea. He entered a great bay which turned out to be the estuary of the Dvina River which runs all the way into the heartland of Russia itself. On its banks Chancellor was accosted by some emissaries of Czar Ivan who took him by sledge the thousand or so miles to Moscow, proving to him that the route could provide a new channel for trade not only with the Russians but with the riches of Persia to the south. The Right Worshipful Companie of Muscovie Merchants of London was born. The Company even established a town on the Dvina, Archangel, as a port to channel the wealth of the expanding Russian Empire into English ships.

In the excitement over this new trade route, the North-East Passage was forgotten, at least temporarily. A few years later Frobisher and then Davis would turn their attentions instead to the west. The Dutch did not give up so easily.

While Chancellor slid along the Dvina towards Moscow, the Roman Catholic Philip II of Spain had just inherited the whole of the Netherlands. He was fiercely opposed by the Protestant nobility of the northern provinces and William I, Prince of Orange, led them in revolt against Spanish rule. In 1588 independence was declared and the Dutch began exploring the seas in defiance of the Spanish monopolies. Six years later they picked up where the English had left off and set sail for the North-East Passage. Their pilot was a man called Willem Barents. Like John Davis he was a remarkable navigator. Unlike Davis he knew the Norse descriptions of Greenland and the northern seas, and had even translated some of them.

His first voyage took him past Novaya Zemlya and into the Kara Sea, where he met fishermen who told him that navigation as far east as the vast Yenisei delta was certainly possible. Buoyed with confidence he returned to Amsterdam and secured funding for seven ships to try again, but the ice that year was heavier and he was forced back. The following year, 1596, he tried a third time. With him was a man named Gerrit de Veer, to whom we owe the best surviving account of their journey.

De Veer describes all three of the expeditions in his, *The true and perfect description of three voyages, so strange and woonderfull, that the like hath never been heard of before.* In an echo of Willoughby and Chancellor's expedition their third and final voyage was captained by a nobleman, Jacob von Heemskerck, with the tried and tested navigator Barents as chief pilot. From Norway they sailed north to try to round Novaya Zemlya at its northern cape, and in due course came in among pieces of sea ice which floated, they said, like swans upon the water. The sea was said to be so green that they thought they must be near Greenland.

On 9 June they sighted an island which was about ten miles in length, mostly flat on top but surrounded by great cliffs and two peaks; one to the east and one to the south. They put ashore to collect eggs and to explore its interior. De Veer says of it: 'In that island wee were in great danger of our liues: for that going vp a great hill of snowe, when we should come down againe, wee thought wee should all break our neckes… for that at the foote of the hill there was many rockes, which wee were likely to haue fallen vpon, yet by God's help wee got safely downe againe.'

With God's help they tried to get back to the ships but were attacked by a polar bear. After successfully killing it they named the whole place 'Bear Island' in its honour.

Barents was heavily criticised by some of the men for taking them so far to the west and into the ice, but he had the confidence of Heemskerck, and after leaving Bear Island they continued on, sailing not east for Novaya Zemlya, but into the north.

*

When we passed Bear Island the sea began to calm, and the sky to clear. One by one the passengers emerged from their cabins. They were from all over Europe, using the boat as a cruise ship from the mainland up to the High Arctic archipelago of Svalbard and back again. Two Italians, holiday refugees from the car factories of Turin, filmed everything they saw. They had both recently been in the far north of Greenland, and wore matching padded jackets decorated with Greenland's flag. They had loved the ambiguity of Greenland, that it was part of both Europe and of North America, but told me they had come in order to see the only High Arctic landscape that wholly belonged to Europe: the mountains and glaciers of Svalbard.

The *Nordstjernen*, or 'North Star,' had once been a coastal steamer trailing the length of Norway between Bergen and the Russian border in Lapland, but was now consigned to the nauseating run across the Barents Sea into the Arctic Ocean. It was an exquisite ship, decked in lacquered hardwoods and polished brass; a relic of a more leisurely and decadent age of travel. The crew and the waitresses who worked on it were fond of it, despite its fading velvet curtains and narrow warrens of gangways. I had been given a tiny cabin right at the bow; its bulkhead ran with the graceful curve of the hull, and the rise and fall of the waves rocked me to sleep.

We had passed 75° north. Night no longer existed; only the endless day of the polar summer. We cruised onwards with our stern to the south, the sun high in the sky and the gulls following in billows. They spun through the currents of air in the ship's wake, sharply silhouetted against the midday sun.

The mountains of Svalbard began to rise over the horizon. The sky was an opaque dome of turquoise arching high above us. Despite it being late summer the snow lay all the way down to the coast, but where the rocks had been exposed the earth looked scarred and barren, scraped by ice. No whales broke the surface of the water, and there was a perfect stillness in the air. There were no smells.

A layer of fog hovered in a dense quilt, wreathing the mountains to the north. It was a compact layer, below and above it the optical quality of the air was unaffected – brittle, sharp and pellucid. White mountains, blue-white glaciers, blue sky; the colours slipped from one into the other in magnificent and timeless austerity.

The ship rounded a cape where a cluster of cabins marked the island's main landing strip. Beyond it lay the harbour of Longyearbyen, the principal settlement of the island of Spitsbergen.

*

Soon after leaving Bear Island Barents and his men sighted land again. High mountains loomed through the mist, and the sea ice lay fast to the beaches. Snow lay in drifts down to the edge of the shore. It was late June. A profusion of whales surfaced between the fragments of ice which floated on the water, looking like shards of shattered marble. The men pushed through the leads of open water in small boats to get to the shore, and tried to get up the rivers to see the interior. The waters were in flood with the summer thaw and pulling hard on the oars they could not row upstream. Along the shoreline they saw many barnacle geese, and de Veer commented that the observation proved that the geese did not grow on trees in Ireland as had previously been believed. They explored several of the fjords of the western and northern coasts of the island, and noticed that as well as whales, there were herds of walrus ready for the taking.

But they were not interested in whales, or in geese, in bears or even in coal, which the new islands had in abundance. They were trying to get to *China*. They thought the whole place pretty dismal, and called it 'Spitsbergen' which means simply 'Pointy Mountains'. After a cursory look around they went back to their ships and set sail east.

Disaster struck on their way through the ice. Their hull was cracked near the coast of Novaya Zemlya and they were forced into their boats, and into the first recorded European wintering in the High Arctic. From their crushed ship they retrieved the fo'c'sle and built a house, and under the direction of their surgeon constructed a Turkish bath to counter the effect of the cold air. The doctor also pressed them to continue to exercise, something which at the time was believed would stave off scurvy. De Veer writes that the men were enjoined, 'to exercise their bodies with running, walking, playing at colfe [golf], and other exercises, thereby to stirre their joints and make them nimble.' For heat and light they burned the fat of the 'cruell beares' which prowled near their hut and which they repeatedly had to shoot. Their wintering house has since been discovered on the bleak shores of Novaya Zemlya. They lived in some style, it was found, if perhaps with little luxury. It was decorated with chiming clocks and engravings of biblical and classical scenes intended for the edification of the people of China.

On 24 January they saw the sun again, fourteen days too soon for the latitude of their hut. They were astonished, and de Veer comments that it was 'cleane contrary to the opinions of all olde and newe writers, yea and contrary to the nature and roundness both of heaven and earth.' They took it as a sign that God would help them escape. They were naïve of the fact that the earth is flattened at the poles, and of thermoclines in the Arctic air which cast mirages high into the sky. The sun actually still lay below the horizon, and their calculations had been correct.

In June their food supply failed, and they realised that they would have to undertake an open boat journey across six hundred miles of the Arctic Ocean if they were going to reach Vardø. Barents himself was very ill, and struggled even to get into the boat.

One of the finest mariners in the world and greatest explorers of the Arctic to have lived, he was not to see his fame spread. While setting sail, still within sight of their wintering house, he begged de Veer to pass him a drink. 'He had no sooner drunke but he was taken with so sodaine a qualme, that he turned his eies in his head and died presently.'

Back in the Netherlands, Maurice of Nassau, son of William of Orange, had finally liberated the Low Countries from the Spanish. In defiance of the Spanish Armada the Dutch fleet had already made it to China and Siam by the Cape of Good Hope. The North-East Passage was no longer so essential for the future of Dutch trade.

In October of that year, 1597, Gerrit de Veer and eleven other survivors dragged themselves back into Amsterdam. It would not take long before news of their discoveries would reach the ears of the English.

*

I walked about the town looking for a room. Near the harbour I met a sad girl from Trondheim who said she had been in Spitsbergen for three years. I asked her what she liked about it; 'Very little,' she replied. She showed me to a cheap hostel made of plywood and painted a sickened off-yellow then waved goodbye, telling me to watch myself. 'The owner eats men like you alive,' she said.

The owner was a chain-smoker of indeterminate age. Her hair was yellow, limply permed, and her face was a battleground in the war against ageing; scored with trenches and caked with make-up. On the walls were studio photographs of her wearing leather and lycra. In one she had a collar around her neck and was crouching in a kennel, in another she was gripping a wire fence in her teeth. Her face cracked in a smile when she saw that I had noticed them. Her eyes sought mine, but I looked away. She ushered me into the living room which stank of stale cigarette smoke and vodka. A couple of empty bottles stood on the table. I filled in her day-book, including the phone numbers of my family back in Scotland; 'In case of an accident,' she explained, 'with the bears.'

To get to my room I cleared a pile of empty cardboard boxes from the corridor, and behind them saw that my door had been punched through near the handle. On the bedside table were gun magazines, truck magazines, soft pornography and a paper wallet of photographs. There were two types of photograph in the wallet: tiny skiing figures dwarfed by an immensity of snow, and drunk leering faces balancing cigarettes in their nostrils. Guns, trucks, pornography and alcohol; I wondered if this then was the reality of Arctic life.

I went for a walk. The town was built in a blunt little valley, its few houses overshadowed by sheer scree slopes on all sides. A river ran through the middle, its bed broad enough to handle the swollen waters of the thaw-season and made of the same grey rubble as the mountains. Utility pipes ran up above ground out of the perma-frost, thickly lagged with insulation and used by the townspeople as bridges to cross the river bed. Two glaciers hung balanced above it, looking as if they were retreating into the mountains. High on the slopes around the town lay the dilapidating remains of the coal industry which had fathered and nurtured it. Gantries which once cabled gondolas of coal to the harbour were rusting and collapsing, shifting stations mounted on spindles of iron were sinking back into the earth.

Sometimes life imitates art, and reality follows the imagination. Martin Behaim, the Nuremberg cartographer whose globe was based on the descriptions of the Greenland-faring Minorite friar, invented the south-west passage to the Indies years before Magel-lan discovered it. Relying on classical authors he reasoned that the known world must have its opposite, known as the Antichthon, which could only lie far into the southern hemisphere. The An-tichthon was well-known to mediaeval Europe. In Canto XXVI of Dante's *Inferno* Ulysses calls upon his men not to forget the trials and terrible dangers that they have survived, and to turn their stern to the east and set sail out past the Pillars of Hercules and into the ocean for the dark southern continent. In Italian his rallying cry has a rolling power, and is still used today by anti-war protesters and humanitarian groups in Italy: 'Considerate la vostra semenza: Fatti non foste a viver come bruti, Ma per seguir virtute e conoscenza.' ('Consider the soil you spring from; you were not made to live the life of beasts, but instead to follow virtue and knowledge.')

After travelling from their homeland to the south for five moons Ulysses saw the sky fill with new stars of the southern pole, and when they looked back to the north they saw that the stars that they knew and loved no longer appeared over the horizon.

To educated cartographers such as Behaim, aware of this European cultural heritage, it was obvious that those two bodies of land – the known and the unknown – would be separated by an immense strait of water into which Ulysses had sailed. So he drew it. When Magellan later found his strait leading out of the southern ocean he already knew that he was on the very edge of the world.

German speculative cartographer, Johann Ruysch, had presciently drawn Spitsbergen in anticipation of Barents' voyage nearly a century before the Dutch revolt against the Spanish. Like Behaim his vision was a fusion of classical and mediaeval ideas: he knew that in the far north there was still supposed to be a land known as Hyperborea, and from the work of the Minorite friar (*Inventio Fortunatae*) he knew that four great islands encircled the North Pole. His world map of 1508 shows the island of Spitsbergen quite clearly; it is called Hyperborei Evrope, 'European Hyperborea.' A great peninsula stretches towards it from Lapland, the eastern shore of which is clearly marked with 'Sancti Odulfi': Saint Olaf's Church in Vardø.

When the Norwegians won control of Spitsbergen in the 1920s they changed its name to Svalbard, which means 'the cold coast', and relegated the name Spitsbergen to the largest island of the archipelago. The Icelandic annals for 1194 had briefly mentioned a 'cold coast' spotted far in the north, and so renaming the island reasserted their Viking sovereignty over it. The naming of land and sea, like the writing of history books, is a powerful tool in the manufacture of identity.

*

There are just over a thousand people who live in Longyearbyen, working in the mines, operating the power station, studying in the university research centre, and working with the tourists. People make the move there to escape from heavy Scandinavian taxes and because they like the idea of living in the Arctic. They stay for all sorts of reasons: lack of bureaucracy, escape from their families, dislike of urban life, inertia, and because they love the landscape. It is a magnificent place to live.

The centre of Longyearbyen was crammed with bright new buildings: an enormous supermarket, four bars, a shopping centre, a nightclub, and even a Thai massage parlour. But despite the garish shop windows and the neon signs the town felt like a village and had an unmistakable sense of standing on a frontier. There was a sign on the only track out of the town warning against polar bears, but it might as well have said, 'Abandon hope all ye who enter here.' Svalbard has the highest concentration of polar bears in the Arctic, and it is normal to carry hunting rifles around the town.

There are some other peculiarities of life in Longyearbyen. No door is ever locked in case you need to make a sudden escape from a bear. There is no theft because there is no way in or out undetected. Everybody knows everybody. In every building, including all the shops, you have to take your shoes off at the door to prevent dragging coal dust and glacial mud through the carpets. Each shop, hotel or public building has a shoe rack and a gun rack next to one another by the door. There is very little violence. It is difficult to get angry or self-righteous when you are standing in your socks.

I walked up the hill out of the town to the old graveyard, a bare scrap of land lined with white wooden crosses. The mountains to the north were cut into sharp outlines, their summits crisp, flat ridges tipped with ice. Their slopes sank in languorous curves, hollowed by glaciers and stepped with seams of resistant rock. The light refracted through the air as if through a prism. It was so clear that it made my eyes ache.

The museum lay below the graveyard, and was a monument to excess and the power of humans to destroy their own environment. It charted the course of the Svalbard whaling industry and its demise from over-whaling; then the trapping industry, and its demise from over-trapping. A replica of the coal industry's former offices filled the top floor, complete with lurid calendar pornography. The information panels below traced the industry's implosion; how too many miners had died and the mines were all too far away from civilisation to be commercially worthwhile. Unlike the whales and the bears, at least at the end of the coal mining industry in Svalbard there had still been some coal left.

In a small art gallery on the hill I spent an afternoon reading through a private library collection. The manager had lived in Fife once, and he unlocked the cabinets for me and brought out the entire published works of the Hakluyt Society concerning the discovery and exploration of Spitsbergen. Among them were the writings of a certain Englishman by the name of William Purchas. They are a fascinating description of the lives that these mariners led, accustomed to a hardship that we now find unimaginable. The dangers of the voyage around the Cape of Good Hope must have been truly horrendous to inspire and galvanise these attempts to find a passage that could avoid it.

The English could not bear that the Dutch had made discoveries in the waters that, since Willoughby, they considered theirs. Within a decade of Barents' voyage the Muscovy Company fitted out a ship for the north once more. Its captain was a mild-mannered man named Henry Hudson, who carried Barents' charts and set his sails for the North Pole. Although he knew that Barents had found an archipelago and named it Spitsbergen, when he reached it he claimed that he was the first, and renamed it Newland. He reached 80°23′north, just beyond the islands' northern limit, but was turned back by the pack ice. He was the first fully to describe the abundance of whales, walruses and seals that were to be found in those waters, and the tales he told on his return opened the door to commercial whaling. Drifting far to the south and west of Spitsbergen he saw the east coast of Greenland, and also discovered a small volcanic island that he called 'Hudson's Tutches' ('Touches'). The island was later rediscovered by a Dutchman, Jan May, and given the name Jan Mayen that it still holds today.

In 1608 Hudson returned to the Arctic and sailed for the North-East Passage, but on reaching the Vaigach straits which lead into the Kara Sea his crew, frightened by the density of the ice, mutinied. Hudson capitulated, showing signs of poor resolve and weakness of character for which the English later stripped him of his command. Being such an experienced mariner he was immediately snapped up by the Dutch, who sent him west. The next year, the summer of 1609, he fought the 'Red Indians' of Maine and Chesapeake, named a river after himself, and penetrated it as far as Albany. At its mouth he laid the foundations of the settlement of New Amsterdam, which would later be renamed New York. He was a remarkable man, who met an unfortunate death. The ice that he had met near Svalbard in 1608 would play a part in his downfall.

By 1610 Elizabeth was dead, Mary, Queen of Scots, beheaded, and the Scots Stewarts had moved to Westminster. James the First of England, the Sixth of Scotland, ruled over both domains. James had already commissioned the translation of his famous Bible. This was the society, poised on the brink of the Enlightenment, which lusted for riches that trade on the high seas, and with China in particular, could bring. That year Hudson was re-commissioned by the English. Dispirited as they were about finding a passage to China by the north-east route and having heard about Hudson's discoveries for the Dutch in North America, he was equipped with a ship and the same crew that had defied him at the straits of the Kara Sea and ordered to sail for the Americas once more. The choice of crew would be his undoing.

He was dispatched in search of the north-west passage, 'through those inlets which Davis saw,' and came upon 'a great and whirling sea,' which he named Hudson's Bay. In the bay he was locked in by ice and forced to winter near modern Churchill in Manitoba. Thunderstorms presaged disaster, scurvy broke out, and by June of the following year it was clear that they did not have enough supplies. The principal mutineer was Robert Juet, the same first mate who had led the rebellion against entering the Kara Sea three years before.

They bound Hudson and forced him and his son, the ship's carpenter and six sick men into a shallop (a type of small, open boat) along with an inadequate supply of shot, an iron pot, and some meal, with which the mutineers hoped to assuage their consciences. The painter-line holding them to the ship was cut and the shallop drifted free. They then, 'let fall the mainsayle, and out with their top-sayles, and fly as from an enemy.' Winters in Hudson's Bay are harsh, but summers can be almost as bleak. None of the men were ever seen again.

*

The following day I walked along a loose track looking for an address, reading signs nailed on posts and hammered into the earth, giving a loose structure to the open building site. Much of Longyearbyen is open gravel, but nearer the shore a few tentative streets were appearing between stacks of timber and bulldozed rubble. Most of the year the town is sanitised and bleached by a mantle of snow, but in the brief summer months the illusion is broken. Pools of mud lay soaking between the derelict shacks and rusting building works.

When I found the house it was neat and blue and two huskies lay on the porch. They panted in the warm sunlight and looked out over the fjord. I knocked on the door and waited. Reggae music boomed out from inside. It took a while for anyone to answer.

Stefano's hair caught the wind like black wool on barbed wire. Clutching a cigarette he stepped out onto the porch, hopping from foot to foot in his clogs and long-johns. Some children walked by and the huskies started to whine, tugging on their chains. 'They're fine with adults,' he explained, 'but children they think of as fast-moving food.'

His house he had built by himself. For four months of the year Svalbard is in total darkness, and he needed something to keep himself busy, he explained. 'Winter is only a problem for people with nothing to do,' he said. He told me a potted history of his life, growing up in Milan, learning mountaineering in the Dolomites, then moving to the Lofoten Islands, the dazzling eruptions of cliffs and sheer rock faces that stand off the Arctic coast of Norway. It was there that he had learned his trade as a mountain guide. It was from Lofoten that he had come to Svalbard, and he had been here six years.

'How long will you stay?' I asked him.

'It's always another year, always another season,' he said. 'Maybe three more years, maybe less. I know there is more to life than Svalbard.' His Lombard accent tumbled with the heavy consonants of Norwegian; you could have flapped a sheet in his 'R's. 'I think I want to go to Perrrru next,' he said.

A ladder of pinewood steps led up onto a second floor, where the walls were painted in dark blue and crimson. Everywhere there were maps: maps of Svalbard, maps of the Alps, maps of Europe and maps of the world. Some of his friends arrived, mountain guides from the tour companies operating out of Longyearbyen. They were Norwegians, Danes and Germans, escapees from what they saw as the clamour of the south. We drank coffee and I listened to them all talk about the life in Svalbard. It was generally acknowledged by them (all young men) that the main problem was the lack of women there. 'But isn't there a university here?' I asked. I had been shown around the research centre and there seemed to be quite a few young female biologists around.

'But where are they all?!' shouted out one of the guides, a German. 'Where do they drink?'

'Not in the pubs, anyway,' said Stefano, and poured himself another coffee. 'They don't want to get involved with smelly guys like us!'

I thought of the sad girl from Trondheim, and why she had come to Svalbard. Maybe she came for love and had found it difficult to contemplate giving up the inevitable advantage that all this choice of men gave her.

I wanted to chat to them about leaving the confines of the town and going walking in the mountains. Everyone had some advice to offer me. 'Remember that bears hunt seals, and seals are a hundred times more aware of their environment than you are. Always be very aware and concentrate on what's happening around you.'

'If you are camping, don't cook any food near the tent, they'll smell food from miles away.'

'A big one will stand about six feet high at the shoulders and run at forty miles an hour, it is like trying to shoot a train.'

'Try to scare it, make a lot of noise, clap your hands, yell.'

'Fire a flare at it.' Stefano produced a flare gun the size of a pen from his pocket. 'But with this you have to get the trajectory right – you must not set it off *behind* the bear.'

One of the Danes spoke up: 'But don't run, then you are definitely prey. Most bears are just curious. They don't know what you are, and they want to find out.' His eyes were unseeing for a moment, as he pictured in his mind episodes and near-misses of the past. 'There are no rules about polar bears, you just have to think about it carefully each time you see one.'

*

I did not feel particularly encouraged. In a bar decked with seal-skins in the centre of town I had a drink and thought about what to do next. I wanted to climb into the mountains, but going alone was not recommended. Beside me a mechanic from the Lofoten Islands slumped in a drunken stupor. Before losing consciousness he had told me he had come to the Arctic because he hated all the 'black people' 'filling up' the south. Covering one wall was a mural of a bear soaking in a widening pool of blood. A crumpled leaflet lay on the bar entitled 'TAKE POLAR BEAR DANGER SERIOUSLY!' On the front of it two bears, muzzles covered in blood, were tearing apart some unidentifiable mammalian remains. It warned me to take nothing less than a big-game hunting rifle outside the main streets of the town, as well as a flare gun, and included the advice: 'Aim at the chest and shoot several times. Then approach the polar bear from behind, and make sure it is dead.'

Drinking on the other side of me was a Englishman called Andy, a DJ from Manchester. He was hired by the nightclub in town to work two nights a week, but the rest of his time was his own. He spoke with the slowness and exaggerated gestures of a man who has lived a long time abroad, speaking English to those who do not speak it often. By sometime after midnight we had agreed to join forces against the army of bears which threatened to be prowling just outside the town's limits. As we staggered out into the glaring sunlight at 3 a.m. he turned to me and asked, 'Where can we get a gun?'

*

Frontier-living calls for frontier laws. The first shop I walked into handed me a high-calibre hunting rifle and eight bear-piercing rounds. 'Have you ever used one of these?' the guy asked me.

'No,' I said.

'Oh well,' he said. 'You'll get the hang of it.'

Andy had been in the army for twelve years. He weighed the rifle lovingly in his hands ('Ah, a classic'), and pocketed the rounds with satisfaction ('Mmm, armour-piercing'). He nonchalantly slung the rifle on his shoulder and we headed into the mountains.

Further into the valley there were abandoned huts and relay-stations that had belonged to the coal mines, now rotten and damp. Their concrete floors were crumbling and their foundations slipping away with the relentless subsidence of the permafrost. Flock of little auks circled our heads, fanning out from their perches on the ledges of the cliffs, and the silence was broken by the whisper of hundreds of their wings beating in time. They banked over us again and again, each time closer. As we walked Andy talked to me about the blunt realities of weapons technology.

'I've seen these things used in Northern Ireland – you could shoot a brick wall with one of these rounds and still kill the guy on the other side…'

The valley narrowed to a ravine, skirting the edge of the glacier which was rent into crevasses, some only visible as slight slumps in the snow. Streams trickled out of the shattered mess of rubble that composed the mountainside, all of it heavily laden with silt, an opaque bluish colour. When mixed with the muddy shale it formed a viscous slurry which flowed down the hillside like lava. It was undrinkable.

'See, these are designed so that when they break the skin, they start to tumble inside, so they cause a lot more internal damage than a usual round which just goes straight through. They were designed by the British to fight the Afghans over a century ago, because the Pushtun tribesmen were so bloody unbeatable.'

On the top of the plateau we looked out to the north, across the fjord to the mountains of Oscar II Land, which makes up a large part of the northern half of Spitsbergen. The sun was anaemic behind the drifting clouds, but tinted them in shades of honey and spilled an ambrosial light onto the highest of the peaks. The mountains were all nunataks, meshed into a sea of glacial ice. Across the plateau I saw three reindeer, but they were so far away that at first glance I mistook them for bears.

'You know, these rounds are illegal technically, but I bet they were made in Europe, maybe even in Britain. But then I guess if you're going to shoot a bear you've got to have just about the most lethal round ever invented…'

Less than a hundred metres from the top the mist came down, disorientating us. It was impossible to go on. The horizon was obliterated and though the air was filled with light it was as if we had been blinded. Rules of perspective disappeared, and the judgment of distance was impossible. We sat down and waited an hour, but it showed no signs of lifting. I had wanted to catch a glimpse of Bell Sound to the south – it had been one of the favourite berths of the whalers – but in this mist it was impossible. We turned and headed back, sliding hundreds of metres in a few minutes on polythene bags.

'When I was in the army we used to use bullets that were designed to stay inside you, after they'd broken into pieces.'

'What?' I asked, 'so that the victims die of wound infections?'

'I suppose so. I never really thought about it,' he said.

The whole landscape was white, so bright it made the eyes water, despite wearing sunglasses. We walked across a plain of snow, only two or three miles wide but covered in a thin crust of re-frozen ice. Every step meant plunging through to the knee or the hip, and crossing the snowfield took hours. Thin ski-tracks left by a man being pulled by dogs ran lightly over the surface ahead of us, the way Amundsen's tracks mocked Scott's party as they approached the South Pole. The next time, I thought, I would bring snow-shoes or skis.

'There is another kind of bullet, whose object is to maim people, but not kill them…'

The plateau had been the scene of tragedy a few years before; two girls had been walking unarmed and were approached by a young male bear. It was probably only about two years old, weighing about 100kg, recently abandoned by its mother and therefore hungry. It caught and killed one of the girls, while the other saved herself by jumping from the cliffs, breaking most of the long bones in her body on the way down.

'The thinking goes that if nine hundred soldiers are running at you, and you kill three hundred of them, the rest will only get angrier. But if you *maim* three hundred, the other six hundred will want to stay to carry them back to safety.'

We reached the end of the plateau. A track ran down to the landing strip, from where a road ran the short distance back to the town. It started to snow. I thanked Andy for the company on the hike and for handling the gun; it had been an educational day.

*

John Davis was dead. He survived Elizabeth, his Queen, by only a couple of years before being run through by a Japanese pirate in the Malacca Straits. The new golden boy of English navigation was a man called William Baffin. He was the first navigator to take a lunar observation at sea, had been a chief pilot in Greenland at the age of 28, and a year later, in 1613, he was commissioned as a chief pilot by the Muscovy Company of London. His mission was to explore the northern whale fisheries more carefully than Hudson had managed.

Baffin died at only 38, shot in the belly by a Portuguese soldier while laying siege to a fort in the Strait of Hormuz. In his short life he explored more territory in the Arctic than any man before him. For two centuries his 'farthest north' was unsurpassed, and on his fifth voyage to the Arctic, in 1616, he went more than 300 miles further than anyone had before and explored the island and the bay to which he gave his name. In his dealings with the Inuit as with his skills in navigation he followed Davis, not Frobisher. His love for the Arctic shines in his prose. The best accounts of his explorations in Spitsbergen are however from the pen of another Muscovy Companyman, Robert Fotherby.

On his second voyage to the northern whale fishery Baffin moored his ship at the north-west corner of Spitsbergen, and together with Fotherby provisioned two shallops with a tent and some food. Together with a handful of men they tried to push between the heavy ice along the northern coast. The full extent of the islands was still unknown; for all Baffin knew they could represent a far-reaching peninsula of Siberia itself. Hopes of a commercially navigable North-East Passage still whispered on the edges of his ambition.

They ran out of food on the expedition, and had to get ashore to hunt some reindeer. The Svalbard reindeer is a closer cousin to the Lapland reindeer than the caribou of Greenland and Canada. It has short legs and is stockily built, and its pelt is the colour of dirty snow, making it well camouflaged. There is a great strandflat peninsula on the northern coast of Spitsbergen called 'Reinsdyrflya' for the herds of the animals that are found on it, and it is likely that it is there that Baffin and Fotherby went hunting. The snow was murderous, sometimes bearing the men's weight, at other times breaking through so that they slipped in to the knee or thigh. They were cold and tired and the weather was deteriorating, but they managed to bring down three bucks. They made a fire from driftwood and broiled their venison. Their spirits were restored.

Further along the shore they reached a bay where Fotherby and two of his companions went for a walk towards the interior of the island, intending to explore it a little. Their account is one of the first descriptions of Arctic glacier travel, undertaken without any climbing equipment. They started walking up a long gradual slope, 'but having gon a while upon it, wee perceived it to be ice.' Further on still there were great chasms in the ice-mountain, which seemed to gape all the way down to the ground below them. Fotherby was fascinated by these crevasses, and broke off some lumps of ice to throw into them. He noted that as they fell they made a noise, 'much like to a peice of glass throwen downe the well within Dover Castle.' He seemed to be unaware of the existence of glaciers at all and continuing his stroll he contemplated their origin, correctly arguing how the snow, never thawing, is gradually compacted by its own weight into ice.

Baffin and Fotherby continued on in their explorations, though the snow fell hard on the sea around them and the surface began to freeze. The wind blew them south into the great strait separating the island of Spitsbergen from Nordaustland, the most northerly island of the Svalbard archipelago. After eighteen hours rowing in a blizzard through a sea curdling into heavy slush they had to turn back to their starting point on the western side of the strait. The northern limits of Svalbard would remain unexplored.

Baffin's next voyage would be back to Greenland, but he left the Northern Whale Fishery fully open for business. The result of Hudson and Baffin's reports was a Dutch, English, Basque and Danish free-for-all. Whaling ships were soon so thick in the fjords of Spitsbergen that they passed gunwale to gunwale, yelling insults at one another. The Dutch, apparently, took great delight in reminding the English that they were ruled by a Scotsman. The Scots were there too, but employed by the Danes as hired ombudsmen to try to extract taxes from the English and the Dutch. The king of Denmark was convinced the islands were part of Greenland and so belonged to him.

The Dutch considered themselves the owners of the land and the seas around it; it had been Barents, after all, who discovered it. Ever sensible and international in perspective, they published lucid arguments for their sovereignty over it but did not fight so much, as fighting interfered with whaling. One of these arguments, by a man called Hessel Gerritszoon Van Assum, has been translated and published by the Hakluyt Society. His thesis has the beautifully informative title of: *History of the country called Spitsbergen. Its discovery, its situation, its animals, with an account of the annoyances which the whalers Basque, Dutch and Flemish, have endured at the hands of the English in the present year 1613. Also a protest against the English, and a refutation of all their frivolous arguments, on which they base a claim to make themselves sole masters of the aforesaid country.*

He lampoons the English for thinking that Spitsbergen and Greenland are parts of one and the same country, asking how can they have rights to it when it is obvious to all intelligent men that the two countries are separate, indeed, 'are further situated from each other than Norway is from Scotland?' Not all the Dutch were so enlightened. Another claim for sovereignty, this time by one Jacob Segersz van der Brugge, describes his bewilderment over describing the country also known as Spitsbergen as green: 'Greenland, being by no means green, and probably named by rule of the contrary, though it should more fitly be Greyland, because it is grey and gruesome.'

Every year brought more whalers, each nation staked out certain beaches and marked them with flags. The great copper pots they used to rend the whales' blubber into oil were left over winter, and on the whole the fighting subsided. Settlements with huts of rubble and wood grew up along the most well-used beaches. The biggest of these was owned by the Dutch; called Smeerenburg or 'Blubber City', it lay on the north-west corner of the archipelago. At its height it had over a thousand inhabitants, and the dubious honour of the world's most northerly red-light district.

*

I did a little more walking in the mountains around Longyearbyen. There were breeding kennels for the huskies high in the hills, and one day I came across a colossal NASA antenna hidden behind a false summit. After a week or so the town and its alcoholics began to depress me; I wanted to get north into the bays of the whalers. I heard of a vessel which was going to make the trip up to the international research village of Ny Ålesund, but then its engine failed and it had to be ignominiously dragged back into harbour by the Russians.

In the end it was the same ship that had brought me, the *Nordstjernen*, that broke me out of Longyearbyen. It had completed its tour, returned to Lapland, disgorged its passengers and returned with another set. I climbed on board with relief, and even managed to get the same cabin.

The sun shone night and day through a diaphanous sky. For three days it was continuously ringed with haloes and rainbows, called *parhelia*, caused by the refraction of the sun through frost crystals high in the polar atmosphere. Four pale brother-suns, 'sun-dogs', shone in cruciate formation, arranged around the central star like the cardinal points of the compass. Barents had seen the same thing here and taken it as a sign of the munificence of God. Columns of light fell from the suns onto the ice below, where they splashed in a cascade. The air was so clear its light was abrasive, rasping on the skin.

The *Nordstjernen* skirted the southern coast of Oscar II Land, frightening the seals. Cliffs jutted up from the beaches like ribs, and a soft blue haze hung over the water. I had been glad not to meet any bears in the mountains around Longyearbyen, but in the end my patience on deck was rewarded. Through my binoculars, from the safety of the ship, I saw a bear pick its way along the shoreline. Its head was held regally aloft, and the fluidity and speed of its movement as it ambled along the beach was terrifying. I was glad that it was not hunting me. Too quickly it was gone, and I was left straining my eyes at every piece of ice and every lump of stone, willing them to transform themselves into bears.

Smeerenburg was gone; its huts had blown into the sea and its buildings had been shattered by frost. The only remains of the town were rings on the beaches where the blubber-rending pots once stood. When the oil and fat were poured from the pots into barrels some fell to the ground, mixing with the gravel and setting into a kind of concrete. The rings around the blubber furnaces stood fast on the gravel, the only legacy of a century of whaling.

Around the coast from Smeerenburg stood a natural harbour, the Magdalenefjord, where the ships used to stop and meet one another, fire their furnaces and bury their dead. The spit of land sheltering the bay was one of the few places where there was enough loose rock to pile over the corpses, and the headland was dotted with their remains. Proper burial is impossible in the permafrost, and carrying the dead back to Europe was unthinkable. Just as I had seen at the Moravian graveyard in Greenland, bones lay scattered over the rocks. Perfectly preserved coffins of thin board sagged under the weight of the few boulders that had been hastily rolled over them more than three centuries before. The whalers had a horror of being dismembered by the bears after death; when forced to winter on the islands they would keep their dead in their huts until spring rather than put them out where the bears could get at them. While we ship's passengers picked over the beach two marksmen stood on a little hill nearby, watching for bears, ready to shoot if for a moment one of the tourists were threatened.

Pieces of brash ice sculpted in smooth organic lines flowed down out of the Arctic Ocean. The water was still relatively warm, thawed by the Gulf Stream and kept mostly free of ice despite being only six hundred miles from the Pole. Around the hull of the ship the heads of walrus bobbed in the water like mooring buoys, dipping their whiskers in the waves, scowling at the ship and its camera-toting passengers. On Moffen Island nearby they lay hauled out on the gravel, their brown bodies catching the sun, like swollen hessian sacks. They had no preference for lying on their fronts or their backs, but lay rolled at every angle. As the ship approached some of them righted themselves and dashed for the water, their bodies rippling with blubber.

The ship trailed along the north coast. Through binoculars I saw the sites where trappers had built their huts, strung out along the northern beaches like pearls in a necklace of isolation. I had read stories written by the men and women who had lived in them; of winters spent in wonder at the beauty of the polar night, the aurora borealis, the stillness and peace that comes from silence. But there are stories too of madness, suicide, individuals broken by their solitude who never regained strength or confidence after enduring the darkness. There is a tale of a hunter living in a hut with his wife who was eight months pregnant. He went out to set his traps, the drift ice blew into the fjord and he could not get back. When he returned to the hut in the spring, several months later, his wife was nursing a healthy baby but had lost her wits. Through fear of the bears, the darkness, her loneliness and isolation, she had cut herself adrift into a psychosis more terrible and unrelenting than any Arctic winter.

More mountains, more glaciers, and for each cape and ice-locked bay I imagined how many untold episodes of bravery and narrow survival had taken place there among the hunters, trappers and whalers. But the coastline was silent under the ceaseless glare of the sun. The sea was clear all the way to Nordaustland where an ice-cap rose from the shore in a great dome. If Fotherby and Baffin had come that year, I thought, they could have reached it with ease. Global warming had done its work here, too. The ship skirted the peninsula of Reinsdyrflya, the scene of their reindeer hunt, and turned around a headland. I had reached 80° north. The Alaskan coast was now closer than London, and there was no more land between myself and the North Pole. I really had reached the edge of Arctic Europe.

And now it was time to turn back, towards Lapland.

*

Winters on Spitsbergen were feared as bringing almost certain death from bears, cold and scurvy. A gunner in the Danish navy called Jón Ólafsson, an Icelander from the Westfjords, wrote about his tour of duty in the north between the years 1615 and 1619. His vessel was based largely off the Finnmark coast in Lapland, but his duties took him frequently up to Svalbard too. He took it for granted that the island was joined to Greenland, and was therefore owned by the Danes. Only the Dutch, he said, refute this and call it 'Spitz Bergen'. He described the monstrous mountains, the night-less days, and the continuous roar of landslides as the summer thaw liberated rubble and ice from the glaciers and mountainsides. He himself contracted scurvy; his skin erupted in boils, and his teeth fell out. He nursed himself back to health, he said, by rubbing his raw gums with salt and tobacco ash until they bled.

In the book he tells the story of an Englishman who lived through a winter alone for a wager of 100 dollars. The man spent the time in one room, singing, playing the viol, writing poems (one reaching 100 stanzas, which he memorised), and reading the Bible. When he tired of that he made heel pieces for black wooden shoes, and filled a whole barrel by the spring. In July his colleagues arrived to find him singing one of his own poems, with three dead polar bears around the house, lying where he had shot them.

The Dutch too took their share of Arctic wintering. Seven men abandoned in 1634-35 were besieged by bears and paralysed by scurvy. In the end they did not even have the strength to raise their guns. They diligently kept up their journals as one by one their bodies succumbed to crippling pains in the loins and belly, 'one did spit blood, and another was afflicted with the bloody flux [dysentery]...' In the spring they were found dead, their bodies frozen solid and their faces twisted in expressions of agony.

The greatest contribution to the literature on the subject was written by an Englishman called Edward Pellham. He was a gunner's mate who with seven others was abandoned one summer by his captain at the end of the whaling season. The weather had turned against the fleet while Pellham and the others were out hunting in Bell Sound, and they had been left behind. His book, *Gods Power and Providence in the preservation of eight Men in Greenland, nine Moneths and twelve Dayes*, published in London in 1631, is an encomium to the beneficence of the God who delivered them.

He begins by describing how the Muscovy Company had been so keen to have permanent settlers on the islands that they had arranged for the liberation of criminals who had been sentenced to death in exchange for spending one winter there. On arriving in Spitsbergen the criminals had been so frightened by the prospect that they chose instead to return to England and face death. Pellham and the others had no such choice. When they realised that they were abandoned without clothes, a house, or sufficient ammunition to protect themselves they stood on the beach in a numbed silence. They said that together they faced death, and from their despair rose hope. Pellham explains that, 'it pleased God to give us Hearts like Men… for the resisting of that Monster of Desperation'. They began to insulate their tent as best they could, placing a smaller lining inside it. They made needles of whalebone and mended their clothes with unravelled rope-yarn. When darkness fell in October and the sea froze they were plagued with visions of their wives and children at home hearing the news of their deaths. Again, God delivered them of these thoughts and showed them the best means of preservation. They restricted themselves to one meal a day, and fasted on Wednesdays and Fridays. The only food they allowed themselves to gnaw on indiscriminately were pieces of blubber rind, 'and these mouldie too… a very loathsome meate, the Scraps of the Fat of the Whale, which are flung away after the Oyle is gotten out of it.' Sometimes they managed to bring down a reindeer, which was cause for great celebration, and throughout the winter they were threatened by the bears: 'twas a measuring cast which should bee eaten first, Wee or the Beares… they had as good hopes to devour us, as wee to kill them'. When their ammunition was all gone they were reduced to lancing the bears with the pikes they used to cull walrus.

The cold stung their flesh and raised it in blisters, their breath itself froze before it left their mouths, and touching any metal object would burn like a flame and pull their skin away in pieces. For the month of December they lost even the dimmest of glows on the horizon, and they feared the end was close. In January they roasted the last of their reindeer meat and were at the end of their provisions, but God sent them a she-bear and her cub which sustained them.

On 25 May two ships from Hull sailed into Bell Sound. The crew rowed ashore and approached the tent with care, expecting to find only frozen bodies shredded by bears and foxes. They were overjoyed to find Pellham and his men inside, praying in preparation for a walrus hunt.

*

The *Nordstjernen* called in at the research village of Ny Ålesund, where scientists from all over Europe studying the rocks, the bears, the ice and the sea live in an international Arctic utopia amidst magnificent glacial scenery. Each day they suit up against the cold, and carrying rifles to protect themselves against the bears, set out on foot, in zodiacs and on snowmobiles into the wilderness around the bay to collect samples. The village itself was grouped around a central hall, run by the Norwegians, where the scientists sat together every mealtime to talk about their work. I had just enough time to call in at the British base run by the National Environmental Research Council. The base commander, Nick Cox, made me very welcome and treated me to a very English cup of tea. There had been a dead whale washed up a few miles down the coast and a congregation of bears had assembled to feast on it. 'Once in a lifetime this happens here,' he said. 'It would be wonderful for you to see it. Are you sure you can't stay on?' But the *Nordstjernen* was due to leave in two hours time and, kicking myself, I explained that I could not afford another ticket back to Norway.

I contented myself instead with sitting in the cafeteria, chatting to him and some of the other scientists about the work that takes place there, one of the most northerly research stations in the world.

The obvious change they pointed out was that the ice in the glaciers around them was retreating. But more worrying was that the area of nearby Arctic Ocean that freezes over each winter was diminishing each year. That has implications for sea level, but also for a property of the earth's surface known as 'albedo'. A climatologist explained it for me. 'A perfect mirror has an albedo of 1.0,' he said. 'The warming trend we are seeing now has begun to drive itself because ice has an albedo of 0.8 but sea water has an albedo of only 0.07, so open sea absorbs about ten times more solar energy than ice.' This trend, a positive feedback cycle, could eventually lead to a 'tipping point' when a new and unpredictable balance will have to be found in the earth's climate.

Another problem is that the permafrost in the Arctic is actually an excellent store of the greenhouse gas CO_2. There are billions of tonnes of it locked up in frozen earth which are being released as that earth melts, forming another positive feedback cycle as the newly released CO_2 itself retains more of the sun's energy.

One of the scientists pointed out one of the peaks behind the settlement, Mount Zeppelin. The Norwegians and Swedes had built a state-of-the-art air sampling laboratory up near the summit. 'People estimate that at the beginning of the Industrial Revolution, in the early nineteenth century, CO_2 was present in the world's atmosphere at about 290 parts per million,' he explained. 'Fifteen years ago the samples they took up there found the figure had risen to about 350. Now it's apparently reached 380. It is rising at a rate of more than three parts per million per year, and that figure too is climbing. No one knows where it will all end, or what effects that will have on our climate. There are no precedents for this kind of rise in CO_2 levels.'

'And it's not just CO_2,' broke in another. 'Methane measurements they take up there are climbing too, and methane is much more dangerous as a greenhouse gas than CO_2.'

'Where is the methane coming from?' I asked.

'All sorts of places, but it's mainly being produced by bacteria in the soil, which are working harder themselves as the earth warms up.'

It did not sound like there was very much to be optimistic about. I asked if they ever became disheartened or depressed about the discoveries they were making. There was an uncomfortable silence. 'That's not really what our job is about,' said one of them, finally. 'We just report the facts and it's up to governments and individuals to listen to those facts or not. This might be a critical time when we might still have a chance to turn things around. The lack of will out there to change, now that's the thing that is depressing.'

※

Before leaving Svalbard the ship made a final call to the Russian settlement of Barentsburg. The International Treaty of Svalbard gave sovereignty of the islands to Norway, but allows any other country's citizens to reside and mine there. The Russians are the only ones to take the Norwegians up on the offer, and their town has eight hundred people. It stands on a steep siding, catching the sun and looking across a bay to a mass of peaks and arêtes in a more beautiful situation than the overshadowed valley of Longyearbyen. One of the harbour buildings was daubed with a message in letters three feet high; a reminder of *glasnost*: 'ВАС ПРИВЕТСТВУЕТ БАРЕНЦБУРГ – 1931-1991'. ('Greetings from Barentsburg – 1931-1991.') In the town centre stout functional communist architecture was arranged around a frowning bust of Lenin. The streets were wide and the windows polished, pot plants lined the windowsills of homes that, though beginning to crumble, were well cared-for. Since the collapse of the Soviet Union the people there had worked for months on end without pay, but there was a longhouse with pigs and cows, and a greenhouse for vegetables. As if the collapse of Soviet communism was not enough of a blow to the community, a few years later a plane had crashed killing over a hundred of the inhabitants. Soon afterwards a mineshaft exploded killing thirty two of their men.

Thick coal-dust swirled in the streets, blackening the walls, powdering my nose and mouth with soot and lying in the creases of my skin. Only the embassy was gleaming. In the museum a world map filled a whole wall, dominated by the former Soviet Empire. Though the Russian Mafia has moved into Barentsburg the people I met were managing to carry on, and some were even doing well. Many had hard currency accounts over the mountain at the Norwegian bank in Longyearbyen, and they still had their pride.

My last night in the High Arctic was spent at a culture show in the town. Three women and two men sang songs from all over the former Soviet Union for the assembled audience of cruise passengers. A hostess explained in faultless English that though there were Russians, Ukrainians, and Kazakhs in their community, they were all brothers and sisters of the Soviet Union. A young classically trained ballerina spun across the stage, and the men played balalaikas and drums. The songs were linked by the hostess' declarations: 'we want to give our hearts to you,' and, 'can you feel the love we have?' The talent among the tiny community was immense, and hidden in their performance there seemed to be a message: 'Yes we are poor, yes our town is falling down, but we are *proud* and *able* and we do not need your sympathy. We need your money.'

A rainbow-coloured sign hung over the culture centre. On it there were scenes of industrial life in the Arctic framing three portraits: two square-jawed miners complete with hard-hats and chains stood by a busty female worker, her hair tied up in a red bandanna. They looked fierce, and their eyes shone with the certainty of Soviet destiny.

*

The last phase of the exploration of Spitsbergen was not carried out by the Dutch, or the English, or the Danes or even the Basques. It was carried out by the Russians.

The whaling industry had all but collapsed by 1700, and though whalers would return in the nineteenth century when their ships and technology improved, for a while the islands lay empty. In the first decades of the eighteenth century, as Peter the Great's reforms forced Russia into the orbit of Europe, Siberian trappers arrived on Spitsbergen. They called themselves *Pomors*, meaning 'those that came by sea'. They were hardy men used to life in the Siberian forests, unintimidated by bears and unafraid of the merciless winters. They lived there for years on end, trapping the bears and the Arctic foxes and shooting the reindeer. One Russian trapper lived for thirty-six years on Bell Sound, where Pellham had narrowly survived his nine months and twelve days. The only legacy that these men left on the islands are solitary and occasional Orthodox iron crosses, propped up by rocks on the beaches and headlands.

They did not confine themselves to the fjords of the northern and western shores. They spread out across the whole archipelago, their solitary personalities and their search for animals driving them farther and farther away from one another. They built huts of driftwood on the remotest and iciest islands to the north and the east. A couple of decades after Alexander Selkirk, or 'Robinson Crusoe', returned to civilisation from his rocky island off the Chilean coast, four Pomors underwent a parallel adventure.

On Edgeøya, one of the islands to the east, four Russian trappers were stranded. They survived by scouring the beaches for driftwood to heat their tiny shack, and hunted with arrowheads made of rusty nails pulled from ship's planking. Like the Inuit they lived on raw meat, and drank reindeer and fox blood to counter scurvy. One of their number who refused to drink blood died of the disease. For six years they survived in this way, gathering what they could to survive in the summers and enduring the bitter winters. When eventually they were rescued they were taken back to Chancellor's port of Archangel at the mouth of the river Dvina, and like him were taken overland from there to Moscow.

The simplicity of their lives in the far north had apparently agreed with them. They were not unreservedly happy about being dragged back into the squalor and bustle of Moscow, and had lost their taste for the luxuries of agricultural society. On returning to Archangel the first thing they discovered was that they had all developed an intense dislike of both alcohol and bread.

*

Following the adventures of the Russian Pomors, the great age of discovery in Svalbard could have been said to be dead. But there was one last discovery to be made, a little more recently. In 2004 an English artist by the name of Hartley laid claim to a new island, discovered after the retreat of the glacial ice-cap due to global warming. Hartley claimed the island was not covered by the international treaty that gave Spitsbergen to Norway, allowing them to rename it Svalbard in the first place. He landed on his discovery, placed a tin can with a written declaration in it and built a cairn over the top. In the time-honoured tradition of mariners and explorers from the Vikings of Greenland to the Victorian explorers, he wanted all those who came after him to understand that it now belonged to him.

The Norwegians were not impressed. 'The ice-cap withdrew and uncovered it,' said an official spokeswoman for the Norwegians. 'Anyway we don't consider it big enough to be an island.'

Hartley has named the new island Nymark, meaning 'new land', and at the size of a football pitch, says it is definitely worth fighting for. The last I heard in the news, he had been petitioning the United Nations for recognition as an independent nation.

The northern reaches of Europe may hold out hope for eccentrics and dreamers that there are still discoveries out there worth making.

*

I sailed south. I had been sitting at the stern of the ship for some time, watching Spitsbergen retreat over the horizon. Beside me on the bench sat a Swedish businessman with wet, red-rimmed eyes. He was drunk. I had said very little for over an hour.

'What am I doing with my life?' he had been asking, repeatedly. 'I am thirty-four years old and I am still looking for the perfect woman.' I shrugged and watched the birds trailing the ship.

Norway and Sweden have the highest divorce rates in Europe: over fifty percent of marriages fail. Another couple on the ship, an engineer and a doctor from Kristiansand, adopted me in an attempt to avoid talking to one another. Every evening I would sit at a table with them while they flung barbed comments at one another and smiled sweetly at me. I thought it would not be long until they joined Scandinavia's most modern statistic.

As we lost latitude the sun fell lower in the sky until at midnight it dropped below the northern horizon once more. By the time I reached Norway there was once again a 'night', though it was short and the Barents Sea bled crimson into it. The ship rounded Nordkapp, 'the North Cape' of Scandinavia. It is a stern buttress of rock standing off the Lappish coast, named by Chancellor on his voyage intended for the East Indies. He thought that the North Cape was the furthest extent of the European mainland, but the cliffs are actually situated on an island, Magerøya, and its most northerly point is in truth a low headland a little to the west of the 'North Cape' itself. Nevertheless, the cliffs of the Nordkapp are more impressive than the tiny spit of land, and so it is those cliffs that Europe has chosen for its end.

The ship circled the island and docked at the little port of Honningsvåg on its southern shore. Reaching Lapland meant that I was approaching the end of my journey. After visiting all those islands on the edge of the ocean, it felt strange to walk somewhere that was so firmly part of the continent of Europe. Even Magerøya is connected by road to the mainland now, and though it lies at 71° north and on Norwegian soil, it is as far east as Istanbul. Norway is such a long country that Oslo now lay half way between me and Rome. Being back on continental Europe I suddenly realised that if I had had a car I could have driven there.

Lapland
TOURISM AND THE END
OF EUROPE

✳

IF ALL ROADS lead to Rome, then all roads lead from it. It kept crop-
ping up everywhere I went on my journey. Himilco, the first Phoenician explorer to reach out of the Mediterranean, probably walked
there. Pytheas too would have known it well. The Irish monks and
the Celtic Church eventually had to capitulate to Rome and it is
a toss-up whether the Vikings considered Rome or Jerusalem the
centre of the world. Until the end of the Middle Ages Rome ruled
Western Christendom. By the fifteenth century the great explorers
were not Roman, but were largely Italians nevertheless: Columbus
was Genoese, Cabot was Venetian, and Amerigo Vespucci, the man
who gave his name to America, was Florentine. In the seventeenth
century Italy produced a forerunner of the next great phase in the
history of exploration: tourism. Like so many travellers I had come
across on this journey he was another undauntable clergyman.

Francesco Negri was forty-one years old when he left Italy. He
thought it reprehensible that Italians knew so little of their own
continent, and set out to explore the 'Land of the Midnight Sun'
of which the shelves of the great libraries of Italy were so silent. He
did not know that books on Svalbard and Finnmark were piling
up in the libraries of London, Copenhagen and Amsterdam. He
travelled alone, and in 1663 reached Denmark. Later that year he
made it across the Arctic Circle as far as the Torne River in Swedish Lapland, at 68° north, but was forced back by poor weather.

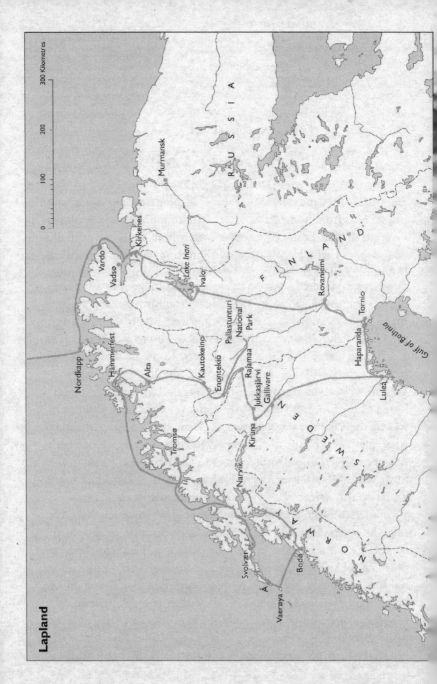

Lapland

He gathered his strength in Stockholm and the following spring he started on the road to Lapland once more. Again the weather deteriorated, but this time he persevered. By the time he reached the North Cape it was winter.

He was not well prepared for his journey, and as the Arctic darkness fell the weather became bitterly cold. The Laplanders he met along the way looked after him and saved his life several times. They must have pitied this ill-prepared Mediterranean priest so far from home. It was not until he approached the North Cape itself that he met someone with whom he could actually converse, in Latin. He described this meeting with the local priest in his account of the journey, written in the form of eight letters to his sponsor of which the final letter deals with Finnmark. On reaching Nordkapp he wrote, 'from the end of the green world': 'Here I am at the North Cape, on the edge of Finnmark, and at the very edge of the world since there are no other inhabited places further north. I am satisfied to have reached this place, and will now return to Denmark and, God willing, to the land of my birth.'

Although his thoughts had turned quickly to home, the landscape of Lapland had taken a firm grip on his imagination, as did the kindness of the Lapp nomads and what he saw as the purity, freedom and simplicity of their lives. In only a few decades Rousseau would resurrect the concept of the 'noble savage' from the Greeks. Negri thought their lives as luxurious as those of the Hyperboreans who lived on in classical myth: 'It is true, the Lapps do not live in palaces, but neither do they need to worry that these might one day fall down on them. With regard to glory and fame they have nothing to fear either, for they have nothing to lose. In all these ways the Lapps are better philosophers than Diogenes, who wanted a whole barrel for himself; for they are happy with even less.'

He had loved the North. For years afterwards he worked on the manuscript of his letters and lobbied the Duke of Tuscany to fund him for another journey to Lapland. In 1698 he died without returning there. Two years later his eight letters were published in Padua under the title of *Viaggio Settentrionale, fatto e descritto,* or, 'Northern Journey, Completed and Described.' Posthumously he had succeeded in his mission; the first book with a reliable description of the northern limits of Europe now stood in the Latin libraries of the continent. The North was no longer the preserve just of whalers, traders, and the navy, but also of independent travellers, who wanted only to see, learn, and travel home again.

After the surge in maritime exploration of the sixteenth and the seventeenth centuries, the flowering of the Enlightenment and the advent of industry brought a new class of explorers towards the edges of the world. Men like Francesco Negri, reaping the benefits of a surge in wealth and leisure, began to arrive singly. They came overland and by sea, clutching satchels of books and yearning to write books of their own. Theirs were not the pilgrimages of the Irish or the emigrations of the Norsemen or the plunder of the merchants and whalers. They did not seek wealth so much as knowledge and new experiences, and in that respect their journeys were perhaps more akin to those undertaken by the Greeks. The history of exploration had, in a sense, come full circle. But something new had been created by the abundance of wealth and the awakening of curiosity in Europe: tourism. It is not without its critics, but by seeking to preserve the customs and landscape of the lands that it visits, at least in some form, while generating an income for local people, tourism has been a welcome arrival. New ways of nurturing it are being developed all over the North.

*

I hitched a lift to the end of Europe. A Saami family driving a spacious Land Cruiser dropped me off. 'Saami' is the name preferred by the ethnic Lapp people of the northern Finland, Sweden, Norway and Russia. 'Lapp' is reckoned an insulting term, long used by southern Scandinavians in their exploitation of their northern neighbours. This family had been on their way to visit relatives in Skarvsvåg, a small fishing village near the cliffs of the North Cape and one of the most northerly settlements in the world. The mother, father and little boy were all slight figures, with pale skin and Asiatic folds above the canthus of their eyes. The father, Nils, produced a wedding photograph from the glove box of their car to illustrate traditional Saami dress for me. In the photograph his wife wore a headdress and gown beaded in rainbows of colours and criss-crossed with elaborate brocades. He too had worn stunning formal dress: a multi-coloured hat with four points, each one stuffed to defy gravity, and slippers of reindeer skin with pointed toes. He asked me if it was true that Scotsmen wore skirts to their weddings and I said that it was, but disappointed him by being unable to produce a photo to prove it. As we drove along they told me all about the ceremony, now fifteen years ago, and took me twenty miles out of their way so that I would not need to walk. At the Nordkapp I climbed out of the car, thanked them, and was promptly confronted by a tollbooth and someone asking me for money. It was the first time in my whole journey that I had been asked to pay to see a part of the landscape.

'What, I have to pay to get to see the cliffs?' I asked, a little incredulously.

'Yeah, sorry.' The man in the booth was a bored college student, probably reaching the end of his three-month summer job. It had been a long season. Folded on the counter in front of him was a copy of Kierkegaard's *Either/Or*, in English.

'How much?' I asked.

If I was surprised by being asked for money, I was amazed by how much he was going to charge me.

'Did you hitch all the way here?' he asked.

'Yes,' I lied.

'Well… don't tell anyone, but I guess you can go in for free.'

Norwegian, Finnish, Swedish and Russian Lapland unravelled behind me in seemingly endless plains of tundra. The climate was still too Arctic for trees to grow, and reindeer grazed among the stunted grasses and the mosses that grew between the rocks. The Barents Sea lay before me, laminated in a thousand shades of blue. It was impossible to tell where the horizon welded the sea to the sky. On the headland in the middle of this magnificent open wilderness stood a monument to tourism and the new economy of the North; the Nordkapp Visitor Centre. On the ground all around it visitors had spelled out messages in the rocks, declaring their undying love for absent partners or celebrating their visit to Europe's end.

There was no soil to pitch my tent, but I weighed the edges with boulders and sat down to watch the sunset. A busload of men and women in formal evening wear pulled up to the car park. In surreal succession they stepped off the bus and walked past me, nodding hello and pulling their dinner jackets and evening gowns tight against the cold wind. I followed them into the private function, and for an hour or two mingled with the rich and beautiful people of northern Norway. Waitresses served me glasses of champagne. I was dressed in waterproof clothes and hiking boots, spattered all over with the glacial mud of Svalbard, but no one gave me a second glance. The Norwegians are a tolerant people. I never did find out what the function was for.

Unlike the other places I had visited so far, Lapland was never 'discovered' by an explorer and then reported back to a literate southern culture; it was always known to the peoples who lived at its southern limits. There is some evidence that the Saami people originally lived much further south in the Scandinavian peninsula before the great Germanic migrations of the fourth, fifth, and sixth centuries pushed them into 'Lapland'. The word 'Lapp' itself is thought to stem from a Finno-Ugric root meaning 'peripheral'. Tacitus called them 'Finns' and described how they made arrowheads from bones. Procopius in the sixth century called them 'Scridfinns', and said, 'they wear only skins sewn with sinew, and the women don't breastfeed, the babies eating only fresh marrow.' In the eighth century a Langobard called Diaconus wrote that in the far north lived the 'Scritobini' who chased animals by bouncing on pieces of bent wood, an early allusion to skiing.

By the rise of the Viking Age they were subjected to heavy taxation and exploitation by the Norsemen. Ohthere, a Viking from northern Norway, sailed to the court of Alfred the Great and described his ruthless hunting and tax-collecting sprees along the Finnmark coast as far as modern Russia. Alfred was so impressed with Ohthere's descriptions that he wrote them into his then on-going translation of Orosius' 'History of the World'. Alfred thought Orosius' fifth-century account of the northern regions of Europe so suspect that he deleted a chapter and inserted the Norseman's description. His amended chapter is now in the British Museum, in Alfred's own handwriting.

The sagas, too, talk of journeys into Lapland and describe the Saami, whom the Vikings considered shamans and sorcerers who were only there to be taxed. The tradition of persecuting them continued throughout the Middle Ages right up until modern times. In turn the Russians, then the Swedes, then the Norwegians, would make incursions into Lapland and redraw their national boundaries. Until fairly recently the Saami carried on exactly as they always had done, unconcerned by the imaginary lines invented in the courts and parliaments of the south, but carried on paying tributes in pelts and fish whenever forced to by the southern armies or their mercenaries. 'Lapland' is more a concept than a country with borders, and although the Saami people have been denied a state of their own by their neighbours it is impossible to compare them as a nation with, say, the Kurds or Tibetans. There are only about 80,000 of them divided between the four countries, half of that number living in Norway. They are now outnumbered twenty to one in their homeland by Scandinavians from the south. As the Danes had done in Greenland the Norwegians initially tried to wipe out their culture; until 1940 it was forbidden for non-Norwegian speakers to buy or lease land. More recently the Norwegians have been trying to make amends. Since 1989 the Saami have had their own parliament, in Karasjok, and now enjoy special privileges and unique passports allowing them greater freedom of movement.

Historically they have always been nomads, migrating with their herds of reindeer from the tundra to the coast and back again as the seasons come and go. Now they herd reindeer with helicopters, and with their new passports they can move in and out of Russia with much greater ease than other Scandinavians. A 'Finnmark Law' has recently been passed in Norway, giving the Saami parliament and the Finnmark administrative council joint responsibility for the land. Most of their area is just open tundra, but together they control 98 per cent of the land in Finnmark. Saami people now have their own TV news and newspapers, their own college in Kautokeino and their own theatre, the Beiwaš, based between Norway and Finland. As I had seen with the Greenlanders, their faith in themselves, and in their own identity, is growing.

*

The morning was dull and overcast, and the first chill of autumn shivered in the air. A busload of retired North Americans pulled into the empty car park. Only a few hours earlier the dignitaries had finally left and now the centre opened up again to receive the tour buses and camper vans that arrived daily from all over Europe. While they were looking around the centre I asked the driver of the first tour bus whether I could hitch a lift. He asked the tour guide, who in turn put it to the group, who had a vote. 'Sure you can come with us!' called out one of the elderly ladies, who wore a pink baseball cap and a matching tracksuit.

Every few kilometres across the tundra plateau the bus stopped to wait for groups of reindeer to get off the road. Nearer the town it pulled up at a roadside Saami tent erected for our benefit, where a man in traditional dress stood by his reindeer waiting to be photographed. The bus driver was Saami and stood by the bus while we tourists filed out, chuckling to himself and shaking his head.

The ports of the northern coast of Norway have been nourished for over a century by the coastal ships that carry cruise passengers and budget tourists, cargo and news between Bergen in the south and Kirkenes in the far north-east at the Russian frontier. The first 'coastal steamer' made the journey in 1893, and though there was a break during the German occupation, ships have called at each of the ports on the route regularly ever since. The villages are linked by air now too, but it is the *Hurtigrute*, the Norwegian name for the 'Express Route', that keeps them alive. In Honningsvåg I waved goodbye to the busload of Americans and climbed on board. This ship was sailing east, towards Russia.

The cliffs of Finnmark slid gently by. Snow clung to the cracks in the rock, obscured from time to time by drifting banks of fog. It started to rain, and then the rain turned to sleet. The ship was the *Nordlys*, 'the Northern Lights'. It was huge and modern, with several decks and none of the comfort or charm of the *Nordstjernen* that had brought me down from Svalbard. It was so much like a hotel that at first I could not even find the way out onto deck. Apparently the passengers preferred to crowd against the windows in the 'viewing lounge,' and I had the deck to myself. There were cabins for the paying cruise passengers, and a single space set aside for people to doss down in. I heard rumours that the owners wanted to spruce up their image, and were considering making it compulsory to book a cabin. Some of the cruise passengers had complained, it was said, at the intrusion of scruffier passengers into their holiday. It remained to be seen whether Norwegian tolerance and egalitarianism would win out over the tourist dollar.

The *Nordlys* docked at a couple more ports on the way east: clusters of bright houses backed by the sombre grey of the cliffs and the tundra. Hardy men in oilskins stood out on the wharves handling cargo, squinting against the sleet and the wind. After a particularly barren stretch of coastline the ship drew into the ancient port of Vardø.

Vardø, or 'Wardhouse,' recurs again and again throughout the history of Lapland. It is a settlement on a small island flung out into the Barents Sea, lying as far to the north as the Arctic coast of Alaska, and as far east as Cairo. It was here that Chancellor rebuilt his ship, to here that Barents' crew dragged themselves out of the frozen hell of Novaya Zemlya, and from here that the Danish navy thrust north to Spitsbergen against the Dutch and English whalers. It is less of a tourist destination than the North Cape, but for centuries it was the principal seat of power in Lapland.

Fishing boats bobbed in the harbour, slowly being covered in a layer of slush. Crowded around them were wooden houses, their paint chipped and peeling, and stacks upon stacks of fish crates. My breath turned to fog in the cold air. The island is shaped like the letter 'H', and the little town curled itself around the thin isthmus. A road led up the hill to the fourteenth-century Vardøhus Festning, 'the Fortress of Wardhouse'. I turned away from the port and climbed my way up to it.

Strung out towards the Arctic, isolated by its climate, the mediaeval Norse wanted to plant a flag at what they saw as the northeastern limit of their domain. But there was more to it than flag waving. When Eirik the Priest-hater was on the throne of Norway the Russians were advancing into the Kola Peninsula and incursions into Finnmark were feared. The first fortress was built to provide a base for defence against these Russians and was completed by Eirik's brother, Håkon V Magnusson. There was another advantage to garrisoning the far north; it made persecuting the Saami a bit easier. St Olaf's Church (that was marked so clearly on Johann Ruysch's map of 1508) was built to Christianise them. Though a border treaty of 1326 brought peace between Russia and Norway, both countries continued relentlessly to tax the indigenous people. After the union of Denmark and Norway (at the end of the fourteenth century) and the ravages of the mediaeval plague years the monarchy lost interest in the far north. But a couple of centuries later, when Greenland fell silent, the more accessible furs and walrus tusks of Lapland became important once again. King Christian IV visited Vardø in 1599, and in 1608 he wrote to its governor, reminding him to be merciless in collecting taxes from the Saami. He writes that it is good to burn a few for witchcraft every year, so as to keep them dispirited; 'Lappish folk by nature and custom are inclined to magic,' he wrote. 'Thou shalt be careful to see that those who are convicted of using magic, after judgement held and sentence pronounced, shall be put to death without mercy.'

Thanks to Jón Ólafsson, the Icelandic gunner who described his voyages with the Danish navy in the waters around Spitsbergen, there is a record of a visit to Vardø around this time. Ólafsson had been chasing pirates around the Kola Peninsula and back into Russia when he docked at its harbour, which he said was dominated by a 'huge castle' surrounded by cannons. He and the other men were given lodging inside, and spent a few days enjoying the hospitality of the last outpost of Danish rule. It was by now seventy years since Chancellor had met Scots merchants there, but it seemed that the Scots still held positions of influence: 'At the time when we came thither on this journey, a nobleman called Hans, of Scots extraction, was governor there... He was eccentric and very unaccountable in his ways, especially when in his cups.'

The Scotsman was John Cunningham, an admiral in the Danish navy who had served under Christian IV. With an English pilot named Hall he had 'rediscovered' Greenland for the Danes in 1605. As a reward he had been made commander of the fortress, ruler of Finnmark, and given the freedom to extract taxes from the Saami who lived there. It was a bleak coastline, a long way from Scotland. I wondered if he was glad to be living so far from his own country, if his eccentricity demanded the space and freedom of Finnmark to run free, or if he had stayed only for the money and power that he wielded there.

*

The present Kommandant fed me caviar from chipped china plates. His house was over two hundred and fifty years old, a relatively modern addition built into the defences of the fortress itself. It was hardly the 'huge castle' that Jón Ólafsson had reported. Cracked beams of ship's timber framed the low ceilings, a hidden clock chimed with infinite patience, and the floors smelled of furniture polish. Portraits representing four centuries of long-gone commanders stared out from the yellowing walls. None of them looked as if they had been happy men.

He had pink cheeks and white hair, and he shuffled between the ancient rooms wearing wool slippers with which he polished the floor. He led me through a few of his favourite pictures, and when he reached two etchings of Nelson's fleet his eyes began to shine. He told me the old story of Nelson's death, that he was pickled in brandy after Trafalgar and buried three months later. When he said the date, 21 October, he looked up to see if I would correct him, but Nelson was his hero, not mine. I did know that Nelson had crippled the Danish fleet, and perhaps that was the secret of the Kommandant's admiration. He was a true Norwegian patriot, and liked to read about the Danish getting their comeuppance.

He was semi-retired; Vardøhus was a peaceful posting as a reward for good service. The right to gather gull eggs on a nearby island was one of his few remaining privileges; he no longer burned Lapps every year or collected any taxes. Surveillance of the enemy was now the job of the dish antennae on the hilltops behind the town, and the cannons were no longer fired at Russian pirates. They still, however, needed to be polished, and every so often to be given a new coat of paint.

'Hans Könning, John Cunningham, Hans Könning,' he muttered, leading me through to the library. From a high shelf he brought down a rough-typed booklet listing each of the Kommandants since the days of Håkon V. In 1490 I read that Diederik Pining, the Hansa pirate sent to guard Icelandic waters against the English in the days of Richard III, had been in command there. For

1619 he found the entry. He translated for me, and I took some notes:

> John Cunningham; known as Hans Kønning since arriving in Denmark from Scotland.
>
> 1622; lived in Bergen although still in control of Finnmark.
>
> 1625 – married Ellen Klauslatter Hundemark in Bodøgard. She remained living there or in Vardøhus at times.
>
> 1651 died. Buried in Sjaelland

Cunningham's rule had bridged the old and the new era of exploration of the North. The first tourist of Lapland had missed him by thirteen years. The brief paragraph threw no more light over the Icelander's description: 'he was eccentric and unaccountable in his ways, especially when in his cups'. The Kommandant smiled in apology, and offered me a drink.

Later the rain on the turf roof slowed to a stop. Outside the sky cleared to the pellucid blue of a Nordic eye. I walked around the tops of the octagonal walls of the fortress, bouncing my feet on the grass and running my fingers over the cannons. They were painted a glossy black and grew warm and sticky in the thin sunlight.

✳

In Vardø I found out that an ancient legend, concerning the irreconcilability of northern and southern peoples, was false.

Before time began there was only the Ocean. When first the waters were divided from the earth, the sisters of Ocean, the Great Rivers, were born. Of these the Nile was the greatest.

The Nile's majesty was known not only for its immensity, but also for its unusual behaviour. Alone of all rivers it rose in summer and fell in winter. Eudoxus of Cnidus, a contemporary of Pytheas and Alexander the Great, reasoned that it must therefore have its source in that alien world of the Antichthon, where everything known and beloved of mankind occurred in its opposite: trees grew downwards, rain fell upwards, and sunlight itself was black as night. Its legend was part of the Greek conviction that the universe must always be in balance. As the Antichthon by necessity lay across a stretch of Ocean, the Nile was thought to traverse an underwater channel from the Other World before popping up in the deserts of Africa. Some disagreed: Ptolemy thought that it arose in a range of hidden mountains with magical properties which he called the Mountains of the Moon, a name later adopted by nineteenth-century explorers of Uganda. When Alexander found crocodiles on the Indus river he thought that the riddle of the Nile had been solved; it source was evidently in India. From India the Antichthon itself could even be seen; its northernmost tip was a headland called Taprobane, now known as Sri Lanka. There lived the Antichthones, a dark-skinned and barbarous people who lived perpetually roasted by the sun. 'It is an alien world,' it was said, 'We cannot live with them, and they cannot live with us.'

In Vardø I met members of Norway's most northerly refugee population: a community of Tamils. Norwegian immigration policy, designed to prevent the growth of ghettos in the cities of the south, disperses asylum seekers and refugees throughout the country. The Tamils had been living in Lapland for over a decade, and for most of them, it had proven a promised land. It had not been easy. Vardø's climate is harsh even by Scandinavian standards, and the Norwegians, though welcoming, can be taciturn and stubbornly reserved. Torn between maintaining the strength of their own community and trying to integrate into Norwegian society some of the refugees have succumbed to drink, depression or neurosis. Most have not. That afternoon in Vardø I walked down the street behind two young Tamil girls on their way home from school. They were chatting with a Norwegian friend, and all three were wearing the Norwegian national dress.

Perhaps the Hyperboreans and the Antichthones can live together after all.

✳

The next day I sailed south to Kirkenes and the Russian border. The town of Kirkenes is distinguished for its iron mines, its proximity to Russia, and the savaging it received under German occupation during the Second World War. The Allies' only supply route to Moscow was to send ships in convoy around Nordkapp and into Murmansk. Hitler suspected that they would try to invade Norway, not France, and his intelligence told him British commandos were busy in Shetland. The long Norwegian coastline with its deep fjords provided refuge for his U-boats, and, when the time was right, might allow an easy route for the invasion of Britain.

By 1944 over thirty thousand German soldiers were posted in Kirkenes. The Soviets carried out over three hundred bombing raids there before it was liberated in October of that year. To add insult to the already considerable injury, the retreating Germans burned whatever buildings remained standing. Consequently its architecture is uninspiring.

In Kirkenes, the atmosphere was heavy with the presence of the Russian border, less than three miles away. Rusting vessels collapsed in the harbour, their home port written on their sides in dirty white: Мурманск, 'Murmansk'. The goods in the town's shops were priced in kroner and in roubles. Wealthy Russians regularly crossed back and forth to buy Western consumer goods. They were immediately recognisable among the Norwegians and the Saami, their clothes cut in the Western fashions of two decades past, their high cheekbones and sharp features marking them out from the locals. There was growing unease in Kirkenes about the numbers of Russians using it as a gateway to the West. I was told there that Norwegian brothels were now staffed entirely by Russian girls, and old Norwegian bachelors regularly took young Russian wives. Norwegian law grants them full citizenship if they stay married for three years, and with the divorce rate as high as it is these marriages of convenience were often as successful as more traditional unions.

In the tourist office I met a new Norwegian who had married for love. He worked behind the counter:

'Snakke du engelsk?' I asked him, 'Do you speak English?'

'Yep, sure I do, where ya from?'

'Scotland.'

'I thought so,' he said. 'I can usually tell. I'm from the States.'

He told me how he had visited Norway one summer, and had never managed to leave again. He had married a Norwegian woman, and for three years had been living in Kirkenes.

He looked out of the window and his eyes misted over for a moment. 'Yep, love sure can take you to the strangest places,' he said finally. 'Anyway, how can I help you?'

'I'm wondering where I should go to see some of the landscape around here. Are there any paths or trails to the border?'

'I know exactly where you should go,' he said, and his face unfolded into a generous smile. 'And you're gonna love it!' He took out a map, and began to show me how I could walk down the Pasvik valley through the forest alongside the frontier. He gave me a pamphlet called 'Conduct and Travel at the Norwegian-Russian Border'. 'That's just to stop you getting into trouble,' he said.

'What kind of trouble could I get into?'

'Don't go up to the Russian border fence if you find it, don't try to speak or wave to anyone you see on the other side,' he replied. 'You know, the usual stuff.'

'Anything else?'

'Have you got a camera?' he asked.

'Yes.'

'Zoom lens?'

'Yes.'

'Well… just keep it out of sight. And don't forget to keep an eye out for the bears.'

*

The bus from Kirkenes down the Pasvik Valley took nearly three hours, stopping at every house to deliver mail, and going down all the side roads to take children back from school. Next to me sat an old Saami woman with a densely lined face and hair tied in braids, wrapped back over her head and held in place with a multicoloured Saami hat. The driver was jovial, smiling all the way, cracking jokes with the children and letting them post some of the letters for him. At one point we drove down a long track to drop a little girl at a homestead. She lived in a large wooden house in a clearing with some vegetable patches, a tractor, dogs and outhouses, with the Russian border visible through the trees across the river. Bicycles were left unlocked at the end of tracks leading off into the forest. Skis stood beside them, waiting for the day when the snows returned, which would not be long now. I felt as if I was entering a world sustained by trees, where unbroken forest extended hundreds of miles. There was a deep sense of peace there, as if the trees themselves gave energy and life to the air.

At the end of the road I got out to walk further in the forest. The whole valley was an intimation of what was to come as I travelled deeper into Lapland: low rolling landscape, intricate networks of silvered lakes and rivers, and endless, evergreen forest. There was a luxuriance of birch, spruce and Scots pine. The forest was dense and comforting, but the trees were widely spaced enough that walking among them was a pleasure. After the sterile sea-air of Svalbard and Finnmark the smell of the moss and the earth was delicious.

*

A voice came to him in a vision: 'Go into an unpopulated, inaccessible country, into a thirsty land, where no man yet lived.'

And so Tryphon, the apostle of Lapland, walked north and west, through the forestlands of Karelia. He left his home in Russia and walked into Sweden. There were no fences in the forest then, in the sixteenth century, no signposts or marks on the earth, and the Finnish nation was still four centuries short of independence. Near the Pasvik valley he stopped, and built a monastery.

The area was a no man's land, and for a few decades he worked among the Saami and the few Finns who lived along the rivers that seeped out of the lakelands to the south. He was living there when Richard Chancellor swept past, on his way to the Dvina and the palaces of Moscow. He was still living there when the Swedes arrived, marching overland, consolidating their control over the region when they heard that the English and the Dutch were sailing in northern waters to catch whales. Tryphon was an Orthodox Christian, and a Russian, so the Swedes killed him. He was one of the first to see the worth in the land, but more were to come.

Only a few years after Tryphon was killed, two men pushed through the swamps from the Baltic to the Barents Sea. They returned to Stockholm for an audience with King Karl IX, to tell him the news that they had wandered in his realm all the way to its furthest point, and they deemed the limit of Sweden to be the Nordkapp itself.

Swedish interest grew; travellers such as Negri were beginning to make the journey north, and the Swedes realised they knew less about the limits of their own country than these tourists. In 1673 another foreigner, a Strasbourg man named Scheffer, published his *Lapponia*, an exploration and discussion in Latin of what was currently known of the northern regions. Elsewhere in Europe interest in Lapland was also on the rise; only a year after Scheffer's book was published it was translated into English by an undergraduate of Christ Church College, Oxford (the translator, Acton Cremer, was set the task as a punishment for 'improperly courting a mistress').

Europe was changing. The Treaty of Westphalia in 1648 had ended the Thirty Years' War and the power of the papacy. In England the Civil War was over and the Cavaliers, based in Oxford, defeated. It was in Cambridge that the next English revolution would begin, and unlike the Civil War, it would send shockwaves through the whole of Europe. Revolutions in thought have no respect for borders.

Isaac Newton was eighteen years old when he entered Trinity College, Cambridge. For four years he immersed himself in the works of the pioneers of the new Science. Cambridge still taught a strict diet of Aristotle, but Newton read promiscuously. Descartes, Kepler, Boyle, Copernicus and Galileo were among his favourites. In the summer of 1665 the Black Death reached England and the university closed. Isaac returned to his mother's home in Lincolnshire, which may or may not have had an apple tree in the garden, and for two years stayed there in quarantine, thinking. When he emerged he had single-handedly redefined physics, and brought order to a world of apparent chaos.

He had invented calculus, years before Leibnitz. He had proved that white light was composed of a spectrum of colours, and had set the foundations for the invention of the reflecting telescope. He had formulated his three laws of motion, and explained the movements of the planets, comets, moon and tides. He wrote his laws concerning gravitation. It would be another twenty years before he would finally set down his vision in his *magnum opus*, *Philosophiae naturalis principia mathematica*, but the intelligentsia of Cambridge, London and the rest of Europe were astonished. In 1669, at just 27 years old, he was elected Professor of Mathematics of Trinity College.

Newton represented a new breed of scholar, a man who refused to take knowledge on trust. Though he had a strong Christian faith he felt it his duty to uncover God's secrets, and he was prepared to turn the whole world into his laboratory. There were many others with a similar attitude, and for an increasing number of them throughout the seventeenth and eighteenth centuries that laboratory would be Lapland.

*

I walked between borders born of a quite different kind of revolution, the one pioneered by Lenin. The Finnish border lay only a few kilometres away. In contrast to the Russian fence it had open gateways built into it, though you were supposed to tell the authorities before you went through them. The Scandinavian governments see no reason to fight over their borders any more. They have done too much fighting in the past. Finland has swapped back and forth between Russia and Sweden for centuries, persecuted and exploited by both. It was Czar Alexander who took Finland from the Swedes during the Napoleonic Wars. For a century the Finns were Russian, until in 1917 the November Revolution reignited their nationalist sensibilities. The Bolsheviks had barely taken their seats in the Winter Palace of Petrograd when the Finns declared their independence. Immediately there was civil war between German- and Russian-backed Finnish nationalists, but the country itself survived united. For the first time in their history the Finns lived in their own nation-state. They stayed on friendlier terms with the Swedes, now that they knew what it was like to live under the Russians.

The forest which straddled all these borders was a place in which to lose oneself. It ran across Lapland and over the Kola Peninsula, through Russian Karelia, across the Dvina basin and into the Urals. Over the Urals it was continuous with the unimaginable vastness of the Siberian forests, the *taiga*. In Siberia the taiga is feared for its immensity; it is said that travellers in it, on realising that they are lost, become paralysed with fear and lose their wits. It is one of the last places in Europe where bears still roam, and occasionally I would come upon their footprints in the moss of a bog, or their spoor by one of the rivers in which they fished. I never met one face to face. The European brown bear, unlike its American cousin, is timid and hides from men.

After only a couple of days I ran out of food and made my way back to the road. I had not intended to stay so long in the forest, but it kept drawing me back. I felt I wanted to go on and on, just walking in the silence through the trees felt like a meditation.

At a clearing by the road I found a campsite, but no sign of anyone in charge. I had just sat down on the step when a car pulled up and a woman with long blonde hair in a ponytail stepped out. She looked to be in her fifties, with large spectacles and a welcoming grin. A tall man in his sixties stepped out on the driver's side. 'How can I help you?' he said, in English.

'I'm just looking to see if there's any food I can buy from you,' I said. 'I thought maybe the campsite had a shop?'

'No, it's closed now, late in the season,' the woman said. 'But let us offer you something to eat.'

They introduced themselves as Birgitte and Jøstein, and invited me in. Over coffee and cakes Birgitte explained that she had moved to the Pasvik valley in the 1970s, from Oslo.

'I came for love,' she explained. 'My ex-husband was from this area, and so I came to be with him. But things didn't work out. In the end it was he that left, and I stayed,' she said, and shrugged. She told me that she loved Lapland for the stillness and the silence of winter. 'And I love the cold, it is a dry cold. And the snow, it is so *clean* here in the winter. I love the cleanliness of it.' She was looking forward to the first snowfalls of autumn.

Jøstein told me that before retirement he had been an engineer in the nickel mines that were still in use in the area. 'I haven't seen any sign of them,' I said to him. 'Where are they?'

'No, it is only across the border now, in Russia, that you will see them. But they are quite obvious there, they make a terrible mess!' He told me he was now retired, but had recently lived in Russia for a year while helping their mining programme. 'They are such a welcoming people, the Russians,' he said. 'So generous, although compared to us in Norway they have so little.' Living so close to Russia he had built up close friendships on the other side of the fence. From the car he retrieved an album of photographs, and showed me photos of his last hunting trip with his Russian friends, across the border in the Kola Peninsula.

'What was this?' I asked, pointing out photos of Jøstein standing in a crowd of skiers, all rosy-cheeked and smiling for the camera.

'That is the three-nation ski race at Petsjamo!' he said, his voice lifting in enthusiasm. 'Once a year they ease all the border controls and we ski between Norway, Finland and Russia. Maybe you can come next year!'

'Now then, you are looking for food, what can we offer you?' Birgitte said. 'I can give you some pasta. But I'm afraid there is no bread.'

'Wait a minute,' said Jøstein. 'I have an idea. Do you have a compass?'

'Yes,' I said.

'Well come with us! We can find you some bread and take you to somewhere that will make you remember the Pasvik valley for many years to come.'

I climbed into the back of the car and they drove me down tracks in the woods, until we pulled up outside an old wooden farmhouse, deep in the forest. Birgitte and I waited in the car while he went inside. 'An old Finnish lady lives in there, has lived in that house since she was born,' she explained. 'She bakes all her own bread and Jøstein goes in to check on her every few days.'

'Why is she Finnish if she was born in that house?' I asked.

'The Finns used to own a corridor along the river here opening out onto the sea,' she explained. 'But because they were allies for a while with Germany in the Second World War the Russians and the Norwegians took the land from them when the war was over. In both Norway and Russia there are people whose language is really Finnish, and they just carried on living where they were when the War came to an end.'

Jøstein emerged a while later waving a homemade frozen loaf. I tried to give him some money but it was refused with a frown, as if I'd been rude to offer. 'I didn't want to leave her,' he said. 'I think she has not long to live.'

Too frail to leave the house, deep in this forest, a Finn caught on the wrong side of the fence at the end of the Second World War. I wondered how she viewed all the changes that had happened in the valley during her lifetime.

'Now,' Jøstein said, starting the car, 'we will take you somewhere special.'

*

At a lake called Ellentjerne, 'Helen's Tarn', they helped me unload my rucksack from the back of the car. The three of us stood and admired the beauty of the scene. The silence was luscious and enveloping there. 'This is my favourite place,' said Birgitte. The lake was a rare chance to see to a horizon of sorts, the view over the water unobstructed by the trees. There were no vantage points in the forest, no bare escarpments from which to look out over the treetops, but it was not claustrophobic. It felt warm and welcoming. Occasionally the stillness of the water was disturbed by grebes and ducks splashing among the reeds, or swans roaring through the water in take-off or landing. 'Don't get lost!' they shouted to me as they drove off.

Over the next few days I walked around the lake, absorbing the thick silence, and going deeper into the forest towards the Russian border. When I reached it I found yellow and black posts marking the end of Norway, and looked across the river where the trees continued in an ocean of green. A solitary waxwing flew over the barbed wire fence. The only sign of a national boundary was an observation tower on the other side, built above the treetops on stilts. Below the towers, I had been told, stretched an electrified fence that ran all the way to the Black Sea. An iron bridge stood over the river. I might have been tempted to cross over, but it looked impassable, crumbling back into the water. I had gone far enough. It was time to head west again, and south, into the heart of Lapland.

From the border post at the end of the road I hitched a lift back up to Kirkenes in the back of a Norwegian army truck. The driver looked barely old enough to smoke, never mind carry a gun and defend Norway against a Russian invasion. I mentioned the bridge to him. 'The Germans put it there,' he told me. 'In the War. They brought it piece by piece from Paris and rebuilt it so that they could get artillery into Russia.'

'And did the Russians blow it up?' I asked.

'No!' he laughed. 'Almost as soon as the Germans built it they had to blow it up again, to stop the Russians coming after them!'

*

A couple of days later I reached Rovaniemi, in Finland. It was an island of concrete in the ocean of forest. Like so many other Lappish towns it had been razed to the ground by the retreating German army, and rebuilt as cheaply as possible. In its hostel I stayed for one night, sharing the room with an engineer from Dresden and two young Australian guys. The engineer planned to send a postcard to his mother from north of the Arctic Circle in each of Finland, Sweden and Norway. He was very excited to have made it into the Arctic at last. His grandfather had fought here, he said. The next day they were all going to visit 'Santa Claus Land', a Finnish initiative on the outskirts of the town which claimed to be the only home of the 'real Santa'. Planes from all over Europe drop into its airport throughout the winter, with extra ones laid on around Christmas. As a boost for the local economy it has been a great success. Its future was uncertain, however. Its busiest weeks are in the run up to Christmas, when well-to-do families would bring their children to feed reindeer, see Santa, and go for sleigh rides in the snow. With the effects of global warming the snow, on which its appeal depended, had started to fail.

The Australian guys, Ray and Brian, told me they were 'doing Scandinavia'. They shivered and said they had not intended to come so far north. They were glad to be able to say to their friends back home that they had made it to the Arctic Circle, but after seeing Santa they were going to straight back south. 'How long will you travel for?' I asked them.

'Another year or two,' Ray replied. 'My sister's getting married in Sydney in two years time and so I'd better make it back for then.'

'I'll just see how it goes,' said Brian.

I told them that I was amazed by the phenomenon of young Australians and Kiwis travelling so far and for so long. I had met guys like them all over the world, and the enthusiasm and stamina they had for going on year after year was impressive.

'Yeah, I guess,' he said. 'But you could say there's too many of us Aussies travelling about. Bloody south-east Asia is full of the buggers.'

'But you guys get *everywhere*,' I said. 'You've got a different attitude to the one that young people have in Europe. Europeans often still have this idea of exploration as being something you can only do in an "undiscovered" place, that it's for mountaintops and the North Pole. I think you've got a better attitude.'

'Well, for me anywhere that's totally new to me is pretty much like exploring,' said Brian. 'Like, I don't know anyone that's been to... em,' he paused for a while, struggling to think of a country where one of his mates had not at some point been. 'North Korea!' he said finally, with a note of triumph. 'Now if I was to make it to North Korea, I reckon I'd feel like a bit of an explorer. What do you reckon Ray?'

'North Korea?' he said. 'I'd just like to spend more time in bloody Sweden. Man, they got the most gorgeous blondes I ever saw in my life!'

*

In the morning I sat on the railway platform in Rovaniemi station. Most of the trains that passed were loaded with timber on its way to the pulp mills; some were hundreds of metres long. A troop transport arrived, loaded with chain-smoking soldiers on their way east to the borderlands with Russia. They piled out onto the platform to smoke and use their mobile phones, and the station was filled with the music of the Finnish language. Norwegian and Swedish are sung rather than spoken, their vowels jump up and down to their consonants in a Germanic staccato; Finnish is more fluid, more complex, and in many ways more beautiful. It repeats itself in short melodies which sound as if they have come from the earth itself. The Finnish language has the cadence and rhythm of streams and rainfall, it sounds the way that drawing circles in the mud with your fingers feels.

The southbound train, when it came, rolled through a narrow corridor of pine trees. Their tops were sharp and pointed, lining the railway line like a stake palisade. In the evening light orange clouds swam in the still green water of passing lakes. Occasional turrets flashed past, of stately homes rising through the treetops like fairy-tale castles. The forest seemed endless.

The Gulf of Bothnia stands like a Gothic arch over the Baltic Sea. I moved around it anticlockwise from Finland into Sweden. Rivers radiate from the Baltic like spokes from a hub, each one riveted to its shores by a town: Oulu, Kemi, Tornio, Luleå, Piteå, their names slowly wheeling through Finnish to Swedish with the curve of the coastline. The towns were all established initially as trading ports for the trappers and fur traders who brought their wares out of the forests; a reminder that once the only way of moving through the forest was by river. Each of their districts was called a *March* or a *Lappmark*; the Torne River and Tornio stand as the most northerly of these. From the apex of the Gulf of Bothnia the Torne waggles back and forth almost due north, and for its first 150 kilometres forms the border between Sweden and Finland. At its mouth the old trading settlement has, like the river, been divided. To the Swedish west it is called Haparanda, and to the Finnish east it is called Tornio. One day I walked across the bridge between the two, and the barriers, like the trees around them, pointed to the sky. No one really bothers about borders there; a census in the seventies had shown that one in four women in Swedish Tornedal had been born in Finland, and one in three Swedish boys had a Finnish girlfriend. Living conditions, education and employment opportunities were all found by the survey to be worse for the Finns. Despite farming the same soil the Finns are still poorer than the Swedes, though that is changing.

From Haparanda I travelled down to Luleå, and from there took another train further into Swedish Lapland. The carriage had 'Trans-Arctic Railway' written on the trestle in faded, grimy lettering.

*

Soaked with the stink of the bogs he had waded, clawing at the mosquitoes that tormented him, terrified by the barbarity of his travelling companions, one of the greatest minds of the eighteenth century stumbled into Luleå.

His name was Carl von Linné, a hot-headed young graduate of medicine, and he had come on a journey of discovery. Like Charles Darwin a century later he was a man of faith as much as a man of science, and like Darwin he possessed astonishing powers of observation. He invented binomial nomenclature, the system still used today whereby every organism on earth is assigned a Latin genus and descriptive name. It is thanks to Linnaeus (the Latinised name by which he became known) that we are *Homo sapiens*, 'the thinking man'. Linnaeus presaged Darwin in other ways; when classifying man he realised that mankind and the apes were indistinguishable in terms of the classifications he used for the rest of the living world. He wrote:

> I demand of you, and of the whole world, that you show me a generic character… by which to distinguish between Man and Ape. I myself most assuredly know of none. I wish somebody would indicate one to me. But, if I had called man an ape, or vice versa, I would have fallen under the ban of all the ecclesiastics. It may be that as a naturalist I ought to have done so.

But in 1731 his solemn scientific future was still ahead of him, and he was just a passionate young man straight out of the cloister-like atmosphere of Uppsala University. His journals burst with the power of his developing mind, medical impressions of the people he meets, and with the universal preoccupations of young men.

In Luleå he is fascinated by a hole bored in the old church walls, used, he reports, 'to judge the glans penis of men who had been rejected by their wives'. He follows this discovery with a discussion on the physiognomy of the women of Lapland: 'The vagina in women does not become more ample when they are fat, more likely narrower; the thinner they are, the larger the vagina.' Further around the coast in Tornio he indulges in a meditation on the relative merits of Finnish and Lappish girls: 'The Finnish girls have big breasts, Lapp girls small ones of the sort a girl keeps unspoilt for her future husband.' In the mountains bordering Norway he meets the beautiful daughter of the local clergyman, and notes in his journal that he must remember to write to her, for she seemed to have taken a liking to him. But he was not only interested in women and the various shapes of their bodies; his observations also touched on the economic potential of the North. The Industrial Revolution was not far off, and it struck Linnaeus as unseemly that all these trees should stand idle over so much of his country. He questioned why the whole lot were not burned for pitch or tar.

The consultations with the local people he met in the forests provide an insight into the medical world of the day. To a woman who has swallowed three frogs that keep her awake with their croaking he recommends tar. For headaches he reports that they put their heads in the smoke of the fire and place mashed spruce needles into their hair. He informs the reader that nosebleeds are secondary to suppressed menstruation, and they are common among those Saami women that work with the Swedish settlers. He notes that pregnant women he meets drink schnapps with pepper to initiate labour, and are rarely afflicted with hysteria.

Like Negri before him, the simplicity and happiness of the lives of the Saami people affected him deeply. It was the developing European preoccupation with the 'noble savage' again. He extolled the virtues of their simple lives; how they possessed great tranquillity, slept and woke as they wished, and seemed to luxuriate in a leisure that the people of the south had long since forgotten. They did not drink alcohol, they rarely smoked, in their tents both men and women walked around naked and unashamed, and it seemed to him that they lived in an unspoilt Eden. As Negri had done he resorted to classical metaphors to adequately describe the bounty of their lives, reminiscent of the Hyperboreans: 'Ovid's description of the Silver Age still holds true among the Lapps. The earth is not gashed by ploughs, nor is there clash of iron weapons; man does not descend into the bowels of the earth, nor is there strife about frontiers; the earth gives everything of its own volition.' At the time of his journey the Finns were being encouraged to settle throughout the north, to bring it into cultivation. This meant forcing the Saami from land their reindeer had grazed for centuries. Two decades later the first borders were drawn, designed to preserve lands to the north and west for the Saami and their reindeer. By the nineteenth century, a few decades later again, these 'borders' had been moved further and were no longer designed as reservations, but instead to prevent the indigenous people moving onto territory now 'owned' by rich townsmen in the south.

But that was still a century away. Lapland was a relatively borderless landscape, the back door of Europe, the home of the Saami, and a playground for the best minds and the idle rich of continental Europe.

※

The forest was charmless from the roadside. The drone of the cars and the wet backwash from the trucks made walking beside it a misery. I did get one lift, from a man who told me that unmanned space rockets were regularly fired from the forests around Kiruna. I asked if he could take me to see the launch site, but he said I wouldn't be able to get through. 'You will probably be arrested as a terrorist!' he said.

It was late afternoon when I walked into Jukkasjärvi. The village was as far north as Negri had managed on his first attempt to get to Nordkapp. Modern Jukkasjärvi is the home of one of Sweden's most bizarre tourist attractions: the Ice Hotel. Every spring before the Torne River starts to thaw, great blocks of its ice are sawn out and piled into a giant walk-in freezer. In November, once the temperature has dropped, the blocks are rolled out and built into a hotel. Its design changes every year so that it is always possible for tourists to visit a new version of it. When temperatures outside drop to the minus thirties, inside it stays relatively comfortable at about 5°C below zero. Guests can sleep in an 'ice-room', on an 'ice-bed' draped with reindeer furs, and snug in a down sleeping bag. The hotel even has its own 'ice church', where the waiting list to be married is apparently quite long, and a bar, where vodka (which will not freeze) is served from glasses made of ice.

In September the hotel was a large puddle on a gravel field, strewn with tangled lengths of the wire used as structural support. The only sign of its rooms were sad little clumps of congealed reindeer fur. Inside the giant freezer nearby there were magnificent ice-sculptures, carved in preparation for the upcoming season. The décor too varies from year to year, and sculptors from all over the world contribute to the hotel's changing image. A polar bear snarled over a cowering Inuit figure clutching a spear; a walrus and a musk-ox stood side by side; and over all of them towered a giant bottle, shaped like a well-known brand of Swedish vodka. The sculptures all glowed with soft blue light. The vast freezer for the iceblocks was open to visitors in order to make the most of the tourists, like me, who came by in the summer when there was little else to see. There were igloos built in the corners for those determined to spend a night sleeping on ice, but the place was deserted. A bored and very earnest girl at the counter told me to come back in the winter. 'That's when the fun is,' she said, and smiled coquettishly; 'have you heard about Swedish saunas…?'

A peculiarity of Jukkasjärvi is the 'Sauna Academy of the Bastue'. Most Scandinavians are addicted to saunas, and many homes, even some of the smallest, have one installed. It is a transnational pastime, a common enthusiasm for Swedes, Finns and Norwegians.

It is also a great way of staying warm in the winter. 'The Bastue' refers to the practice of being switched by birch branches while in the sauna, which is supposed to invigorate the skin and add to the sauna experience. I knew she was implying that saunas, which are traditionally mixed, are pretexts for unlicensed orgies. But I also knew from previous visits to Finland that she was spinning me a tourist's line. The British, the Americans and many continental Europeans have a reserve about public nudity that the Scandinavians do not, and Swedes and Finns in particular take great pleasure in poking fun at uptight or over-imaginative tourists who either refuse to enter the saunas, or worse, go to them in search of sexual adventure.

I left the giant freezer and the puddles and walked down to the end of the village. Standing among a grove of birch trees by the side of the river stood an old wooden church. Four hundred years before the Ice Hotel was built it was the only tourist attraction between the Baltic and the North Cape. For those who could not face the three hundred more miles of swamp, forest and tundra to reach the latter, it came to represent the very edge of Europe. For a few of those 'first tourists', leaving a marker at the church was thought to be sufficient proof of travelling far enough into the north to be able to return south again with dignity. Like the modern travellers who want to send postcards from the Arctic Circle it saved having to make that final, gruelling journey across the tundra to the Nordkapp. Linnaeus had signed the guest book of the church in Jukkasjärvi, as had many other tourists whose accounts I had read, and I wanted to do the same. But there was one marker in particular that I wanted to see.

*

Inside the church the walls were painted with the pure whitewash of Swedish Lutheranism. A garish modern triptych over the altar celebrated the life of a man called Læstadius, considered the Lutheran proselytiser of the Saami. He was a Saami himself, a Lutheran minister trained in the south who travelled to his homelands to convert his people. On the triptych a dark-eyed Jesus dripped blood on the earth, from which sprang bunches of flowers in bright primary colours. In the pew nearest the altar a solitary woman sat weeping. In the foyer I found the inscription I had come so far to read.

GALLIA NOS GENVIT, VIDIT NOS AFRICA, GANGEM HAVSIMVS, EVROPAM QVE OCVLIS LVSTRAVIMVS OMNEM GASIBVS ET VARIIS ACTI TERRA QVE MARI QVE STETTIMVS HUC TANDEM MOBIS VRI DEFVIT ORBIS. DE FERCOVRT ● DE CORBERON ● REGNARD AVGVST 1681

It was branded with hot irons into a wooden plaque made from a Saami sledge. 'Raised in Gaul, we have seen Africa, drunk of the sacred waters of the Ganges, and seen the whole of Europe; Fate has driven us across land and sea, and now we stand here at the pole, where the world ends. De Fercourt, De Corberon, Regnard, August 1681.'

Jean-Francois Regnard was a rich kid on a grand tour of the Old World. He was twenty when he inherited a fortune from his father, a wealthy Parisian merchant, and set off at once for Italy. Six years of adventuring later he reached Jukkasjärvi. In his satchel he carried a copy of Scheffer's *Lapponia*, and later wrote a book himself about his travels in the North. In it he describes how he and his companions went as far as the Torne River just west of the little church, and decided they had gone quite far enough. They climbed to the top of a promontory and looked out to the north and west. To make himself seem a little more intrepid he had to use some artistic license in describing the panorama before him.: 'Here we concluded our northward journey and raised the tent poles… When we were up there we saw Lapland in the west and the Arctic Ocean to its full extent as far as North Cape. This, gentlemen, can be called touching the Earth's axis and being at the end of the world.'

Regnard returned home via Poland, Turkey, Hungary and Germany. On arriving in France he bought himself a position in government. Soon afterwards he moved out to his estate of Grillon in the department of Seine-et-Oise where he lived as a country gentleman. In later life he became a successful playwright, but his Lapland book lay unpublished until after his death in 1709. Publishers had started to notice a trend in the public appetite for a strange new genre known as 'travel writing'. It began in 1697 with the publication of William Dampier's *New Voyage Round the World*, and would continue to accelerate throughout the century. It was still only the super-rich and sponsored who could tour the globe, but ever-cheaper printing presses meant that now those who did not have the time or the inclination to travel could read the accounts of those who did.

*

Back in the forest, wandering along the roadside, I followed the borderlands north again. The further I travelled from the towns the kinder and the more open the people seemed to be. Lasse Malmström was one of the kindest, and the most enthusiastic. He pulled up beside me on a rainy afternoon when most drivers would have carried on. 'I used to do what you are doing,' he explained, 'and it's good to treat people how you'd like to be treated yourself.' He and his three sons drove a spacious van, and on the trailer was a brand new snowmobile for the coming winter. Lasse had his own business running a cross-country ski centre, and the snowmobile would groom his tracks for him. 'But you must come and see our place!' he cried.

'Where do you live?' I asked, taking out my map and leaning forward between the seats for him to show me.

'Where we are going is not on any map. I will take you places where no tourist ever set foot!'

We passed through village after village, small clusters of buildings against the impassive forest, their names soft murmurs of Finnish and Saami despite the Swedish sovereignty of the lands: Keräntöjärvi, Parkalompolo, Muonionalusta. As we drove, Lasse told me the villages' different claims to fame as tourist attractions: 'That one has the largest sundial in the world!' he exclaimed. 'That one has a paddle steamer all the way from the Mississippi!'

But Lasse was worried; despite the attractions he did not have as many bookings for the coming winter season as he would have liked. He was trying to dream up new ways of attracting them. He lived on an island in a river that separated Finland from Sweden, and his ski centre he had called *Rajamaa*, 'Borderland'. He cursed the bureaucrats of the south for placing borders on rivers. 'Rivers are where people live!' he cried, 'not where they should be divided!' He was a Swede, his wife was a Finn, and his children spoke both languages with ease. The youngest was fifteen, and was keen to talk in English. Next year he would move to the residential school in Kiruna, and next year would not come quickly enough. He was bored by the forest.

After Lasse announced my presence to his wife an extra place was set for dinner and she brought out the best meal I had seen since the *Nordstjernen*, a mountain of spaghetti. We talked of borders, and of the European Union. Norway is not a member, and the people of Finnmark are far better for it, he told me. Finland and Sweden are tied to rules and regulations which work for Brussels, but not the thin population and precarious economy of Lapland.

'I wondered if you could help me with something,' he asked after dinner. 'After that I promise I'll take you over the border into Finland.'

'Of course,' I told him. 'Whatever you like.'

He was preparing some publicity material for his ski centre, and wanted some help with a translation. We sat in his little office and I wrote out a key for his map of the area, explaining what each of the symbols represent in English. The phone rang, his face became very serious. A worried look came into his eyes, and then faded. By the time he came off the phone he was beaming with happiness. 'The Estonian Cross-Country ski team are going to train here this winter!' he said, his smile widening as he spoke.

'What does that mean?' I asked him.

'Even if we don't get too many tourists, it will be a great season after all!'

His wife and sons came through to see what the noise was about. 'Get the bottle of champagne,' he said to them. 'We're all going to celebrate!'

*

Adventurers and men of letters continued travelling to Lapland throughout the eighteenth century. In 1718 Aubry de la Motraye, a Frenchman but 'a subject of Great Britain' travelled throughout the forest with the Saami on their reindeer migrations. He said that their nomadic lives and their generosity reminded him of the Tartars, with whom he had also lived for a while. He compared the milk of the reindeer with the mares' milk he drank on the steppes of central Asia.

Five years after Linnaeus staggered out of the swamps two more advocates of the new science arrived. Pierre de Maupertuis was the greatest proponent of Newtonian science in France. Newton had proposed that the earth was not round after all, but was actually an 'oblate spheroid', flattened at the poles. With Anders Celsius, the Professor of Astronomy at Uppsala University and inventor of the temperature scale, de Maupertuis set out into Lapland to prove Newton right. In the hills above Jukkasjärvi the men took measurements that proved the earth really *was* flatter in Lapland. Science was still a gentleman's activity, it was still possible to make new discoveries in widely ranging disciplines, and later in his career de Maupertuis gave up on geography and turned to biology. He was the first to realise that the human embryo goes through a process of development and differentiation. Before his revelation it was assumed that semen contained many tiny perfectly formed *homunculi*, which required only to be nurtured in the womb.

Public fascination with travel and the exotic proliferated. In London the last quarter of the eighteenth century saw the establishment of the British Linnaean Society and the African Society, to encourage interest in both botany and travel. Asian and African colonialism gathered pace after the American colonies were lost. Cheap editions of the voyages of Captain James Cook became available, and it seemed that everyone with means wanted to explore the unknown. Even today most maps of Europe still cut Scandinavia off at the latitude of Oslo and Stockholm; Lapland provided an ideal destination for those who wanted a bit of adventure, but not *too* much. It was remote and austere, but it was still very much a part of Europe.

Louis Philippe, the bourgeois king, also sought refuge in Lapland. He was there in 1795, aged just 22. The godson of Louis XVI and Marie-Antoinette, he escaped there from revolutionary France and a legend in northern Sweden persists that he left a blue-blooded bastard in the forests near the Jukkasjärvi. There were other consequences of the French Revolution, much farther reaching. The Napoleonic Wars were to redraw the map of the North. It was because of Napoleon that Sweden lost Finland to Russia, and it was after his defeat at Waterloo that Norway was gifted to the Swedes. The Torne River became the border between Russia and the West, as the Pasvik would be a century later.

The *Pax Brittanica* which followed Waterloo made exploration even easier. Britain turned its attention abroad. With mercantilism over, the seas were free for trade. In London the Palestine Association, 'for the exploration of Syria and the Holy Land,' had been formed in 1804; now other distinguished societies joined it. In 1828 the Zoological Society, in 1830 the Geographical Society, and in 1831 the British Association for the Advancement of Science. After the defeat of Napoleon the British Navy had less to do, and so under Sir John Barrow, secretary to the Admiralty, they were sent to all the corners of the earth. His men travelled across the deserts of Africa and through the Arctic archipelagos of Canada. He himself journeyed extensively in China and elsewhere in Asia. All in their quest to make the world British.

As the might of the British Empire grew, the travel accounts of its subjects in Lapland become more and more pompous, and less and less enamoured of the Saami and the simplicity of their lives.

After a lengthy and outraged discourse on the smell of fish in the fishing villages, one writer takes issue with the apparent weakness of his Saami porters: 'Our luggage was not heavy; two Negro carriers on the Congo or the Gold Coast would have capered with it,' he says. He is appalled by the apparent immorality of mixed saunas, while commenting that 'female personal beauty of any sort is not brought to any high stage of cultivation.'

The First Marquess of Dufferin, later Governor General of Canada, then Viceroy of India, the man who would orchestrate peace with Afghanistan and the annexation of Upper Burma, visited Lapland in 1856 as part of a tour of Iceland and Spitsbergen. His private yacht *Foam* put in at the harbour of Hammerfest on the Finnmark coast. He found the Saami ugly, but 'not unintelligent'. According to the developing science of ethnology, he outlined the contemporary theory that the Lapps were related genealogically and linguistically to the Australian aborigines. As mankind 'bubbled up' out of central Asia, he explains, the inferior races were driven to the extremes of the world, thus making the Saami first cousins with the 'Polynesian Niggers'. He finds their customs barbarous, but amusing.

It is unclear if he realised that the British Isles lie farther from central Asia than Lapland. One wonders what the Saami made of all these distinguished and cultivated guests.

*

'I used to stand by the road, waving packets of cigarettes,' she said. 'That's the only way I could get a lift.'

She would never smoke them, she was much too clean-living for that. But picking up foreigners in the Chinese Autonomous Region of Tibet was illegal, and cigarettes were her only bargaining power.

'It used to drive me crazy! Seeing trucks go by, and picking up some local people there on the road ahead of me, but they wouldn't stop for me.'

She was small and neat with blonde hair and blue eyes. Her name was Susanne, and in her home town of Umeå she would have been lost in a crowd. But in China she had been far more conspicuous.

'Trucks never stop for me,' I complained. 'They only seem to stop for women.'

'It's *only* trucks that stop for me,' she said. 'I wish it wasn't. That's the guy who brought me down out of Norway this afternoon.' She jerked a thumb back over her shoulder, where a thin moustached man sat behind a clutch of empty beer bottles. He was staring at us.

I tried to picture her waiting by the roadsides of Tibet with her yellow hair and outsized rucksack, jumping up and down for each truck that went past, a tiny dot of Europe on that immense landscape.

The truck driver stood up and lurched to one side. He looked as if he was summoning the courage to make a rash proposition. She turned round to me with some urgency and asked, 'Where are you staying?'

There is a thin spit of Finnish territory which points an accusing finger to the West, running between the forests of Sweden and the tundra of Norway. In the middle of this narrow corridor lies Enontekiö, and I was staying in its campsite. It is a languorous stretch of a town, only a few houses wide but over two kilometres long. It was a quiet place, but like so many other villages I had passed through in the north, warmly so. The presence of the trees was inescapable, they breathed on the peripheries both of the settlement and the lives of its people. Even in death they did not escape. The forest crowded the little cemetery in the centre of the village, roots snaking over the surface and digging deep into the soil. Through the roots of the birch, spruce and pine, the people of Enontekiö find immortality. The campsite too was more trees than grass. My tent stood between them by the river bank.

'I'll go and sit by the river while you change your clothes and get into your sleeping bag,' I said.

'You can sit where you like,' she replied. 'I trust you. It's strange, but I have often found that people who travel the same way as me are the most reliable of all.'

I lay in the half-light listening to her talk of approaching the Nepalese border from the north, the poverty of Lhasa, the closed Kingdom of Bhutan, the Qinghai plateau. The branches of the forest swayed in the breeze, and when I slept I dreamt of the wind that blows from the Taklamakan Desert.

When I awoke I was back among the trees of Lapland. I was very happy to see them.

✻

Little children all over Europe are told that Santa Claus lives in Lapland. This leaves the children of Lapland justifiably asking their parents, 'Where *exactly* does he live?'

The answer? On top of the Pallastunturi National Park.

Pallastunturi rises from the Finnish forest like a muted Uluru from the Australian desert. It soars over the treetops. Immense folds of brown and grey stone, smoothed by the Ice Ages, stand high above the forest plains. Most of the interior of Lapland is so flat that its mountains are a novelty, and a tourist attraction. The park, or 'Pallas Ounastunturin kansallispuisto' as it is mellifluously known in Finnish, is a ski resort. Pigga and Antte, a couple I had met in the bar in Enontekiö, invited me on a trip to see where Santa *really* lives.

They lived on the outskirts of the village where the path to their house meandered between the pines. Antte worked as a policeman, and Pigga was a teacher of the Saami language. They had lived there a year, they said, but had never visited the bar. The first night they did so they were so surprised to find a Scotsman there that they decided it must be a sign that they should get out more, and they decided to invite me to go camping with them for the weekend.

The sky was the pure blue of gentians, and a few wisps of cirrus formed high above Norway to the north. From the summit of the range the forest stretched to every horizon in a sea of velvety green, jewelled with lakes. The soft undulations of the landscape were like the slow swell of waves. Marching up out of Sweden a procession of cumulus clouds cast shadows on the forest, forming patchwork patterns of light that melted and reformed in ceaseless motion.

To the north beyond the horizon the forest ran into tundra, and from tundra into the Arctic Ocean. From the top of Pallastunturi there was no sign that people had ever lived, or would ever live, in the forest. I laid out all my maps on the summit, weighed them down with stones and orientated them correctly to get my bearings: that way was Jukkasjärvi, that way to Pasvik and Murmansk, that way to Rovaniemi and that way to the North Cape. But trying to put markers and pointers on the forest was to take something from its beauty. Its beauty was its immensity and its *borderlessness*, its uniformity and its timelessness. It was unphotographable.

From the east the cumulus clouds were being pushed aside by a slate-grey cumulonimbus, a giant storm cloud. Lightning flashed down onto the trees below us, and the timing of the thunder advanced. Antte grew nervous; we were on the highest point for hundreds of miles in every direction. 'We should think about getting down,' he said calmly, with characteristic Finnish understatement. Ten minutes later the lightning sparked and bounced over the rocks at the summit as we ran for the shelter of the valley below.

The rain washed freshness into the air. The forest seemed renewed. Every twig sparkled with raindrops, and a wet, loamy smell rose from the earth. The following day, after a breakfast of Norwegian shrimps, Pigga drove me into Norway. She worked at the college in Kautokeino, fifty miles north of Enontekiö. In the borderlands, she said, it was common to live in one country and work in another. Outside the window I watched the pine give way to sparse birch, and then to tundra. She talked, and I listened.

She was a Finnish Saami from Utsjoki, another border town further east, and grew up speaking Finnish, Saami and Norwegian interchangeably. Like Nils had done back at the Nordkapp she showed me a photo taken on her wedding day in which she wore the magnificent traditional dress of her people. Antte was a Finn, not a Saami, and in the photograph he stood by her side in funereal black. He was learning her language, she said, but it is very complex. It is Finno-Ugric, loosely related to Finnish and the languages of the Siberian nomads, but its consonants are far harsher. It is filled with sibilant *dhz* and *cz* sounds which give it a Slavic flavour.

Neither of them had ever been outside Scandinavia. They preferred to live on the edge of Europe. At the time I met them they were planning to drive to Rome. Several months after I had returned home I received a postcard from the French Riviera. They loved the sunshine, they said, but had yearned for home. They had missed the trees of Enontekiö.

*

Petrol stations are good places to hitch. People feel kinder when they have a full belly and a full tank of petrol.

My driver was Saami, and he said he was going all the way to Hammerfest. He was short and sprightly and when he smiled his eyes disappeared in the folds of his face. He offered me two options: I could ride on the mound of reindeer skins in the back of the van, or I could sit up front and keep him company. I rode up front. People are more interesting than reindeer skins.

He said he was a 'businessman'. He made full use of his Saami passport for 'trade purposes'.

'All these borders are a good thing,' he said, 'they make opportunities for business.' His eyes narrowed and his voice slowed when he said the word 'business'; you could tell it was one of his favourite words. He was a good businessman, and he liked making risky deals.

'Who do you do most business with?' I asked him.

'I like all the people, but the Norwegians are friendliest, the Swedes they want everything on a fax, and the Finns they try to con you,' he said. 'But the worst are the Russians!' he broke into a high-pitched giggle. 'Some of them even try to get me to send them money before I see their merchandise!'

He had bought a load of reindeer cheap from Russia after the collapse of the Soviet Union, and he had a long story about being conned by the Murmansk mafia.

'But I think most of all, I like to sell to the Norwegians.'

'Why?' I asked him.

He turned to me and gave me an impish grin. 'Because they have got so much money!'

'Haven't they got the highest taxes of all the countries?' I asked, but he just looked back at me with a surprised expression. Of course he had never paid them.

*

In Hammerfest the falling snow melted gently into drizzle. I pitched my tent on a hill overlooking the town. Reindeer grazed around me as I cooked my dinner. The view looked out onto the island of Sørøya, where rows of grey cliffs squatted in the mist.

For years Hammerfest had been considered the most northerly town in the world, but a few decades ago was surpassed by Honningsvåg, thanks to the North Cape and the tour buses. The town councillors had fought back; next to the harbour there was a refurbished 'Royal and Ancient Polar Bear Society' building, ready to offer cruise passengers lifelong membership and an official-looking certificate for a couple of hundred kroner. Further into the town there was an oriental pagoda built to celebrate the two hundredth anniversary of the founding of the society. There are numerous descriptions of Hammerfest by tourists passing through over those two centuries, none of them complimentary. I read one that was offended by its smell of blubber and fish, while another commented that its lunatic asylum was the biggest building north of the Arctic Circle. It's clear that the writer thought this was a sign of the madness that the town seemed to induce, rather than a mark of a civilised approach to mental illness.

I spent an evening wandering around Hammerfest. The port was grimy and heavy with rusting cargo containers. Cars roared through the main street, and I was the only person who seemed to walk anywhere. I did not want to fall into the same trap as the previous visitors, and was looking for something to like about it. I found it in the local cinema.

The local operatic society was putting on a show of songs from the 1920s to the 1980s there, and in the interval I chatted to a young man who worked as a psychiatric nurse in the local hospital. He was wearing a dinner suit and spats, and had a feather boa hung around his neck. He told me that there were no more 'lunatics' in Lapland; the local psychiatrists had a small ward in the hospital but most people were looked after in the community. I asked him where I could find the old asylum, but he did not know. 'It was probably destroyed by the Germans,' he said, 'like everything else.'

I told him about the books that I had read that never seemed to be very impressed with Hammerfest. 'But these people, they don't know what it is that they are looking for,' he said. 'I came here from Oslo because it is so beautiful here, there are mountains to ski in and the people live life so much more gently. And look at what I am wearing!' He lifted up the feather boa and raised his eyebrows. 'Would I ever have ended up doing something like this, having so much fun, if I had stayed in Oslo?' The question was presumably rhetorical. 'I don't think so,' he said.

Another writer to have visited the town, and written of it in more poetic terms, was W. H. Auden. He was a seeker after the silence and the stillness of the North, and by the time he came to Hammerfest he had already written a book describing his travels around Iceland with Louis MacNeice. Back then, in the 1930s, Europe was sliding towards fascism, and in a road-side restaurant Auden had met Hermann Göring's brother. Göring was the chief of the Gestapo at the time. 'He didn't look in the least like his brother,' Auden commented, 'but rather academic.' Sixteen years after the War ended he came to Hammerfest on a pilgrimage. It was a place he had been drawn to in atlases since childhood, 'the northernmost township on earth,' he called it in his poem written after the visit. He had a distinctly Greek viewpoint, opposite to that of the Victorian adventurers. For him the North represented all that was furthest from civilisation, and therefore beautiful and untainted. In a poem about his stay he described how he pottered through the streets of the town and slept through sunny nights. He felt he had travelled into another world, where social mores had changed. He had gone beyond 'the Moral Circle,' and he mourned the devastation wrought by the War. The only building left standing in 1945 had been the church.

I walked around the churchyard. A few of the graves had clear plastic protective covers over them. Condensation had formed underneath the plastic, and the stones looked as though they had been weeping.

✳

The photograph is grainy, but still recognisable as Hammerfest. The hill I had camped on behind the town is just within the frame to the right. Tin-roofed houses clamber up its slopes. Fishermen's warehouses stand out along the wharf, and a fine yacht floats in the harbour, decked in Norwegian flags. The whole town was out to celebrate the homecoming of the Norwegian nation's favourite son.

The photograph was in a book published in London in 1898. It was taken on Monday 17 August 1896, from the deck of the *Hurtigrute* steamer on its way into harbour from Vardø. The photographer was Fridtjof Nansen, on his return from the North Pole.

I had caught up with him again, the man who achieved the limits of exploration of the North. It was fitting to cross his path once more on my way back home.

Nansen had proven with his crossing of Greenland that he was one of the few men in history who have had the hubris to take on world opinion. With his expedition to the Arctic he became acclaimed as the greatest pioneer of what was later known as the heroic age of exploration; the last phase in the history of discovery in the Arctic and the beginning of exploration of the Antarctic. From 1893 to 1896 he developed revolutionary methods of travel, hauled sledges over hundreds of miles of pack-ice, sailed across the Arctic Ocean in improvised kayaks, and wintered in a hut on the shores of Franz Josef Land. In Hammerfest he faced the scrutiny of the European media and was reunited with his wife, who had begun to fear he was dead. She had not heard from him in over three years.

In June of 1893 he and his crew had left the Oslofjord, and by September were frozen into the ice of the Laptev Sea to the north of Siberia. They drifted on their specially designed ice-strengthened ship the *Fram* that winter, for the whole of the following year, and for the following winter. In March 1895 Nansen realised he was drifting no nearer to the Pole, but only west towards Spitsbergen. With another consummate skier, Hjalmar Johansen, he decided to make a dash for the Pole.

The ice was intolerable. The pressure on it had mangled and wrenched it into ridges so high that the sledges had to be carried over them. They had dogs, but not enough of them. On 8 April Nansen wrote in his diary, 'this continual lifting of the sledges over every irregularity is enough to tire out giants.' Two days later he gave up. They had reached 86°14′ north, and had not seen land further north than Russian Franz Josef Land back at 82°. The Arctic seemed to be an ocean surrounded by land after all. He did not think there were any more Hyperborean lands to discover.

They had a banquet of chocolate and hot whey to celebrate

reaching farther north on the globe than anyone had before them, then turned back. They knew they had no hope of finding the *Fram* again after such a tortuous journey; their only hope was to make for Franz Josef Land and the northern coast of Spitsbergen. Nansen slept in one morning and forgot to wind his watch. With the sun high above them both day and night and no accurate knowledge of the time they had no way of calculating their longitude. Nansen had to guess.

They barely made it to Franz Josef Land before autumn, and used the last days of sunlight to build a small shelter from stones and the frozen hides of walruses they had slaughtered. The men had little in common; when Nansen described the six months of darkness he said, 'our life was so monotonous that there was nothing to write about. The same thoughts came and went day after day; there was no more variety in them than in our conversation.' Sometimes it would become calm and clear, and he and Johansen would walk out on the ice under meteor showers and the aurora borealis. The glow from the southern horizon at noon seemed to Nansen like the flames of Muspelheim, the Norse fire-world from which Óðin had made the earth.

They had nothing to read but an almanac, and both men grew to love it as their only token of civilisation. They ate only frozen chunks of walrus and polar bear, and spent hours fantasising about food. Again and again they discussed how they would spend the following winter if they survived to return to their families. But on the whole they were happy.

'It was a strange life, and in many ways it put our patience to a severe test; but it was not so unendurable as one might suppose... Our spirits were good the whole time; we looked serenely towards the future, and rejoiced in the thought of all the delights it had in store for us. We did not even have recourse to quarrelling to while away the time,' he wrote.

In May the ice had melted sufficiently for them to start out once more. They had been living in the hut of walrus skin for eight months. They knew that they would have to go west to reach Spits-bergen, and so they assembled their kayaks and set up their sails once again. A little over a fortnight later they were rescued by an-other gentleman adventurer.

Frederick George Jackson was a little more spirited than most. He had actually applied to join the *Fram* expedition four years be-fore, but been refused because he was not Norwegian. As a wealthy man he resolved instead to make his own bid for the Pole, and that spring was in Franz Josef Land reconnoitring the land for a pos-sible sledge journey north. He had been frustrated to find that the land extended only a little past 82°. It was Jackson's relief ship, the *Windward*, that took Nansen and Johansen back to Vardø and their beloved Norway.

He had only been in Hammerfest three days when he received a telegram from Otto Sverdrup, captain of the *Fram*. He too had broken out of the pack that summer, and had just arrived in port a few miles to the west. The telegram read: '*Fram* arrived in good condition. All well on board. Shall start at once for Tromsø. Wel-come home.'

The beak-nosed figure of Roald Amundsen frowned over Tromsø harbour. His eyes gazed out towards the north, as if contemplating his Arctic adventures. He was not a pleasant man, and the majority of Norwegians are not particularly proud of him. His statue stood alone. Gulls stood on his head, and his aquiline profile was streaked with guano.

Amundsen initially trained to become a doctor. A son of high-ly ambitious parents, he went to medical school to please them. When they died half way through his course he quit, and con-centrated his mind instead on how to find funding to become a polar explorer. He studied for, and eventually obtained, his master's ticket. Between 1905 and 1907 he captained a vessel that located the north magnetic pole, and completed the first navigation of the

North-West Passage. Like Nansen he used his time among the Inuit to learn their survival skills and how to handle sledge dogs. By the time he got back to Norway he felt he was ready for an assault on the Pole. In their common cause of Norwegian Nationalism Nansen gifted Amundsen the use of the *Fram*, and by 1909 he was ready to sail north.

Disastrous news arrived at their departure with a telegram claiming that Robert Peary, an American, had already reached the Pole. Peary's claim was later discredited, but Amundsen had to think fast. His funding was at stake, and so, telling no one else but his crew, he instead decided to sail south, to see if he could beat the British expedition to the South Pole led by Robert Falcon Scott instead. The tale of Amundsen and Scott's race to the Pole is known to both British and Norwegian schoolchildren, in different versions. But what is not often retold is how when Amundsen reached it, on 14 December 1911, he wrote in his diary, 'no man has ever stood at the spot so diametrically opposed to the object of his real desires.' He still preferred the Arctic.

At this point Amundsen could have turned his attentions elsewhere, and rested on his laurels. Nansen had realised when he was getting too old for the heroic age of exploration, and quit while he was ahead. After his bid for the North Pole he had gone into politics and eventually settled in London as the Norwegian Ambassador (where he was rumoured to have had an affair with Lady Scott while her husband was freezing to death on an Antarctic ice shelf). He represented the League of Nations in the 1920s, organised famine relief for post-revolutionary Russia, and was involved in negotiating the resettlement of Greek and Turkish nationals following their war of 1920-22. Polar exploration for him was just one element of his monstrous ambition. But for Amundsen, getting to the Pole was all, even if it meant becoming a tourist to do so.

An attempt to freeze into the ice and drift to the North Pole failed, as it had done for Nansen, and so in 1926 he grabbed at a new opportunity. An Italian, Umberto Nobile, was experimenting with the new technology of airships. With Norwegian backing he piloted Amundsen and a rich American financier called Lincoln Ellsworth from Svalbard over the North Pole to Alaska. Together they dropped three flags onto the Pole itself: an Italian tricolour, a Stars and Stripes, and a Norwegian cross. It was too dangerous to try to land, but they did verify once and for all that there were no more lands to discover on their way across the Arctic Ocean. The heroic age of exploration was over. It was enough to find a rich backer and be flown wherever you wanted.

Amundsen and Nobile squabbled for the honour of being first at the Pole, and in 1928 Nobile tried another attempt, this time funded entirely by the Italians. Three hours from take-off the airship went down. Amundsen, unable to let go of his drive for glory, or perhaps motivated by remorse for the way he had behaved in his squabbles with Nobile, took off from Tromsø in a French plane to look for him. Nobile was rescued, but Amundsen was never heard from again, and his plane was never found.

In Tromsø I stayed for a while with Mads Gilbert, the Professor of Anaesthesia and Emergency Medicine there. He was a close friend of a former colleague of mine in Edinburgh, who had told me to get in touch if I was ever in Lapland. For a week or so I enjoyed the feeling of being back among busy streets and letting myself slowly readjust to the idea that my journey was coming to an end. Tromsø manages to combine the cosmopolitan vibrance of a university town with the austere beauty of living on the edge of the Arctic. It is built on an island, sandwiched between the crystalline glacial scenery of the Lyngen Peninsula and the soft green fringes of the Atlantic sea-board, still warmed by waters which flow all the way from the Caribbean. In its bars I met people who were genuinely worried about climate change. One woman told me that if the Gulf Stream did divert, her whole town would freeze to death. On the hillsides around it many of the birch trees were already bare.

They stood silhouetted by the snow which had begun to lie on the wintering earth.

My host, Mads, had made me especially welcome, though I had never met him before. When I arrived he gave me the keys of his house and his car, and sent me off exploring the countryside. He also arranged for me to see first-hand the work of the emergency hospital services in that remote and isolated part of Norway. I flew on hospital transfers all over Finnmark, and went out in the helicopter ambulance to rescue stranded mountaineers deep in the Lyngen Alps. While in Tromsø Mads' work as a professor keeps him busy, but his career has taken him all over the world. Together with Hans Husum and Torben Wisborg he has founded the Trauma Care Foundation, an organisation dedicated to helping victims of trauma, including land-mines, in countries as far apart as Mozambique, Iraq, Cambodia and Afghanistan. 'We are the smallest NGO in the world,' he joked. 'But that way we actually get things done!' The Foundation is committed to providing low-cost training in trauma first aid, and to preventing reliance on Western expertise and technology. He told me stories of working in some of the harshest and most dangerous places on the planet. Gesturing out of the window at the magnificent mountains that surround the town, he said that it was only by being able to return to this 'mountain fastness' that he managed to keep going in his Foundation work. I am grateful for the discussions we had during my stay there, his reflections on the life he has chosen to lead, and our conversations about the choices open to all of us to try to improve, rather than inflict more damage on, the world around us.

*

I kept on moving south. All along the coast there were fishing villages hunkering down to the shoreline, backed by spectacular Alpine mountains. Islands stood out to sea like scattered jewels, encrusted with foam as the power of the westerly ocean swell broke over them. The *Hurtigrute* snaked through ever-narrower fjords and straits, past the islands of Kvaløya, Senja, the Vesterålen archipelago, until it came alongside the Lofoten Islands.

Lofoten is a place apart, a chain of islands that hover between reality and myth. Impossibly steep mountains erupt out of the sea in a series of peaks and gulleys that do not seem to belong to this world. The sheer granite slopes look polished and brittle. The summits teeter over great scooped-out walls of rock, as if the islands were sculpted by giants. When the sky clears, rays of sunlight slide between the summits, like shafts of golden light falling into a cathedral.

I hitched slowly down the spine of the islands, preferring to walk away from the road into the mountains when the light or the landscape demanded it. Since the days of the Vikings the islanders have made their fortune from the migrations of cod through their waters, and every village I passed was announced at its outskirts by rows of wooden racks used to dry the cod harvest, destined mainly for Spain and Italy. Some of them were draped with fish that rustled softly in the wind, dripping their oil onto the ground. The grass below them was a lurid green, in sharp contrast to the muted landscape.

In the evenings the sun slid unhurriedly towards the horizon on a gentler incline than we are used to in the south. As it dropped to the west the eastern sky would well up with lavender and lilac light. There were only a few hours each night when the sky grew dark enough to see the stars, and one magical night I managed to see the flood of the aurora borealis. I had not seen them since Shetland, way back in May. The sky had been too light since then.

The tail of Lofoten dripped into the sea just beyond a little village called simply 'Å'. The road ended in a turning circle for coaches and a noticeboard for tourists. It was late in the season, and I seemed to be the only one left. Beyond the noticeboards the headland ran down to the water's edge where a serration of impassable cliffs stretched the last few kilometres. Across a small strait stood the island of Mosken, the tidal rips caused by the underwater channels so severe that they cause whirlpools. Mosken stood guard over the most famous whirlpool of them all, the original 'Maelstrøm'. Negri was disappointed to find it so tame, but Jules Verne was more impressed; he imagined it sucking a ship twenty thousand leagues beneath the sea. Beyond it lay the last two islands of the Lofoten chain, Værøya and Røst.

Watching the water in vain for any signs of a whirlpool, I took a ferry over to Værøya and spent my last days in Lapland walking around the island in circles, thinking about my journey and sleeping by its shores. I did not want to leave.

*

The Great War of 1914-1918 sent its ripples out even to these furthest reaches of Lapland. It was thought to be the War to end all wars. It was hoped that Europe had learned its lesson. Never again, it was said, would there be such naivety, never again such enthusiasm for bloodshed, never again the carnage of the fields of the Somme. But the harsh terms of German surrender forced it into an economic quagmire which proved fertile soil for the new politics of National Socialism, or Nazism.

Fifteen years after the Treaty of Versailles Adolf Hitler was named Chancellor of Germany. Within two months he had secured a four-year term of dictatorial powers. Within a year he had withdrawn Germany from the League of Nations. By August 1934 he had assumed the presidency, and named himself the *Führer* of the Third Reich. He deprived all Jews of citizenship, and in defiance of the Treaty began to ship armaments into the Rhineland. With a flying ace from the Great War called Hermann Göring he set to work on his four-year plan to re-establish the dignity that he believed the German people had lost.

Britain and France watched warily, hoping to keep peace by complying with German expansionism. First the annexation of Austria, then the occupation of Sudetenland, then the dismemberment of Czechoslovakia. Until the invasion of Poland they were still hoping to avoid war.

The beleaguered intellectuals of the Czech nation had not been so optimistic. They had lived under the threat from Germany throughout the twenties and thirties and their history, like that of Finland, is one of being overpowered alternately from the west and from the east. In 1923 the Czech playwright Karel Čapek earned international acclaim with *R.U.R.*, a play that warned of the dehumanising potential of an increasingly mechanised and industrial society. To give voice to this new threat, he had to invent a new language, and in it he coined the term 'robot'. In 1936 he published his social satire on the rise of totalitarianism, *The War with the Newts*. At the time the threat from Germany was darkening, and Čapek felt oppressed. Like Auden in Iceland the same year, he decided to journey into the North in order to breathe more freely. The description of his trip to Lapland is published in English under the title, *Travels in the North: Exemplified by the Author's Own Drawings*. For Čapek, Lapland was a refuge from the hell he saw breeding in the south. As he travelled by boat from Denmark to Sweden and then by rail through Norway he felt increasingly released from the dark cloud of Nazism. But it was never far from his mind.

Čapek was to be the last of the travellers I would follow in the North. He travelled in the Europe of my parents' and grandparents' generation and he saw a society there in many ways similar to our own. I would follow him last because he saw Lapland just before the historical upheaval of the Second World War (the consequences of which are still being played out), and because of all the travellers and explorers that had accompanied me since Shetland, when he comes to describe the beauty and the value of the northern fringes of Europe, he speaks for me too.

From Bergen he took the *Hurtigrute* to Lofoten. Its scenery made a profound impression on him, and of all the landscapes he travelled through he loved it best. 'A bouquet of mountains: you can't express it in any other way; and here you can see that the world blossomed in granite before it could flower in bird-cherry and lilac… it gives you more the impression of something brimming over, of terrible abundance and exuberance.'

From Lofoten he journeyed on to the North Cape, but the barren tundra made him think only of death, and his mind turned once more to the destruction of all that he loved far away in Bohemia. His journey was a pilgrimage, he said. He had gone into the North to be reminded of the sublime in nature, to remember that it transcends the meanness and pettiness of humanity.

The colonial empires of the European states stretched right around the world. British schoolchildren looked in atlases and marvelled that 'half the world is pink'. France administered the whole of West Africa. The Dutch and Belgians too had their share, but the old ways were passing on and a new era in global history was about to begin. The world was shrinking. The power of the United States grew every year, and the Great Bear of Stalin's Soviet Union growled over Europe, which is only a peninsula of Asia, after all.

Even on the eve of war Čapek still could not see the new order, did not anticipate that Europe could not face the new threat alone. Near the North Cape he came upon a boat-load of American tourists, and his comments give voice to an opinion commonly held at the time, and a sentiment that is unfortunately still uttered today. 'What do they want here, after all? The end of Europe, that's our affair; let them go and have a look at the end of America, if there is one; and if there isn't, let them make one for themselves.'

He travelled, he said, to have a last look at God's peace, but now it was time to go back home, 'where men were at their busiest', and where the Europe he loved was coming to an end. He died in 1938, just in time.

*

From the rail-head at Narvik it was seventeen hours by train to Stockholm. The line had been built during the War to channel iron ore from supposedly 'neutral' Sweden to German ships waiting in Narvik's occupied harbour. The assistance the Swedes gave to the Nazis is one of the many reasons Norwegians still distrust them. Outside the window the forest was black; black as charcoal, as pitch, as the slag of the iron ore that had been mined beneath it. The train rumbled south, and I passed over the Arctic Circle for the eighth and final time on my journey. It dropped out of the forests to slide along the shores of the Baltic. As we moved south each settlement that we passed seemed busier, gaudier, and dirtier than the last.

In Stockholm there were bikers with swastikas tattooed on their shaved scalps. On the outskirts of town, on the way to old Upp-sala, I found the university campus and its library. There were no barriers, no ID checks, and with the liberalism characteristic of the Scandinavians the lectures were open to all. I heard an American from Harvard discourse on Nietzsche, and how National Socialism had twisted his rhetoric of the 'blonde beast' to include the Japa-nese, who were also to be considered an Aryan race. The Swedes were all blonde. They listened politely, and afterwards asked in-sightful questions in articulate English.

When their society seemed threatened by corruption, greed and violence, the Greeks looked to the North. Modern writers such as Karel Čapek and W. H. Auden turned to it for the same reasons, voicing a need that many of us in the south still feel. The northern fringes of Europe were once the edge of the world, a back-country of the imagination where reality and myth intertwined. Now with the growth of tourism these magnificent spaces have become acces-sible to us all. I thought of all the people I had met on my journey who had a deep love for the North and the peace that they found there. Of Paul Whitworth in Shetland, painting in blizzards and from his open boat while the North Atlantic storms raged. Of Peter and Berlina in Faroe, and how pleased they were to get home from their holidays in continental Europe. Of Anna and Ólafur in Iceland, starting new careers in London but always finding ways to take their lives back home. Of Jukku and Maria in Greenland, gazing forward to a future free of the constraints of colonial rule.

Of Stefano and the tour guides in Svalbard, taking tourists out in safety to a world of polar bears and glaciers. Of Birgitte and Jøstein in Norway, Pigga and Antte in Finland, and Lasse and Kaisu Malmström in Sweden, who had all gone far out of their way in order to take me to a part of their country that they loved, so that I might love it too.

In the two and half thousand years since Pytheas made his voyage there have been shifts in Europe that to him would have seemed wildest fantasy. The northern countries no longer seem so primitive and barbaric as they once did to the Greek world. Following their centuries as the spawning grounds of Viking raiders the Scandinavian countries have developed a fierce ethic of social responsibility. Their health, education and social security systems are now the envy of the world, while those of Greece and the Mediterranean world struggle to keep up. Thanks to oil discoveries and robust state support for industry and enterprise they are now very rich countries (with taxes to match). In a recent survey examining the proportion of GNP spent on charity and foreign aid among developed countries, Norway, Sweden and Denmark came out on top.

Arctic Europe has changed a great deal in two and half thousand years. The threat posed by global warming seems to be the greatest challenge it currently faces. Part of its beauty lies in the seeming timelessness of its landscapes, but on my journey I had seen that that 'timelessness' was more fragile than it appeared. The Arctic is changing, and changing fast.

But its landscapes still give the traveller a magnificent sense of the sublime in nature. As his train sped south towards central Europe, Čapek tried to put this into words:

> And then there is still another journey, or pilgrimage, North; this makes for nothing else but just the North; because there are birch trees and forests there, because grass grows there, and plenty of blessed water is sparkling there; because there

is a silvery coolness there, and dewy mist, and altogether a
beauty that is more tender and more severe than any other...
no flaming South is so copious, and buxom, so juicy with
sap and dew, so blessed with poverty and beauty, as the land
of the midnight sun.

From Stockholm I took a bus to Oslo, and from there a train over
the mountains to Bergen. From Bergen I caught a ferry west across
the North Sea to Shetland. I was almost back home.

Epilogue

WHERE DID MANKIND'S search for new lands begin? From where did men and women first look to the North as an escape, a solution to their discontent, a resource to be plundered, an untainted landscape, a refuge from the world, a curiosity, a bargaining pawn, a new homeland?

In Edinburgh I could not settle down, but walked the streets thinking of all the places where my journey would have to take me if it was to go full circle, if it was really to come to an end. My journey had begun in the tropics, and now I felt that in order really to be complete it would have to return there. My experience was by now much greater and I felt that I was ready to go back, perhaps to hospital wards like the one described at the beginning of this book. Having explored so much of Arctic Europe gave me the impression that this time I would feel more grounded when I came up against the heat and the disease of the south.

Just before leaving, I could not resist one more trip to the North.

*

Rain trickled across the window, distorting the landscape. Low grey clouds smothered the earth. The fields with their puddles and their damp steaming cattle gave way to rolling uplands, and then to the oceanic swell of the Cairngorms.

In Inverness I changed trains. I crossed over the fertile earth of the Black Isle and into Sutherland: Viking country. From Lairg the postman with the largest district in Britain drove me fifty miles, and dropped me off at the harbour of Kinlochbervie on the shores of the Atlantic Ocean. There were no vessels in the harbour, and

302

the Seaman's Mission was empty. I walked north across peat moors which clung like blackened and wounded skin to the bare hills behind the village. It was the following afternoon when I reached Cape Wrath.

Cape Wrath is the last headland of the island of Britain. Some claim that honour for John o' Groats, but John o' Groats has coach-tour cafés and souvenir shops, Orkney lies within spitting distance across the narrow Pentland Firth, and the mainland reaches out to it like a supplicant hand. It is at Cape Wrath that the British mainland ends abruptly, and stares down the ocean without flinching. Only a solitary dirt track of fifteen miles leads to it, but it is a crossroads of worlds: the end and the beginning of the North. Its name has nothing to do with anger; it comes from the Old Norse *hvarf*, meaning 'the place to turn' or 'the place to reach safety'. The English word 'wharf' has the same root. Although the Vikings named Sutherland as their 'southerly land' it was only when they doubled Cape Wrath that they felt they had really arrived in the South. It is not clear which direction they preferred; whether it was on travelling north or on travelling south that they felt that they could relax.

I set up my tent on the cliffs, took out my stove, and sat down to make some dinner. Grey seals rolled among the waves below me, and fulmars spun and hovered on the up-draughts. My back curved neatly into the soft turf and the ocean glittered into the northern horizon.

Chronology

c. 600 BCE	Phoenician explorers sail into the Atlantic and reach Britain
c. 330 BCE	Pytheas the Greek sails as far as Shetland and probably Iceland
83	Agricola's troops circumnavigate Britain
c. 550	St Brendan and other Irish monks sail to Faroe and Iceland
c. 780	'Viking' raids out of Scandinavia begin to attack the shores of Europe
825	Dicuil writes his 'Book of the Measure of the Earth'
874	Ingolf Arnarson, a Norwegian, settles Iceland
986	Eirik the Red discovers 'Greenland' and settlers begin to arrive
c. 1000	Leif Eiriksson ('the Lucky') finds North America
1112	First Bishop of Greenland, Eirik Gnupsson, appointed
1378	Plague years in Europe. Great Schism begins, dividing the Mediaeval Church
1400	Norse settlement of Greenland starts to founder
1517	Beginning of Reformation in Europe
1553	Richard Chancellor finds the White Sea of Russia
1578	Martin Frobisher 'discovers' Greenland and claims it for England
1596	Willem Barents discovers Svalbard and names it 'Spitzbergen'
1606	Henry Hudson reaches 80° 23´ north, renaming Spitzbergen 'Newland'
1664	First 'tourist', Francesco Negri, reaches Lapland from Italy
1681	Three Frenchmen led by J. F. Regnard include Lapland in their 'Grand Tour'
1697	Publication of first 'travel book', Dampier's *New Voyage Round the World*
1736	Anders Celsius travels to Lapland to prove Newtonian science correct
1898	Fridtjof Nansen returns to Lapland from an attempt on the North Pole
1945	Many towns in Lapland destroyed by the retreating German army
2000+	Tourism forms increasingly large part of modern economies all across Arctic Europe

Thanks

There's a line in one of J.D. Salinger's stories where a character gives his brother some writerly advice along the lines of: *you loved to read books long before you thought of writing them, so go ahead and write the book you would most enjoy reading*. It's good advice: *True North* was my first book, my first attempt to write anything for publication, and my intention was to create a book I'd want to take down from a bookshop shelf, keep at my bedside, pack into a rucksack as holiday reading. Thanks are due to many people who helped me get it into the bookshops: Seán Costello, my editor, immediately saw what I was trying to achieve with this book and patiently guided it through to publication despite my inconvenient absence for the whole period of preparing the first edition. Tom Johnstone oversaw the book's transition to Polygon from Mercat Press, and made a potentially rough crossing slide smoothly. Thanks to Annie Tindley for her support, advice, performing the role of agent, and having an incomparable sense of the importance of a good index. Will Whitely read the first draft with a child on each knee, somehow managing to provide his unapologetically honest and always welcome opinions (those children are now grown up). Michelle Lowe, Nick Hay and Katie Hay helped with logistics in the lead-up to publication. Sara Wheeler gave me the support and encouragement to embark on the writing of *True North*, and advice about approaching publishers. The British Antarctic Survey Medical Unit were kind enough to give me a job at Halley Research Station with enough time and space on my hands to get the book drafted. Paul Torode read the earliest drafts down there and gave me some valuable suggestions. The late Gunnie Moberg and Tam MacPhail in Orkney gave me the benefit of both their knowledge of the Faroes and their ideas about the typescript. Phil Stewart in Islamabad, and Donald and Philippa Johnson in Western Australia, opened their homes, computers and refrigerators to my wife and me, allowing me to get the first edition of *True North* completed in time for the printers. It's a pleasure to see it re-issued as a Canon for another generation of readers, and appreciation for making that happen is due to the generosity of Edward Crossan and Jenny Brown, as well as the dreamteam at Canongate – most notably Leila Cruickshank and Francis Bickmore.

Thanks are also due to the many hospitable, warm-hearted people that I met all over Arctic Europe, from Shetland to Greenland to Svalbard and back again. They invited me into their homes, drove me hundreds of miles in their cars, and talked to me of their lives, their histories, their hopes and their worries for the future. Without their kindness this book might have become just a history of Europe's discovery of its own northern limits, and I hope the reader, to whom I owe my final note of thanks, will be able to take more away from it than that.

Notes on Sources

SHETLAND

p.4:

Homer, *The Odyssey*, translated by T. E. Lawrence. Book XI. (London, 1932)

p.5:

Pindar, *Pythian X*, quoted from a translation in: Romm, J. S., *The Edges of the Earth in Ancient Thought* (Princeton, 1994)

p.6:

Strabo, *The Geography*, translated by H. Hamilton and W. Falconer. 3 vols. (London, 1854)

p.15:

Tacitus, *Agricola*, translated by H. Mattingly (Harmondsworth, 1948)

p.20:

The Sagas of the Icelanders, including *Egil's Saga*, translated by Bernard Scudder (London, 2000)

p.20:

Orkneyinga Saga, translated by Hermann Pálsson and Paul Edwards (London, 1978)

ALSO OF INTEREST:

The Bible, Ezekiel, Chapter 27, verses 3-12 (for a contemporary description of the might and sailing reach of the Phoenician trading Empire in the sixth century BCE)

Cunliffe, B. *The Extraordinary Voyage of Pytheas the Greek* (Harmondsworth, 2001)

Herodotus, *The Histories* (Oxford, 1998)

Whiteaker, I., 'The Problem of Pytheas' Thule', *Classical Journal*, 77 (1981)

THE FAROE ISLANDS

pp.46, 47, 48, 51:

The Age of Bede, including *The Voyage of St Brendan*, translated by J. F. Webb (London, 1965)

p.50:

Jackson, Kenneth Hurlestone, *A Celtic Miscellany* (Harmondsworth, 1971)

pp.65, 66, 67:
Dicuil, *De Mensura orbis terrae*, reprinted and translated in Beamish, N., *The Discovery of America by the Northmen* (London, 1851)

ALSO OF INTEREST:

Heinesen, William, *The Lost Musicians* (London, 2006), translated by Glyn Jones. (A tale by a master Faroese novelist of Torshavn life in the early twentieth century.)

Kjørsvik Schei, Liv & Moberg, Gunnie, *The Faroe Islands* (London, 1991)

Severin, Tim, *The Brendan Voyage* (London, 1978).

ICELAND

pp.73, 92, 93:
Cook, A. S., 'Ibn Fadlan's Account of Scandinavian Merchants on the Volga in 922,' *Journal of English and German Philology* (1923)

p.78:
Sturluson, Snorri, *Prose Edda*, translated by Jean Young (Berkeley, 2002)

pp.79:
Jordanes the Ostrogoth, translation from Nansen, Fridtjof, *In Northern Mists* (London, 1911)

pp.84, 87:
The Sagas of the Icelanders, *Egil's Saga* ibid.

p.85:
'The Anglo-Saxon Chronicle, 937', translation from Magnusson, Magnus, *The Vikings* (Stroud, 2003)

p.86:
Magnusson, Magnus, ibid.

p.94:
Diamond, Jared, *Collapse: How Societies Choose to Fail or Survive* (London, 2005)

p.95, 96:
For a fuller discussion of Pytheas, and for the quotations from Geminus of Rhodes, Pliny, and Strabo used on this page, see: Whiteaker, I., 'The Problem of Pytheas' Thule,' *Classical Journal*, 77 (1981)

pp.100–104, 106–108:
The Sagas of the Icelanders, including 'The Saga of Gunnlaug Serpent-Tongue,' translated by Katrina C. Attwood (London, 2000)

p.103:
John of Wallingford, quoted in Magnusson, M., ibid.

p.115:
Adam of Bremen, *Gesta Hammaburgensis ecclesiae pontificum*, available through Columbia University Press (2002)

p.116:
Tacitus, *Germania*, translated by H. Mattingly (Harmondsworth, 1948)

pp.117, 118, 119:
The Sagas of the Icelanders: including *The Saga of Hrafnkel, Frey's Goði*, translated by Terry Gunnell (London, 2000)

pp.125–127:
The Age of Bede, including *The Voyage of St Brendan*, ibid.

p.136:
King Harald's Saga, translated by Magnus Magnusson and Hermann Pálsson (London, 1966)

ALSO OF INTEREST:

Jones, Gwyn, *The Norse Atlantic Saga, Being the Norse Voyages of Discovery and Settlement to Iceland, Greenland and America* (London, 1964)

GREENLAND

p.141:
Fridriksson, Sturla, 'Grass and Grass Utilization in Iceland', *Ecology*, 53:5 (1972)

p.144:
Virgil, *Georgics*, and the banners of Charles V, quoted from the translation of Romm, J. S., *The Edges of the Earth in Ancient Thought* (Princeton, 1992)

p.150:
The Age of Bede, including *The Voyage of St Brendan*, ibid.

pp.151, 163, 164:
The Sagas of the Icelanders, including *The Saga of the Greenlanders* and *Eirik the Red's Saga*, both translated by Keneva Kunz (London, 2000)

p.155:
The Meregarto, this translation from Fridtjof Nansen's *In Northern Mists*, ibid.

p.155:
Adam of Bremen, ibid.

p.158:
Translations of 'The King's Mirror' taken from Nansen, *In Northern Mists*, ibid.

p.176:
Taylor, E. G. R. 'A Letter Dated 1577 From Mercator to John Dee', *Imago Mundi*, Vol. XIII (1956), pp.56-8

p.185:
Nansen, Fridtjof, *Across Greenland on Skis*, translation taken from Roland Huntford's biography of Nansen, *Nansen* (London, 1997)

p.187:
Bardarson, I. (ed. Jónsson, F.) 'Det gamle Grønlands beskrivelse af Ívar Bárðarson (Ivar Bårdssön)' (Copenhagen, 1930); Manuscript AM 777 a 4to.

p.196:
Shakespeare, William, *Henry V* in Wells, S. and Taylor, G. (eds), *Shakespeare: the Complete Works* (Oxford, 1988)

p.196:
Seaver, Kirsten, *The Frozen Echo: Greenland and the Exploration of North America ca AD 1000-1500* (Stanford, 1996)

p.201:
Egede, Hans, *A Description of Greenland* (London, 1745)

p.202:
Hakluyt's 'Chronicle for the year 1502', quoted from the publications of the Hakluyt Society (Glasgow, 1903-05)

pp.205–207:
Hakluyt, R., *The Principal Navigations, Voyages, Traffiques, and Discoveries of the English Nation*, Vol. XII, part I. Hakluyt Society, Ex Ser. 12 vols (Glasgow, 1903-1905)

p.207:
Davis, John, *The Hydrographical Description of the Earth* (London, 1595). (I used an online version published by ebooks@adelaide, the University of Adelaide. The printed book carries the publisher's information for those keen to get their hands on one: 'Imprinted at London by Thomas Dawson, living by the Three Cranes in the Vinetree, and are there to be sold. 1595.')

p.208:

Davis, John, *The Seaman's Secrets* (London, 1594). (I used an online version of this book transcribed by the McAllen Library in Texas, www.mcallen.lib.tx.us.)

ALSO OF INTEREST:

Aubrey, John, *Aubrey's Brief Lives* (Harmondsworth, 1972)

Fristrup, Borge, 'Some Characteristic Problems in Present-day Greenland,' in Wonders, W. C. (ed.), *The Arctic Circle: Aspects of the North from the Circumpolar Nations* (Don Mills, Ontario, 1976)

Ingstad, Helge, *Land under the Pole Star* (London, 1966)

Skeie, John, *Greenland: The Dispute between Norway and Denmark* (London, 1932)

Rink, Henry, *Tales and Traditions of the Eskimo* (London, 1875); translated by the author and with illustrations by the Greenlander Aron of Kangeq

SVALBARD

pp.213, 216, 217:

de Veer, Gerrit, *The Third Voyage Northward to the Kingdoms of Cathaia and China in Anno 1596.* Hakluyt Society, 1876 (New York, 1964)

p.219:

Dante, *La Divina Commedia* (Florence, 1845); author's translation

p.219:

Johann Ruysch, World Map, from Ptolemy's Geography. Published 1507 and 1508, Rome. James Ford Bell Library, University of Minnesota

p.222, 223, 230:

Purchas' writings, taken largely from Hakluyt Society, Series 2 Vol. XI (Glasgow, 1902). Also notes from publications of the Hakluyt Society: *Three Voyages by the North-East* (London, 1853); *The Voyages and Works of Davis* (London, 1880); *The Voyages of William Baffin* (London, 1881). (For more information, see www.hakluyt.com.)

p.231:

Van Assum, Hessel Gerritszoon, *History of the Country Called Spitsbergen*, Hakluyt Society, Series 2, Volume XI (1902)

pp.232, 236:

Van der Brugge, Jacob Segersz, *Journal or Day Book kept by seven sailors during their wintering on Spitsbergen in Mauritious Bay, situated in Greenland, 1634*, Hakluyt Society, Series 2 Volume XI (1902)

p.236:

Ólafsson, J., *The Life of the Icelander Jón Ólafsson, Traveller to the Indies*, Hakluyt Society, 2nd series No. LIII (1923)

p.237:

Pellham, Edward, *Gods Power and Providence in the preservation of eight Men in Greenland, nine Moneths and twelve Dayes* (London, 1631); reprinted New York, 1968

ALSO OF INTEREST:

Brown, R. N. Rudmose, *Spitsbergen, an Account of Exploration, Hunting, the Mineral Riches & Future Potentialities of an Arctic Archipelago* (London, 1920)

Scoresby F. R. S., William, *The Polar Ice* (London, 1815)

LAPLAND

p.247:

Negri, Francesco, *Viaggio Settentrionale, fatto e descritto* (Padua, 1700); author's translation

p.250, 251:

quotations taken from Nansen, Fridtjof, *In Northern Mists*, ibid.

p.236:

Ólafsson, J., ibid.

p.271:

Linnaeus, Carl, *Systema Natura* (Haarlem, 1788), edited by J. F. Gemlin

pp.272, 273:

Linnaeus, Carl, *Iter Lapponicum* [The Lapland Journey] (1732), translated and edited by Peter Graves (Edinburgh, 1995)

p.276:

Regnard, J. F., *Voyage de Laponie* (Paris, 1709)

p.281:

Hyne, Cutcliffe, *Through Arctic Lapland* (London, 1898)

p.281:
Dufferin, Lord, *Letters from High Latitudes; being some account of a voyage in the schooner yacht 'Foam' to Iceland, Jan Mayen & Spitzbergen in 1856.* (London, 1857)

p.288:
Auden W. H., and MacNeice, Louis, *Letters from Iceland* (London, 1937)

pp.289–291:
Nansen, Fridtjof, *Farthest North, Being the record of a voyage of exploration of the ship Fram 1893-96 and of a fifteen months' sleigh journey by Dr Nansen and Liet. Johansen with an appendix by Otto Sverdrup Captain of the Fram*, 2 vols. (London, 1898)

pp.297, 298, 300:
Capek Karel, *Travels in the North: Exemplified by the Author's Own Drawings and Translated by M&R Weatherall* (London, 1939)

ALSO OF INTEREST:

Butler, Frank Hedges, *Through Lapland with Skis and Reindeer with Some Account of Ancient Lapland and the Murman Coast* (London, 1917)

Fleming, Fergus, *Barrow's Boys* (London, 1999)

Mead, W. R., *The Scandinavian Northlands*, Problem Regions of Europe series (Oxford, 1974)

Rae, Edward, *The White Sea Peninsula: A Journey in Russian Lapland and Karelia* (London, 1881)

Index